CHAPLAINS

# Take a leap of faith

Not all Chaplains jump out of aircraft but if you'd like to take your ministry to new heights why not become an Army Chaplain?
Working side by side with the world's youngest and most dynamic workforce, you'll become a valued member of our team.
For further information contact,
MOD Chaplains (A) Trenchard Lines,
Upavon, Pewsey, Wiltshire SN9 6BE
**www.army.mod.uk/chaps**
**or call 08457 300 111 and quote ref: CSG**

ARMY
CHAPLAINS

YEAR B

_Year B._ (handwritten)

# The Canterbury Preacher's Companion 2006

_Sermons for Sundays, Holy Days,
Festivals and Special Occasions
Year B_

Edited by Dr J. Critchlow

CANTERBURY
PRESS
Norwich

© Canterbury Press 2005

First published in 2005 by the Canterbury Press Norwich
(a publishing imprint of Hymns Ancient & Modern Limited,
a registered charity)
9–17 St Albans Place, London N1 0NX

www.scm-canterburypress.co.uk

British Library Cataloguing in Publication data

A catalogue record for this book is available
from the British Library


Scripture quotations are mainly drawn from the
Revised Standard Version Bible © 1952 and 1971
by the Division of Christian Education of the
National Council of Churches of Christ in the USA


ISBN 1-85311-637-8

Typeset by Rowland Phototypesetting Ltd,
Bury St Edmunds, Suffolk
Printed and bound by
St Edmundsbury Press Ltd,
Bury St Edmunds, Suffolk

# Contents

Unless otherwise stated, the readings are according to the *Common Worship* Calendar and Lectionary, authorized for use in the Church of England.

xi

xv

# YOUR ADVERTISEMENT
## in front of over 400,000 Anglicans —
## 'the ordinary people in the pews'

That's right: you could be advertising to more than 400,000 readers of these two much-loved and long-established parish magazine insets.

*The Sign* has been in publication for nearly a hundred years. *Home Words* even longer. Together, but independently of each other, they help parishes to improve the look and content of their own local magazines.

So, once a month you have the chance to advertise nationally, but in a local publication. All the benefits that come through local, trustworthy and sought-after parish magazines are transferred to you and your advertisement.

Both magazine insets accept advertising from anyone, from individuals to large businesses and charities. You can advertise a holiday letting, or make a charity appeal — anything that is relevant to parishioners.

Want to know more?
Simply make contact:
Stephen Dutton
The Sign & Home Words
c/o Church Times
33 Upper Street
LONDON N1 0PN
Tel. 020 7359 4570    Fax 020 7359 8132
email: stephen@churchtimes.co.uk

**FREE SAMPLES available for potential advertisers; also for parishes who might want to use the insets in their own magazines**

xvii

The readings in this section are taken from Brother Tristram SSF, *Exciting Holiness* (Canterbury Press, 1997); Robert Atwell, *Celebrating the Saints* (Canterbury Press, 1998).

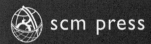 

# First Sunday of Advent  27 November 2005
*Principal Service*  **In Glad Remembrance** Isa. 64:1–9;
Ps. 80:1–8, [18–20]; 1 Cor. 1:3–9; Mark 13:24–37

> *'No eye has seen any God besides you, who works for those who wait for him. You meet those who gladly do right, those who remember you in your ways.' Isaiah 64:4b–5a*

## Cosmic upheaval

Today's texts look back to the exciting time of creation, and forward to the even more exciting End of Time. And where do we come in all of this? We, who are caught up somewhere in-between the cosmic upheaval? We, who stand again at the beginning of a new Christian year? God, the Supreme Encourager, is urging us to learn from the past, to anticipate the thrilling future – and, meanwhile, to do what is right, not merely out of a sense of duty, still less grudgingly, but with gladness. There has been upheaval on a cosmic scale, and today there are still little earthquakes, little meteorites, little disturbances . . . the foretaste of more to come; but the End is not yet. We are to keep steady for Jesus, our mind set on his Great Commission. If we accomplish the work we have envisaged, well and good. If we are called Home – or the End comes – before we have done everything we want to, well, we shall not need to do it.

## A month of remembering

We are still in November, the month when for a variety of reasons we remember the saints in glory, the faithful departed and those who have fallen in war. So now, at the end of the month, we could begin this new year in no better way than by gladly remembering God, in all the ways he deals with us. We could begin to count our blessings; we shall run out of time before we come to an end of them, but that's no reason not to begin the exercise! For all of us, there will be things for which we find it hard to give thanks: yet even in these, there is God. One day we may know the how, the

I

why and the wherefore – or perhaps by then it will not matter. Paul's command is pretty all-embracing: 'giving thanks to God the Father at all times and for everything in the name of our Lord Jesus Christ' (Eph. 5:20); we'd need help to misunderstand it.

## God's at work

God 'works for those who wait for him', says Isaiah (64:4). Advent is surely a time of waiting – but are we going to leave all the working to God? As ever, God's invitation: 'Come now, let us argue it out' (Isa. 1:18), is sounding this Advent. Can we answer the divine summons? Can we draw aside, if only briefly, from the oh-so-busy run-up to Christmas, and get serious with the Lord? What is he asking of us, this Advent Sunday? Only one hour of worship? Only a few minutes of prayer? Only a brief respite in the secular busyness? 'Come now, let's get together and talk this thing through!' God is saying. We are approaching the celebration of the greatest birth of all time, when God played his part so mightily, so convincingly, so lovingly. Come now, what are we going to do about it?

## Lacking for nothing

Paul, in today's epistle, helps us to focus on one important aspect of our faith: spiritual gifts (1 Cor. 1:7). How are we using the gifts God has given us? Have we let any go through neglect? Are we firing on more spiritual cylinders than was the case a year ago? (Oh, my, with all we have on our minds just now, can we even remember our spiritual state of last Advent Sunday? Well, God has given us memory-recall, if we will only use it.) 'God is faithful', Paul reminds us (1 Cor. 1:9). That means, he's still in the business of sharing out his gifts, which doesn't impoverish him one iota, but enriches us beyond calculation. The folk around us – at work, at home, at church – are we giving them cause to bless God for our spiritual gifts? Or vice versa? Not the high-profile gifts alone – the preaching, teaching, healing, prophesying . . . – but the love, joy, peace, patience, kindness, generosity, faithfulness, gentleness and self-control that are the hallmarks of a practising Christian? These are the precious bastion between us and the advances of Satan . . . and if the devil can persuade us that Christmas is merely a vacation, he will.

### Family Service Input

Encourage the young folk to make Christmas cards featuring the church services and events, for distribution throughout the parish.

### Suggested Hymns

Come, thou long-expected Jesus; Hark! a thrilling voice is sounding; O come, O come, Emmanuel; The advent of our King.

## First Sunday of Advent
*Second Service*   **The Jesus Gospel** Ps. 25; Isa. 1:1–20; Matt. 21:1–13

> *'Learn to do good; seek justice, rescue the oppressed, defend the orphan, plead for the widow.' Isaiah 1:17*

### Feather-ruffling, in a good cause

In both the Old and New Testament readings, we have divine feather-ruffling going on: God the Father verbally chastising Israel for backsliding, and God the Son causing mayhem in the entrepreneurial area of the Jerusalem temple (again, it's Israel, the 'chosen race', who is at fault). She had everything going for her: God's especial favour, providence and love. Yet, time and again, Israel let herself slide out of synch with the Almighty – not every Israelite, but more than a few – and so the nation as a whole needed to hear, and hopefully heed, the divine warnings.

### On the home front

Today, on a personal level, how is our standing with God? We may be going through a hard and anxious time, finding it difficult to keep faith with a God who doesn't seem close, who doesn't give us the answers we're looking for. Well-meaning friends may try to tell us that God tests his closest friends more than those who are less ardent, not so loyal – but that's pretty cold comfort, when we're in anguish with no other prospect in view. At times like this, it's often much better to remember four little words of Jesus from his Great Sermon: 'Your heavenly Father KNOWS' (Matt. 6:32). Whatever the angst, he knows. And he has been there already, so he knows how he is going to bring us through the angst and out the other end: we don't know how, but God knows. And none of us is smart enough (or dumb enough, depending on how we look at it) to come up with a problem too big for the Lord to handle: we just cannot do it; let's face our limitations!

## Our own feather-ruffling

A man was visiting his friend in the hospital. The patient was feeling really low after getting a poor diagnosis of his condition from the doctor that morning. 'You must take control,' his visitor urged. 'Fight this illness with the power of Jesus' name. Send the pain back to the devil who gave it you – hit Satan where it hurts!' 'I'm feeling too bad to rough up anyone,' the patient groaned.

When Jesus healed a woman who had been doubled up for 18 years with a spinal disease, he laid the blame for her condition where it was due: at Satan's door (Luke 13:16). This Advent, God is calling us to use the power of his Son's great name, in our fight against evil of any kind: mental, physical and spiritual. Jesus came to earth, not to cheer humankind for thirty-odd years and then leave us to muddle along on our own; when he returned to his Father, he made loving provision for us – his Holy Spirit. He knew – better than we ever could – that without his Spirit we'd never make it in the fight against Satan. But with this all-powerful, divine provision, we can – if we will – give the devil an awfully hard time.

## If we will

If we choose, simply by being ordinarily mediocre in our faith, we can give Satan an easy ride. But who in his right mind would want to do that? If we're not ruffling the devil's feathers, chances are we're not doing too much work for Jesus either.

## Our responsibility

It's our responsibility. If we don't 'do good, seek justice, rescue the oppressed, defend the orphan [and] plead for the widow', Satan won't lift a finger to help. But when we do put God's command into action, the devil will come against us every which way he can.

Today, as a new Church year begins, the choice is ours. We can, if we choose, make a difference – a big difference.

Hark! the glad sound; On Jordan's bank the Baptist's cry; O for a faith that will not shrink; Sleepers, wake! the watchcry pealeth.

## Second Sunday of Advent  4 December
*Principal Service*  **Give – And Take** Isa. 40:1–11; Ps. 85. [1–2] 8–13; 2 Pet. 3:8–15a; Mark 1:1–8

> *'John the baptizer appeared in the wilderness, proclaiming a baptism of repentance for the forgiveness of sins.' Mark 1:4*

### A serious undertaking

'I take – he undertakes', runs an old gospel chorus. If we take God at his word, he undertakes to see us through. If we repent of our sins, he undertakes to forgive us. Is that it? Not quite: we thereby undertake to forgive others; and in the proportion that we forgive ... Aaah! that is where we are pulled up short. John the Baptist preached the rudiments of forgiveness; Jesus followed up with the actuality: 'Forgive us our debts, as we also have forgiven our debtors' (Matt. 6:12) – as we have forgiven, not once, twice or even seven times, but seventy-seven ... (and who's counting?) (Matt. 18:22). If we take God's forgiveness, we need to give forgiveness to others – not grudgingly, for the Lord loves a cheerful giver (2 Cor. 9:7).

### An eternity of hope

Can we, as Christians, imagine the sheer relief that John's preaching (and later Jesus' gospel) brought to folk who had for centuries been conditioned to animals being sacrificed on their behalf? Probably not. In fact, we pray the Lord's Prayer so often, we probably don't realize its full impact. Jesus didn't bring merely a ray of hope and new life, but a whole eternity: chance upon chance to 'start over', no matter how low we have fallen: to come boldly (as sons and daughters of the King) to the throne of grace, and to find there grace to help in time of need.

## Promises kept

God has undertaken to keep all his promises – and, if you are inspired to search, there are hundreds of them in the Bible. In today's epistle, Peter homes in on this faithfulness of the Lord: 'in accordance with his promise, we wait for new heavens and a new earth . . . [and] while you are waiting for these things, strive to be found by him at peace, without spot or blemish; and regard the patience of our Lord as salvation (2 Pet. 3:13–15). While we're waiting, we're already saved. How's that for divine encouragement!

## Patience spawns forgiveness

The more we exercise the Holy Spirit's gift of patience, the quicker we shall be to forgive; and the more our forgiveness grows, the more we shall rely on God's forgiveness. This is divine alchemy at work – and, being divine, it does work. Don't waste time bringing logic, reason and commonsense to bear on it: just believe in God's capability.

Our forgiveness of others means cultivating a Jesus-inspired 'forgettery' of injustices once we've forgiven: to forgive but not forget is really not forgiving at all. If God were to work to such rules in his dealings with us, not one of us would make it to eternal life. Our patience will not be forty-second cousin to God's; but the more we tap into our Holy Spirit reserves, the greater our exercise of it will grow. The Lord's patience is phenomenal: it must be, or who would ever be saved? It is his grace, his unmerited favour, that stands between us and spiritual annihilation: GOD-GIVEN GRACE. And let's thank God, this Advent, that it is God-given – for grace is something that the devil cannot get his hands on.

## In prospect

What are we waiting for? Simply (!), Peter tells us, 'new heavens and a new earth'. Next time circumstances try to get you down, or to get your attention off God, remember this glorious prospect. Think of the loveliest flower, the most dramatic sunset, the sight of a shimmering rainbow, the summer dew on the fresh green grass . . . and try to imagine new heavens and a new earth. Lovelier? More dramatic? Surely, for when did God ever lower his standards? But those who will be a part of the new order will be those who have forgiven, and have been forgiven: it's the divinely fair principle of 'give – and take'.

6

## Advent Word-Search

| R | W | A | I | T | I | N | G | K | A | L | O | B | T | P |
|---|---|---|---|---|---|---|---|---|---|---|---|---|---|---|
| P | I | G | G | N | I | H | C | A | E | R | P | S | S | S |
| A | H | V | F | I | E | J | D | N | C | M | I | E | A | A |
| T | E | J | E | A | R | T | H | Q | O | T | Y | V | L | Q |
| I | R | W | K | R | T | P | S | N | P | T | M | E | V | M |
| E | E | H | T | I | J | M | R | A | I | E | R | N | A | L |
| N | V | N | L | A | S | O | B | N | C | O | N | T | T | L |
| C | E | E | B | G | C | E | R | A | P | D | Q | Y | I | K |
| E | S | V | E | F | A | E | R | D | F | R | E | S | O | K |
| C | R | A | B | T | T | G | T | G | A | D | V | E | N | T |
| A | E | E | N | E | I | W | H | S | I | N | Q | V | H | I |
| D | P | H | E | M | M | A | N | U | E | L | R | E | S | J |
| F | O | R | G | I | V | E | N | E | S | S | P | N | F | G |
| J | W | I | L | D | E | R | N | E | S | S | E | O | D | N |
| A | W | B | T | E | C | N | A | T | N | E | P | E | R | C |

| | |
|---|---|
| RIVER JORDAN | PREACHING |
| JOHN THE BAPTIST | PATIENCE |
| ADVENT | EMMANUEL |
| FORGIVENESS | WILDERNESS |
| REPENTANCE | WITNESS |
| HEAVEN | SALVATION |
| EARTH | ETERNITY |
| SEVENTY SEVEN | PERSEVERE |
| WAITING | GRACE |

*(The words hidden in the word-search squares may be read vertically, horizontally, diagonally – forwards and backwards. A letter may be used in more than one word.)*

### Family Service Input

Encourage the young folk to complete the Advent Word-Search. If time permits, expand the various themes.

### Suggested Hymns

Hail to the Lord's anointed; Hills of the north, rejoice; Judge eternal, throned in splendour; The kingdom of God is justice and joy.

## Second Sunday of Advent
*Second Service* **Prescription for Harmony** Ps. 40; 1 Kings 22:1–28; Rom. 15:4–13 [Matt. 11:2–11]

> '*May the God of steadfastness and encouragement grant you to live in harmony with one another, in accordance with Christ Jesus.*' Romans 15:5

### Doubly encouraging

It's a 'belt-and-braces' job of divine encouragement. God himself is the Supreme Encourager – encouragement shines out from all he does and who he is. And he backs up this great attribute 'by the encouragement of the scriptures' (v. 4). After going to such lengths, how it must sadden our Lord, when we slouch (spiritually if not physically) through life like streaks of misery, grumbling and groaning from one crisis to the next. 'Look out! Look up! Look onward!' the Supreme Encourager is urging. It was because people in general had become so gloomily preoccupied by circumstances that the birth of Jesus passed unremarked in a Bethlehem concentrating instead on a Roman census. While the empire that was Rome has long since ceased to exist, the effects of that birth have gone from strength to strength.

### How do we see God?

Well, how do we see God today? As a prop? As an ever-listening ear for our woes? As a provider of what we believe we need? Or as a loving Encourager? Does he thrill us, cheer us, inspire us, embolden us, to turn the world (or even parts of it) upside down for Jesus? In return for all he gives us, are we encouraging him, by giving him joy, our brightest time, the best of our time and talents? Do we share our pleasures as well as our pains with him? An earthly father would soon feel hurt if all his children could give him were moans and groans. Advent may come at a time of the year when the days are short and the sunshine at a premium, but our capacity to be encouraged and to encourage should continue unabated.

## Scriptural encouragement

The encouragement of scripture is one of God's most precious gifts. Men like William Tyndale have lost their lives to give us God's word in our mother tongue. Many Christians – for example, in remote areas of China – who find access to printed scriptures difficult, have been given grace to commit whole books of the Bible to memory. The more we have of God's word, the more encouragement we are packing under our belt. Once there, we can use it, or let it lie dormant. The choice is ours, but surely only a moron would look such encouragement in the eye, and say, 'Thanks, but no thanks.'

## Passing it on

Passing on the encouragement of God – by word of mouth or example – is vital. We often think of Eliphaz, Bildad and Zophar as pretty gloomy 'comforters' of Job; yet even Bildad had some words of encouragement. 'Your words', he told the suffering Job, 'have supported those who were stumbling' (Job 4:4). Can anyone say the same of our words of encouragement? 'Your words have kept men on their feet.' What a wonderful affirmation of another's worth! The more we can pass on the encouragement of scriptures to others, the more it will grow. Make no mistake: many, many people outside the Church (and not a few inside) are hungry for what scripture has to say on the great issues of the day: on life, death, the Hereafter; on sin, sickness and tragedy; on joy – and particularly what it is, and how to get it and how to keep it. Folk don't necessarily want to come to church each Sunday for this encouragement; but mention you're starting a 'Praise and Prayer Group', or similar, in your front room on a Wednesday morning – and they'll be there.

'If the mountain won't come to Mahomet . . .'

## Making a difference

Christians are getting ready to celebrate Christ's Nativity. The rest of the world is preparing for a vacation. If we will, we can make a difference in the disproportionate ratio. If we will, we have what it takes (what God has provided) to make not only all the difference in the world – but also in the next – for someone.

## Suggested Hymns

How firm a foundation; Love divine, all loves excelling; O God, our help in ages past; The Lord will come and not be slow.

## Third Sunday of Advent   11 December
*Principal Service*   **What Do You Say?** Isa. 61:1–4, 8–11; Ps. 126 or Canticle: Magnificat; 1 Thess. 5:16–24; John 1:6–8, 19–28

> *'Then [the priests and levites] said to [John], "Who are you? . . . What do you say about yourself?"' John 1:22*

## A popular subject

It's generally recognized – human nature being the egocentric animal it is – that the most popular talking-point is ourselves. The recipient doesn't need to be a psychiatrist or doctor; we can usually wax eloquent on the subject to whoever is on the receiving end. John the Baptist was given a golden opportunity to bolster his image, to make a name for himself in the annals of prophecy. He convincingly declined the offer, and instead pointed the questioners away from himself, and to Jesus. (As history has shown, John's humility and self-effacement nevertheless ensured him an honoured place in prophetic annals, and worldwide fame.)

## The Forerunner

John's title, his mission, and he himself – all were unique. It's hardly surprising that this very individuality surprised and wrong-footed many of his questioners. There had been prophets before – men of God, who lived as ascetically as John; men who proclaimed the uncompromised word of God; men who indeed also had looked ahead to the Messiah. But John was different. From his birth – miraculous, in that he was born to elderly parents – his mission had been foretold: 'You, Child, will be called the prophet of the Most High; for you will go before the Lord to prepare his ways.' So had declared the old priest Zechariah, when the miraculous conception had progressed to birth and circumcision (Luke 1:76).

## Today's prophets

Do we look askance at some of the prophets of today? No, because prophecy as it had been understood for centuries of pre-Messiahship passed away with John. The Messiah has come, has conquered, and has left an apostleship – a discipleship – which we have inherited. As the gospel spreads ever further with an ever-increasing apostleship, there will be a variety of styles, of presentation and witness. It would be ingenuous to expect or demand complete uniformity either between denominations or even in particular denominations. If we feel the word of God is being compromised, we should speak out. But if another disciple is actually furthering the work of God, who are we to criticize if his methods differ from our own? The first apostles made this mistake with a 'different' disciple, only to be told by Jesus: 'Do not stop him, for no one who does a deed of power in my name will be able soon afterwards to speak evil of me. Whoever is not against us, is for us' (Mark 9:39). Those who bolster their own ego, will very quickly be seen for the imposters they are. We shall know them by their works.

## Identity in lights

The more we concentrate on Jesus, the less concerned we shall become about getting our name up in lights. God himself is light, and in him is no darkness at all. There is no neon sign made that can come anywhere near the pure light of God's word. Are we shining the Bible-beams of light as far and as fast as we can? If we pray God for more opportunities to extend this illumination, we must be prepared for the Lord to take us seriously: even 'scatter-shot' prayers find a mark with the ever-listening, ever-encouraging Almighty.

## Serious praying

'Pray without ceasing', Paul commands, in today's epistle (1 Thess. 5:17). That's seriously committing. Can we go so far? Do we care about anything enough? Do we, for instance, care that while we've been attending worship today, hundreds, maybe thousands, across the world have been dying without knowledge of Jesus? It may take our spiritual breath away – but the sheer divine power of prayer means that IF WE CARE, we can lift even these – unknown in name, creed, culture or colour – to God.

And the time starts now.

### Family Service Input

Encourage the young folk to make a collage of news items from around the world, to use as a prayer focus in the coming weeks.

### Suggested Hymns

Be thou my vision; Jesus shall reign where'er the sun; On Jordan's bank; Tell out, my soul, the greatness of the Lord.

# Third Sunday of Advent
*Second Service*   **Perfect Peace** Ps. 68:1–8, [9–19]; Mal. 3:1—4; 4; Phil. 4:4–7 [Matt. 14:1–12]

> *'And the peace of God, which surpasses all understanding, will guard your hearts and your minds in Christ Jesus.'*
> *Philippians 4:7*

## God of contrast

Yet God is not all peace! Malachi tells us 'he is like a refiner's fire and like fullers' soap' (Mal. 3:2). He comes to burn what is combustible; to refine what is his by annihilating what is Satan's; and to emerge with prime quality material white and 'glistering' (to borrow the lovely AV word, see 1 Chron. 29:2; Job 20:25; Luke 9:29), as befits eternity with God. He will perform all this, while at the same time offering a peace that cannot be understood, but which enables a human by faith to take heart in even the most troubling situations. It is God at his most awesome, yet the God who could (as we are soon to celebrate) mask his divinity and be born as a child: God at his most exciting and encouraging – and God who must surely wonder at the hard-heartedness and apathy that can turn away deluded by lesser things.

## Cardiac protection

The media tell us that cardiac disease of one sort or another is the world's greatest killer. The reasons given range from stress and obesity, to poverty and heredity, with innumerable peripheral factors thrown in for good measure. But Paul tells us in all seriousness that God is offering us the ultimate antidote – yes, a spiritual antidote, but one that has also direct and substantial physical benefits: his peace, to guard our hearts and our minds – a peace that is Jesus. If we have Jesus (as Spirit) in our hearts, his name on our lips, and his resurrection power in our lives, the inference is that we shall not be wearing out any doctor's surgery mat. The peace of God will percolate right through our bodies; and while we shall not be impervious (in a stoical, unfeeling sense) to any situation, its deleterious effects will not harm us. It's often poorly perceived by the Church, how closely we are being watched and analysed by non-believers: the more we have of God's peace, the more cause we shall give these questioners and categorizers food for thought.

## How is it?

How is it (they wonder) that Christians are not floored by anxiety that lays non-believers low? How is it that Christians can stand by a grave and really believe the parting is only temporary? How is it that the Church, with seemingly little support, keeps going? How is it that wherever the Bible spreads, many things change for the better? How is it that people pray, and great things happen? How is it that miracles – which surely 'went out of fashion' 2,000 years ago – are happening today in those parts of the world where Jesus is being preached? How is it . . . ? Let us never underestimate the impact that Christians – from a handful worshipping in a tiny village church, to thousands gathered at an open-air convention somewhere in Africa – are having on the rest of the world. From very small examples to mega-events, we are spreading the precious peace of God. And, since it's so wonderful it passes a Christian's understanding, a non-believer isn't going to grasp its full import, either. But our 'entrance exam' for eternity doesn't require a 250,000-word thesis on God's peace. We shall either have it, or not. We shall have either used it in this life, or not. We shall have shared it with others, or . . .

## When Peace came down

God's Peace came down at Christmas. Cradled in a manger, it shone – it 'glistered' – in a world darkened by unbelief, disbelief, non-belief and ignorance. It will come again this Christmas, to a world not quite so dark – a world lightened already by 2,000 years of the slow but sure spread of God's peace; but to a world still desperately in need of more.

### *Suggested Hymns*

I'll praise my Maker while I've breath; Peace, perfect peace, in this dark world of sin; Shepherd divine, our wants relieve; Spirit divine, attend our prayers.

## Fourth Sunday of Advent   18 December
*Principal Service*   **The Long-term View** 2 Sam. 7:1–11,16; Canticle: Magnificat or Ps. 89:1–4, 19–26; Rom. 16:25–27; Luke 1:26–38

> *'He will be great, and will be called the Son of the Most High, and the Lord God will give to him the throne of his ancestor David. He will reign over the house of Jacob for ever, and of his kingdom there will be no end.' Luke 1:32–33*

### Extraordinary news

A nine-month pregnancy, as normal – but with eternity in view! This young virgin is to bear the ruler of an everlasting kingdom. What must Mary have felt, as she hurried over the hills to share her news with Elizabeth! How her thoughts must have raced: 'the throne of David' – would Jerusalem, then, go on, 'for ever'?

We know, as the Gospels unfold, that Gabriel was talking of no earthly kingdom – not even of an unending heavenly kingdom, as may have been supposed – for there will be 'a new heaven and a new earth' (Rev. 21:1). The new order began, in what seemed a most inauspicious way, in a Bethlehem stable; and, once started, it cannot stop. God has promised, and he cannot be untrue to himself.

## Rethinking the monarchy

But the Jews found it all but impossible to rethink the Jerusalem monarchy. David had been a very human, very earthly, ruler: by no means perfect, but a king to whom people could relate and behind whom they could stand. His pugilistic enthusiasm had reclaimed land and extended new boundaries, making possible the so-called 'Golden Age' of Solomon. Inevitably, the people hankered after such material peace and prosperity. Yet the child to be born of a virgin was a greater King, a greater Man – for he was God.

## Our Christmas understanding

At Christmas, we relate to a baby in a manger with little difficulty, for a child is something familiar and uncomplicated. And God is inviting us to come as children to relate to our Brother. But this Christmas is not the birth of Jesus: it's a commemoration of the birth. Two millennia have rolled along in between, and history cannot be erased. We come, in awe and wonder, to celebrate a birth – but we also know the child as Lord, Redeemer, King and Saviour. And this extra knowledge, the realization of who Christ is and what he has done and all that he means in our lives, makes this 'birthday' so special, so much more than the celebration of a little child: it's a new birth, certainly – but the new birth of an everlasting king of an eternal kingdom.

Can we take all that in? No. But, as we draw close to the child at the centre of it all, we can pray that he will increase our understanding. We can pray that more of his limitless love will be translated into our hearts and transformed into service, witness and sharing. We can pray that those for whom Christmas does not include Christ, will be brought to a knowledge of this love – and, if we are brave enough, we can pray that God will use us in that work.

## For Mary, Mother of our Lord

And, on this last Sunday before the great day, can we not pray for Mary, whose 'fiat' made possible the unique birth. God would have initiated the saving of the world by some other means, had Mary not accepted the challenge. But she who 'had found favour with God' used that grace in his service. If God calls us to some work which we feel is too great (or too small), and we pass up the opportunity, he will get the work accomplished by someone else – but it will not be quite the same, because he had originally designed it for us, and us for it. With Mary's courageous 'fiat' in our focus today, can we pray for a greater spiritual awareness of what God may be saying, doing, asking in our lives?

## My gospel

God is 'able to strengthen you', Paul told the Romans, in today's epistle, 'according to MY GOSPEL' (Rom. 16:25). The gospel of Jesus is so personal, because it is delivered by our Lord himself, and in the mouths and hearts and lives of his followers. He is MY Saviour, MY Lord – and the responsibility of proclaiming the good news is MINE.

### Family Service Input

Encourage the young people to share the pre-Christmas news items from the current press, and to discuss how the Church and parish may become involved.

### Suggested Hymns

At the name of Jesus; Hark! the glad sound; O come, O come, Emmanuel; To the name of our salvation.

## Fourth Sunday of Advent
### Second Service   Coming to Dwell Ps. 113 [131];
Zech. 2:10–13; Luke 1:39–55

> 'Sing and rejoice, O daughter Zion! For lo, I will come and dwell in your midst, says the Lord. Many nations shall join themselves to the Lord on that day . . .' Zechariah. 2:10–11a

## Only the shepherds

And on the day that Jesus came to dwell with us, only the shepherds took notice of the singing and rejoicing of the angels. By contrast, much of today's world celebrates Christmas, though many of the celebrants still don't acknowledge Christ. The Lord came, not on a fleeting visit, but to dwell, to abide with us. Even when he returned to glory, he sent his Holy Spirit to continue the abiding, in those who will receive him.

> *Not a brief glance, I beg, a passing word,*
> *But as thou dwell'st with thy disciples, Lord;*
> *Familiar, condescending, patient, free,*
> *Come not to sojourn, but abide with me.*
>
> *Come not in terrors, as the King of kings,*
> *But kind and good, with healing in thy wings;*
> *Tears for all woes, a heart for every plea;*
> *Come, Friend of sinners, thus abide with me.*
> (Henry Francis Lyte)

Unostentatiously, unannounced except to the shepherds, the Saviour arrived: the Saviour of the world. It was no new concept; the prophets had foretold the evangelization of the world (e.g. Isa. 52:15; Jer. 1:5; Ezek. 26:3), even before Zechariah. The Jews had treasured the old scriptures for centuries – and it was to the Jews that Jesus came, honouring the divine promise of ages past. The tragedy was, that this 'chosen people' not only refused to accept the implementation of international salvation when it came knocking on their door, but also for the most part refused to acknowledge the person of the Saviour in their midst. What more could God do?

## And still today

And it is still the case today – when, for example, miracles happen: the sick are healed, the dead are raised. Does it make worldwide news? No, the headlines are those to which the *Heavenly Mercury* or the *Eternal Telegraph* would never give space. God is working in the world today with the same power, the same zeal, as ever – and humanity bends over backwards in an effort not to see, or to explain away the divine operations. If Jesus came to earth again, who would heed the angels' rejoicing? Well, he is coming, in a few days' time – and millions of people will doubtless manage to celebrate Christmas without Christ.

## But we shall come!

But for millions more – ourselves included – it will be a Christian celebration: a time of joy, when for a while the pressures of daily life can be put aside. There is, for us, an 'otherness' about Christmas. Much of the business of the world takes a break (for whatever reason), and the overall 'hum' of commerce sinks to a whisper. We forget the Footsie, the Dow Jones and the Hang Seng; most of us don't even miss the daily updates of the currency markets. As the world calms down, then, can we not do all that is possible to fill the airwaves with the great 'News of the Day'?

No – for that is not how it was, 2,000 years ago. It's in the mystery, not the megaphonic blast, of Christmas, that lies its message: God coming in a whisper, with the greatest news of all time. It is so, throughout the Christian story. The Almighty could have ushered in our Saviour with shattering, multi-cosmic force; he could compel people to believe; he could exterminate all opposition to the gospel message . . .

He could.

God is able.

But he chooses to give us the freedom of choice. And we, this Christmas, will not compel anyone to believe. But God, through us, may choose to work a miracle in someone's life . . .

. . . Providing we don't get in his way.

### Suggested Hymns

Behold, the mountain of the Lord; Jesus, the name high over all; Long ago, prophets knew; The Lord will come, and not be slow.

## Christmas Eve  24 December
*Morning Eucharist*  **God's Tender Mercy** 2 Sam. 7:1–5, 8–11, 16; Ps. 89:2, 19–27; Acts 13:16–26; Luke 1:67–79

> *'By the tender mercy of our God the dawn from on high will break upon us, to give light to those who sit in darkness and in*

18

*the shadow of death, to guide our feet into the way of peace.'*
*Luke 1:78–79*

## Light out of darkness

Those who did not believe they were in darkness were the ones who also chose not to see the light that God was bringing. And those who could not accept that they were on unsteady ground, would not accept either the guidance of God into the way of peace. It is not our perceived need that is necessarily the most important, but God's recognition of our real need, and his answer to the problem. We have been brought to this Christmas because in some way, in the will of God, we need it; at some point over this season, if we are spiritually alert, God will show us the how and the why; it may be more light for our own way to God, or it may be an enlightening of something that we can do to help another's life. Christmas is not only for the children, the homeless, the visitor within our home or church: it's for everyone. Jesus comes – as he came to Bethlehem – for all, bringing 'good news of great joy for ALL the people' (Luke 2:10).

## Divine light

Physical darkness comes down early at Christmas, even though the daylight has already begun to lengthen towards spring. But the divine light of the Christmas Jesus shines on, through night and day, year in year out. It can never be extinguished. Even at Calvary, when Satan believed that he had annihilated the light, it came back and shone with resurrection brilliance three days later. And once it has shone into our lives, we have it for evermore. At Bethlehem, the light came so quietly and unobtrusively, so mysteriously, that the angels needed to lighten the night sky to make the news known – not to the grandees in the temple at Jerusalem, but to shepherds on duty guarding their flocks. The Good Shepherd – as was perhaps most natural – had other shepherds as his first visitors, the sound of sheep as his earliest lullaby.

## As a shepherd

He came quietly to earth, as a shepherd quietly and without fuss meets up with his flock. And the light he brought was great enough to push back and overcome the world's darkness.

And that's a lot of darkness.

We may look at little Bethlehem – which has since been in the news so often because of war and terror, rather than peace and joy – and wonder why God chose that particular place. An elderly Chinese pastor was asked, some years ago: 'What do you think would have happened, if Christ had been born in Beijing instead of Bethlehem?' And he replied, sadly: 'I believe we would have thought the news so precious, we'd have kept it to ourselves.' God was not willing for the Christmas news to be contained in Bethlehem. We don't know how, but the Magi in their far-off countries had heard – and they became, so far as we can tell from the Bible record, the first Gentiles to celebrate the birth of Jesus.

### Tender loving care

Just a few short hours away from Christmas Day, can we reflect on God's tender loving care – his gracious mercy – that made it all possible. We know that humanity had veered off the track, and that the world needed the correction and guidance of a Saviour. But this is Christmas: let's focus on the sheer love that could leave glory to accomplish the work; love that forewent power and freedom, to take on the confines of physical form and earthly limitations. It was the best event in this world since creation – and worth the best celebration we can make!

### *Suggested Hymns*

Behold, the mountain of the Lord; Hark! a thrilling voice is sounding; Hark! the glad sound, the Saviour comes; Sleepers, wake! the watchcry pealeth.

## Christmas Day   25 December
*Midnight or early Eucharist*   **God's Gift** Isa. 52:7–10; Ps. 98; Hab. 1:1–4 [5–12]; John 1:1–14

> *'But to all who received him, who believed in his name, he gave power to become children of God; who were born, not of blood or of the will of the flesh or of the will of men, but of God.' John 1:12–13*

## A time for giving

A birthday is a time for giving. We take, or send, presents to the person whose special day it is, but, if we are honest, we realize that in the baby, young person or adult, we have a much greater gift than the item we've so carefully wrapped up in tinsel and coloured paper. Friendship – yes, we thank the Lord for that. Kinship – that, too, is something precious, to be cherished. But, above all else – even though we may not put it into words – are we not saying with our present, that we value the gift of LIFE, whether it's a new, young life, or a life full of years and shared memories?

## Life to and for the world

And so it is with Christmas. Life in Jesus has come into the world. Life of the Saviour has come for the world. Life in a tiny child, which will never be snuffed out. The wonder of Christmas is that all of that can be held in a young mother's arms. We come to worship this baby, with our presents of love, of time, talents, dedication and commitment; our sorrow for what we have done wrong, our prayers for God's forgiveness; and our intentions to lead a better, more Christ-centred life in the future.

These are our gifts; the very best that we can offer; and our Lord will honour them because they are given with love.

But, just look at what we receive from him! Free and full salvation, the fruit of his Spirit (love, joy, peace . . . ) and LIFE – real, everlasting life! God, in his magnificent unfairness, has tipped the scales heavily in our favour!

## Generosity abounding

It's generosity on a divine scale, and it increases the more we put God's gifts to work. We tell each other that 'Christmas is a time for giving' – and so it is. But let's not forget that God gives the most, every time. Jesus came to give – and he is still giving. That's not to say that he doesn't like to receive – he is gracious in the reception of all that we bring for him. We need to reflect that today is also Christmas in heaven. If the angels set the heavens ringing with joy one night 2,000 years ago, we may be sure the bells of heaven are sounding loud and clear today, as millions of Christians send the message round the world: 'Christ is born today!' And every time a Christian lifts up his heart and voice in Christmas joy, won't our Saviour smile and believe his incarnation was worth the effort?

## Divine power

One of the precious gifts of the Christmas Jesus is power (John 1:12); power to become sons and daughters of God; power to inherit eternity, as the heirs of the King; power to 'progress' from being servants to friends – friends of the child who looks out at us today from the manger. We may choose not to use this power – but if we are to fulfil our calling, we should use it to the full. It means we can meet, and defeat, Satan. It means that we shall be tested, but we shall win through. It means that we can walk tall in the name of Jesus, and fear nothing and no one.

There is a caveat: this power is available only to those who believe in Jesus. Would our churches be full if it was made an indictable offence to hold Christian beliefs? Or would the courts be derelict for lack of evidence? How deep, how genuine, is our faith? Christmas, when the Christ-child is giving us so much, is a good time to come clean about our own commitment. Whatever we bring to the little child today, he is looking out most for true heart-worship.

Can we pray for grace to give our Lord the best Christmas present of our lives?

### *Suggested Hymns*

Angels from the realms of glory; Hark! the herald-angels sing; It came upon the midnight clear; O come, all ye faithful.

# Christmas Day   25 December
## *In the Day: Principal Service*   **Don't Be Afraid!**
Isa. 9:2–7; Ps. 96; Titus 2:11–14; Luke 2:1–14 [15–20]

> 'But the angel said to [the shepherds], "Do not be afraid, for see – I am bringing you good news of great joy for all the people: to you is born this day in the city of David a Saviour, who is the Messiah, the Lord."' Luke 2:10–11

## All joy

We don't associate fear with Christmas. To us, the story is all joy – but then, we know it so well; and we know what it led to, and how Jesus is still at work in our lives. To the shepherds, everything was new and strange – and wonderful. We mustn't let our familiarity with the event deprive us of our wonder. To have the heavens carolling in joy, and angels lighting up the night sky, would be to experience orchestration and pyrotechnics on such a scale that the shepherds would have been superhuman not to have been afraid. But God knew the antidote to fear: quickly the angel gave the men something practical to do – he sent them into Bethlehem to find the cause of the jubilation. We're not told how long they searched, but they were successful! We can surely imagine that if they had needed to ask at every house, they would not have given up until they found Jesus.

## Our own search

How diligent has been our search for the Saviour this Christmas? Have we looked for him in the worried, the unemployed, the homeless, the undernourished, the lonely? Or, have we waited for him to come to us, as a model-child on a bed of straw, with candles and crib and carols? The shepherds had to go and find him; later, the Magi travelled many miles to visit him . . .

## The Christ of Christmas

We keep alive the age-old story, with the child in the manger. But the Christ of Christmas is much more surely and vibrantly in our hearts. How he shines out from there, with light so powerful it can illuminate every soul on earth (and in heaven), is up to us. The more we show the Christmas Christ to others, the more the Christmas angels will sing and shine.

'Christ for the world!' we sing, and may God cause us to mean it. In prayer this Christmas, we can encompass the globe, lifting up fellow-believers and non-believers alike. Someone, half a world away, may suddenly be aware that God is moving in their lives, pleading with them to break with drugs, to abandon crime, to set priorities straight that have become skewed . . . they may never know why, yet someone, somewhere, has been lifting them in prayer to God. And, as a soul is brought to the Lord, angels across the halls of heaven sing in jubilation.

Wouldn't you love to be the one responsible for that heavenly joy?

## The Christmas present

We bring our gifts – Christ gives us himself – all his power, love, mercy, grace, compassion, energy and commitment, not to use for ourselves but for others. Thirty or so years on from the nativity, this same Christmas Christ is to gather his friends, and a multitude of onlookers, around him on a mountain slope; and he is going to tell them, with serious conviction: 'Don't worry about what you'll eat, or drink, or wear. Your heavenly Father knows all you need. You just concentrate on the kingdom of heaven, and God will take care of you' (see Matt. 6:31f.). One cannot have a kingdom without subjects – and it's our God-given work to help the population figures of God's kingdom rise.

Christmas is a wonderful time for evangelizing, as we explain the reason for the season – and leave the outcome prayerfully with God.

Who knows how many more folk the shepherds told, that night and thereafter? Who knows if one or more of those men (or their children) were in Jerusalem thirty-odd years later, when after a weekend of uncertainty and confusion, the Christmas Christ became the Easter Jesus?

Who knows the harvest that may come from the seeds we sow this Christmas?

### Suggested Hymns

A Child this day is born; Christians, awake!; What Child is this?; While shepherds watched.

# Christmas Day
*Second Service* **The Jesus Blueprint** Ps. 8; Isa. 65:17–25; Phil. 2:5–11 or Luke 2:1–20

> *'Let the same mind be in you that was in Christ Jesus, who, though he was in the form of God, did not regard equality with God as something to be exploited, but emptied himself, taking the form of a slave, being born in human likeness.'*
> *Philippians 2:5–7*

## Found like Christ

This is our blueprint: to have the mind of Jesus – thinking, praying, speaking and acting like him. It's a tall order (even at Christmas, bolstered up as we are by the joy and wonder of it all), but God would not have called, chosen and commissioned us unless he thought we could rise – in the strength of Jesus – to the occasion. The advantage is, *inter alia*, while we are concentrating on being like Jesus, we don't have too much time to listen to Satan – which is infuriating for the devil, but let's lose no sleep over that.

## Peter & Co

The firm of Peter & Co., with 12 stalwarts on its books (though one proved a broken reed), struggled with this challenge for the three years or so of Jesus' ministry. They were constantly being wrong-footed, forever worrying about each new (or imagined) development, time after time saying the wrong thing . . .

Not, one would think, learning to be like Jesus very effectively. Yet, come the resurrection, they began to make real progress; and after the ascension and the empowering of the Holy Spirit at Pentecost, those men were so like Jesus, that folk noticed (Acts 4:13). Their spiritual laryngitis had changed into holy boldness, their fear into supercharged faith.

## What Jesus continues to say

Jesus continues to encourage us today – yes, even at Christmas: ESPECIALLY at Christmas. Meeting us with the single-minded innocence and straightforwardness of a child, he says with wonderful simplicity, 'Be like me. Your hands are mine, to help others; your tongue is mine, to speak my words; your heart is mine, to show my love. Grow more like me every day, and you will then make my Christmas in another's heart each day.'

Could we give Jesus a better birthday gift than this?

> *We'll bring him hearts that love him,*
> *We'll bring him thankful praise,*
> *And young souls meekly striving*
> *To walk in holy ways.*
>
> (Anon.)

At Christmas, even to so-called 'grown-ups' sing children's songs with gusto. If at any time this disturbs us, may we recall the twentieth-century German theologian, Karl Barth. Eminent professor as he was, one day he was asked what he considered the most profound truth in the Christian faith. The great man thought for a moment, and then replied:

> *'Jesus loves me, this I know –*
> *for the Bible tells me so.'*

With the uncomplicatedness of a child, Jesus grew up proclaiming the simple truth: love as you want to be loved; forgive as you want to be forgiven. Put God first, and self last – and everything else will fall into place.

Simple? Yes. Too simple? Yes – for many it has proved too simple by far. The birth in a stable was so simple that most people took no notice. By contrast, the resurrection was so remarkable, most people didn't believe it.

## The same today

It's the same today; we shall leave this Christmas service and return to a world that is still outside the Church in a long-standing alliance of apathy and non-belief. And surely the best present we can give to our Christmas Lord, is to show the apathetic, non-believing masses that we care about them in Christ's name.

Our commission is as clear as ever it was: we make it as complicated as we choose.

## *Suggested Hymns*

Ding dong, merrily on high; Go, tell it on the mountains; O, little town of Bethlehem; The first nowell.

## Second Sunday of Christmas (or, The Naming and Circumcision of Jesus, q.v.)   1 January 2006
*Principal Service*   **Treasured Words** Isa. 61:10—62:3; Ps. 148; Gal. 4:4–7; Luke 2:15–21

> *'When [the shepherds] saw this, they made known what had been told them about the child; and all who heard it were amazed at what the shepherds told them. But Mary treasured all these words and pondered them in her heart.'* Luke 2:17–19

### All who heard

The inference is either that the shepherds had collected some reinforcements in their search for the Holy Family, or that by the time they reached the place others had already gathered there. At any rate, it would seem they had quite an audience, as they recounted the heavenly vision. Was it news to Mary, that she had given birth to 'a Saviour, who is the Messiah, the Lord' (v. 11)? Nine months before, what had Gabriel told her? 'You will name him Jesus. He will be great, and will be called the Son of the Most High, and the Lord God will give to him the throne of his ancestor David. He will reign over the house of Jacob for ever, and of his kingdom there will be no end . . . he will be holy; he will be called Son of God' (Luke 1:32–35). Gradually the picture of the child she had borne was being made clearer to Mary, as God through his angels gave her more information; and, predictably enough, Luke tells us how Mary treasured this information, pondering it, memorizing it, and storing it carefully and lovingly in her heart.

That her treasuring bore rich spiritual fruit, is seen in her confidence 30 years later, at the wedding-feast in Cana. When Jesus at first refused to be drawn into solving the problem of no wine, Mary calmly overrode his protestation, and ordered the servants to do whatever her Son required (John 2:5)! Almost certainly she would not at the Nativity have appreciated their full import – but she had mulled over, and prayed over, the words of the angels, trusting that God would make known to her their meaning in his good time.

### Waiting on God

'Waiting on God' is an expression not too frequently heard nowadays. So often we like to be 'up and running' with God's work

27

# Christmas Crossword

each day. But there are times when the old Roman proverb '*festina lente*' ('hurry slowly') is more apposite. Were we sure we heard God aright? Did we mess up his message? Wouldn't it, with hindsight, have been better to 'pray through' what he was telling us? Many a time that wonderful gift of hindsight will indicate that 'hurrying slowly' would have meant a much better job being done.

Probably we're all keyed-up still, in the Christmas festivities, and the days are passing by at a rate of knots. Can we, however, take time out to catch up with what God is trying to tell us? On any reading of the Gospels, Jesus was never in a frantic hurry to do or say anything. To go calmly and with spiritual poise and equilibrium through each day, a Christian needs to focus on Jesus' modus operandi. And surely Mary, as she looked at the precious child in

## Clues Across

1. . . . . . . in excelsis Deo! (6)
4. Simpler. (6)
7. Convent sister. (3)
8. Herod. (4)
9. Hours and minutes. (4)
10. Increase. (3)
12. View. (3)
13. Gabriel. (5)
15. Christmas food. (5)
17. It unlocks. (3)
19. Not well. (3)
20. Christmas evergreen. (3)
22. The Lord's day. (6)
23. Need for drink. (6)
26. Seventh letter of Greek alphabet. (3)
28. Feel 9 across. (3)
29. Much . . . about nothing. (3)
30. Silent Night. (5)
31. Try hard. (5)
32. Found in some crackers. (3)
34. Before. (3)
36. Land measure. (4)
37. Declared. (4)
39. Cereal grain. (3)
40. They tend the sick. (6)
41. When turkey's eaten. (6)

## Clues Down

1. Gift of wise men. (4)
2. A mighty tree. (3)
3. Angels are this! (7)
4. Deserve. (7)
5. Skate on it. (3)
6. White Christmas flower. (4)
11. Dec. 25th, Christmas . . . (3)
12. Pigs' home. (3)
14. Mightier. (7)
16. Encourage. (7)
18. Praise. (5)
21. Made simpler. (5)
24. Stumbles. (7)
25. . . . . . . . Virgin Mary. (7)
27. Pretend. (3)
29. Consumed. (3)
33. So be it. (4)
35. The lion's voice. (4)
36. We breathe it. (3)
38. One of the Israelite tribes. (3)

*See page 31 for solution*

---

her arms, would realize that the census-packed Bethlehem, the long search for a room and the scratch accommodation to which it had led, had together not been able to halt the purposes of God. But even her lessons were not learned overnight: when Jesus was twelve, and had been taken to Jerusalem for his bar mitzvah, he stayed behind in the temple. At the end of three days' anxious searching, Mary's patience had worn thin – but Jesus, with calm spiritual poise gently chided her: 'Didn't you know that I must be in my Father's house?' (Luke 2:49).

As another modern Christmas tries to catch us in its rush, can we not draw aside for extra time to have communion with our Father, and in so doing follow surely the best of examples?

### Family Service Input

Encourage the young folk to work on the Christmas crossword, involving the more mature members as necessary.

### Suggested Hymns

Father God, I wonder how I managed to exist; Love came down at Christmas; Once in royal David's city; Thou didst leave thy throne.

## Second Sunday of Christmas
### Second Service    Divine Strength Ps. 132; Isa. 35; Col. 1:9–20 or Luke 2:41–52

> *'May you be made strong with all the strength that comes from [the Lord's] glorious power, and may you be prepared to endure everything with patience, while joyfully giving thanks to the Father.' Colossians 1:11–12a*

### God's sort is best

There is strength, and strength. There's the sort that we call brute force, which storms through everything, often leaving a trail of devastation in its wake. And there's God's sort, which enables us to exercise not only patience in everything, but joyful gratitude as well. It's the sort of strength that baffles Satan, who can cope better with the other sort that creates havoc. So who would settle for less than the best? Well, very often, a lot of people – for Satan's not the only fellow who finds God's strength hard to understand. Because it doesn't seem sufficiently 'macho', we decide that a bit of brute force is needed to supply the lack – and too often end up worse off than before. It was the quiet strength of God that gave Jesus courage to go forward to his passion 'for the sake of the joy that was set before him' (Heb. 12:2) – the joy not only of what he knew would come once the passion was over, but also a deep satisfaction that he was presently in the will of God.

### Overriding our circumstances

This divine strength doesn't invariably change circumstances, but it overrides them. We are not the servants of our situations, but their masters. The anxiety may be there, the pain may be awful, the misunderstanding and misrepresentation may hurt us dreadfully, but with God's strength inside us, we know that even these trials will pass. With God's assurance of that 'way out' (1 Cor. 10:13), we know our testing is only temporary.

## Joy infused

Nehemiah, under God, accomplished the rebuilding of the Jerusalem walls (a mammoth task, and fraught with enemy opposition and intrigue) on the premiss that 'the joy of the Lord is [our] strength' (Neh. 8:10). And our winning through depends no less on this joy being infused to such a degree that our strength may abound. If we soldier on in stoical indifference, where's the joy? We shall merely be sapping ourselves of the strength on divine offer. Take the cheering words of Richard Rolle to heart, on this New Year's Day:

> *Praised be you, my king,*
> *And thanked be you, my king,*
> *And blessed be you, my king,*
> *Jesu, all my joying,*
> *Of all your gifts most good;*
> *Who for me spilled your blood,*
> *And died upon the rood;*
> *Now give me grace to sing*
> *The song of your praising.*
>
> ('Jesu my Joying',
> from *The Form of Living*, 7)

---

**Solution**

Across: 1. Gloria. 4. Easier. 7. Nun. 8. King. 9. Time. 10. Add. 12. See. 13. Angel. 15. Treat. 17. Key. 19. Ill. 20. Yew. 22. Sunday. 23. Thirst. 26. Eta. 28. Ail. 29. Ado. 30. Carol. 31. Event. 32. Hat. 34. Ere. 36. Acre. 37. Said. 39. Rye. 40. Nurses. 41. Dinner.

Down: 1. Gold. 2. Oak. 3. Angelic. 4. Entitle. 5. Ice. 6. Rose. 11. Day. 12. Sty. 14. Greater. 16. Enthuse. 18. Exult. 21. Eased. 24. Falters. 25. Blessed. 27. Act. 29. Ate. 33. Amen. 35. Roar. 36. Air. 38. Dan.

## A large helping

God is the most generous giver of all: Paul tells his friends, they can 'be made strong with ALL the strength that comes from [the Lord's] glorious power' (Col. 1:11). Do we know how much strength this is? Well, for starters, it knows how to break out of a tomb; to heal any sickness and any disease; to command the forces of nature . . . Just for starters.

We cannot 'out-ask' God. If we pray for strength, let's have a fair idea of what we're asking for, and what may happen. Dare we risk it? Come on, let's be brave! God knows we need his strength, or Satan will have us for dinner.

## A new year

We need the Lord's strength, not only to face this new year, but to make of it the very best we can for Jesus; to share his gospel with more folk than ever before; to give more time for God's work; to use more of the talents he has given us to greater effect in his service . . . Yes, we need his strength, or our good resolutions will drop into the mists of time before the ink is dry.

## *Suggested Hymns*

Angels from the realms of glory; In the bleak midwinter; Give me oil in my lamp; Strengthen for service, Lord, the hands.

# Baptism of Christ (First Sunday of Epiphany)
## 8 January
### *Principal Service*   The Importance of Baptism
Gen. 1:1–5; Ps. 29; Acts 19:1–7; Mark 1:4–11

> *'John the Baptizer appeared in the wilderness, proclaiming a baptism of repentance for the forgiveness of sins . . . In those days, Jesus came from Nazareth of Galilee, and was baptized by John in the Jordan.' Mark 1:4, 9*

## Sign of repentance?

John had been preaching that baptism was a visible sign of repentance – and men and women certainly needed that. But Jesus, the Sinless One, surely had no such need? Yet he insisted that John should baptize him, publicly. He humbled himself, putting his sinless self in our sinful stead. Anything that was required of humankind, to bring humanity into an 'at-one-ment' with God, Jesus would undergo, so that at no time it could be said that God required of us what he had not required of Jesus, or that Jesus did not/does not touch our life-experience at every point. He had come to share our lives, and if that included baptism, he would be baptized. For him, it was not a sign of repentance – he had committed no sin – but a sign of alignment with our physical and spiritual condition.

## The two baptisms

Two baptisms were required of Christians: baptism by water (John's baptism) and baptism by the Holy Spirit (the baptism of Jesus). The first took place at the Jordan – and at many locations since; the second took place at Pentecost – and on many Pentecosts since. The baptism by water was, literally, the watershed between the old sinful life and the new life in Christ; the second equipped the Christians with the gifts and power of the Spirit, to get up and get out and get on with God's work. The Eastern Orthodox Church has traditionally linked the two; we in the Western Church tend to separate them, usually by at least seven years.

## A visible message

Any baptism provides a visible message that the person or persons being baptized have made (or have had made for them) a choice for God. One of the key themes of Jesus' teaching was that of giving and showing light for the world: a Christian by virtue of his calling is to share his faith. If he keeps it quiet, he is not being true to his calling. When Jesus ordered John to baptize him, openly, he was making a virtual declaration of intent – and God, in his wisdom, followed this up by driving (v. 12) our Lord into the wilderness for a sabbatical that culminated in a convincing defeat for Satan. Thus prepared – mentally, physically and spiritually – Jesus could begin his ministry proper.

## The question of repentance

If by baptism we are demonstrating the repentance of our sins, surely a case could be made for 'death-bed' baptism, similar to the anointing called by Catholics 'Extreme Unction'? Why be baptized early in life (often in infancy), before we have sinned? Of course, in some parts of the Church, infant baptism is discouraged for this very reason. Yet surely it's better to have been baptized early – to have had solemn promises undertaken for us by our parents and godparents, from whom also is demanded an affirmation of repentance – than to wait until circumstances may intervene and cause death before the rite has been undertaken? It's surely preferable to have the vows made on our behalf at or soon after birth, and then when we are old enough to understand and make our own, to follow up the water-baptism with Spirit-baptism (confirmation, with the laying-on of hands). Both rites are important, for one was undergone by Christ and the other was instituted.

## This declaration of intent

The baptism of Jesus in the Jordan that day, was as much an act of 'repentance' on our behalf, as a declaration of intent to fight sin. And so it needs to be with us, whether we make our own vows, or they are made on our behalf. Armed with the formal 'decision for God' that baptism brings, it's a virtual 'declaration of war' against Satan. Once the cross has been traced on us, it can never be erased; baptism can never be undone. This is a mark of its solemnity, as well as its joy. At baptism, we enter into a covenant-relationship with God. As life goes on, we may be orphaned, widowed, even abandoned by our family and friends, but we can never truly 'walk alone', because our covenant partner remembers forever how his Son, too, was baptized – and partners in so solemn and joyful an undertaking eternally stick together.

### Family Service Input

Encourage the making of baptism cards for the parish/deanery, for subsequent baptisms and/or baptism anniversaries.

### Suggested Hymns

Breathe on me, Breath of God; Christ, who once among us; In token that thou shalt not fear; O Breath of Life, come sweeping.

## Baptism of Christ
*Second Service*   **By Grace** Ps. 46 [47]; Isa. 42:1–9; Eph. 2:1–10 [Matt. 3:13–17]

> *'For by grace you have been saved through faith, and this is not your own doing; it is the gift of God – not the result of works, so that no one may boast.' Ephesians 2:8–9*

### 'That charming sound'

Paul mentions 'grace' three times in this reading. If anyone knew what grace (= God's unmerited favour) was, it was surely Paul, rescued from a life of dedicated persecution to one of even more dedicated preaching and missionary zeal. He struggles to put into words the magnificent unfairness of God: we are saved through faith – our faith, our decision to believe. Yet the capacity to decide, the ability to believe, is not ours, but God's gift to us. Remember this, Paul is saying, in case you are tempted to give yourselves the credit. Give God the glory, for without his grace you'd be lost.

> *Grace! 'tis a charming sound,*
> *Harmonious to the ear;*
> *Heaven with the echo shall resound*
> *And all the earth shall hear;*
> *'Twas grace that wrote my name*
> *In life's eternal book:*
> *'Twas grace that gave me to the Lamb,*
> *Who all my sorrows took.*
> (Philip Doddridge, 1702–51)

It's God's grace that brings us to baptism, God's grace that leads us to repent, God's grace that forgives our sins, and by God's grace that we can pick ourselves up and 'start over'. Completely undeserved, unearned and unmerited. Does that make us feel unworthy? It shouldn't: before we tapped into God's grace, we

35

were unworthy, but our covenant partner from baptism onwards has invested us with his worthiness, his grace. We are new people. We have been 'born again'. Forget any modern hang-ups about that expression 'born again'. We ARE. Jesus said we have to be (John 3:3, 7). Just accept it.

## Works are still important

Nothing that we have done or can do, can earn us God's unmerited favour. Yet nowhere in the Bible does the Lord say that all we need to do is nothing. He is expending precious oxygen on us for a purpose. He has given us his spiritual gifts to put to good use. There's a large chunk of the world still that doesn't yet know anything of the Bible. We have oodles of work staring us in the face, and the time for getting on with it starts now. But all we do needs to be offered to God, as our DUTY for all that he has already done for us and given us. Does that make our life's work sound like a long series of mortgage repayments? Well, that's probably a pretty good way of describing the 'work of faith'. God has financed us; he has given us life and sufficient opportunities to put his gifts to the best use we can. Yes, and when our mortgage is paid, our eternal home will be ours: furnished already, it's prepared and waiting. Can we not go full steam ahead with God's work? Yes, we can – unencumbered by the load of sin, because that load was borne, that ransom price was paid in full, at Calvary.

Fantastic? No, just a five-letter word: GRACE.

> Oh, I would not be an idler in the vineyard of the Lord.
> With the Christ the vineyard-labour I would share;
> Into hearts that know not Jesus I would speak the saving
>     word;
> Let me take the blessed joy of the gospel there.
> (Revd Elisha A. Hoffman)

Paying a mortgage is a duty, but it's also a pleasure, for there is the anticipation of the reward at the end of the exercise. So it is with our work for God, but there's even more joy with this, because the Lord is far removed from a nameless, faceless, unfeeling money-lender: his love and caring concern undergirds all our experiences; his feelings for us run so deep, two millennia before we were born (but when he already knew us), he gave all he had to save us and make a relationship with him possible.

Anything we can ever do for him in return, falls so far short of parity, that only one thing makes it all possible: that five-letter word, GRACE.

If a scholar of John Newton's ilk found this 'amazing', let's not keep ourselves awake with worry if we don't fully understand it.

> *Amazing grace! how sweet the sound*
> *That saved a wretch like me!*


### Suggested Hymns

Amazing grace; God of mercy, God of grace; To God be the glory; When all thy mercies, O my God.


# Second Sunday of Epiphany   15 January
*Principal Service*   **God Goes Looking** 1 Sam. 3:1–10 [11–20]; Ps. 139:1–5, 12–18; Rev. 5:1–10; John 1:41–51

> *'The next day Jesus decided to go to Galilee. He found Philip and said to him, "Follow me."'* John 1:41


### Priorities

Jesus was not merely out for a walk. Wasn't he looking for recruits? Wasn't the fact that he needed to train evangelists uppermost in his mind? He knew that such a lot needed to be accomplished in a very short time: time enough to accomplish all he had to do, but no time to waste. Three years was not too long to train men who would be so genned-up as well as fired-up, that they would travel miles over land and sea with the preaching and healing that was necessary to get the Church up and running. His priorities established, Jesus therefore was looking for suitable material. A recruitment team today may not have looked twice at the twelve whom Jesus chose, but the Lord needed to look only once at each man. 'Diamonds in the rough', we might have said of Peter, who was highly strung and impulsive to the point of saying the wrong thing time and again . . . or Thomas, who was courageous when physical danger loomed, but nervous to believe anything without proof . . . or James and John, impetuous and ambitious . . . or Judas, who seemed inordinately interested in money . . . No, we should not have highlighted any of these as potential preachers, teachers and healers, who would fear nothing and no one, be they in downtown Jerusalem or in the law-courts of Ephesus, Rome or Athens.

## Time for reflection

With the excitement of Christmas and the wonder of Epiphany behind us, in this relatively quiet time before Candlemas, it is surely appropriate to reflect on our own calling. It may be many years since Jesus 'found' us; make no mistake – he did the finding, we did not. 'You did not choose me, but I chose you,' says Jesus (John 15:16). As soon as we 'wise up' on this, our calling is put into a right perspective. Jesus, as in today's reading, was not merely out for a walk and happened on us. He came looking. Why? Because we could be made the people he knows we can be: not because we were already qualified for the job. Any brilliant notions of our ability to qualify for such a wonderful work as being a 'Christian', should be given decent burial. We were no more suitable than Peter and the others, but Jesus could see our potential. We have not yet realized that potential, or we should be already in glory; but under the Lordship of Christ, we're getting there – and, with God's grace, in Christ we'll make it.

## Christian tolerance

It means that because we're so far from perfect, we need to show Christian tolerance with any perceived shortcomings in others. Peter & Co. were used to being looked down on as unlettered fisherfolk. Yet this patronizing attitude actually helped once they began to preach, for their eloquence was at such variance with their background. And still today folk are quick to categorize – and still today, often desperately inaccurate in their assessments.

So, why did Jesus choose the likes of us to be his voice, his hands, his heart to the world? We may be able to answer this to some extent, by reflecting on how he has changed our lives since he chose us. If we can review our progress, and marvel at what he has done through us – the things we have said, or the places we have gone to – well, he has been having his way with us. If we are still doing, saying and going as we did before his call, are we listening to Jesus, or to someone else? The callings of the disciples that are recorded in the gospels all demand an immediate response. Once Jesus has found his recruit, he does not, as the Irish say, 'put it on the long finger'.

### Family Service Input

Encourage the young folk to list/discuss what they like doing best – and how these things can best be used in God's service.

### Suggested Hymns

Alleluya, sing to Jesus; I, the Lord of sea and sky; Jesus calls us, o'er the tumult; Will you come and follow me if I but call your name?

## Second Sunday of Epiphany
*Second Service*   **On Our Behalf** Ps. 96; Isa. 60:9–22; Heb. 6:17—7:10 [Matt. 8:5–13]

> *'We have this hope, a sure and steadfast anchor of the soul, a hope that enters the inner shrine behind the curtain, where Jesus, a forerunner on our behalf has entered, having become a high priest for ever according to the order of Melchizedek.'*
> *Hebrews 6:19–20*

### Our forerunner

It's something akin to the monarch's son, the crown prince, presenting our credentials at the palace gate, so that we can be admitted as honoured guests to the royal banquet or garden-party. We have been vouched for by a personage so well qualified by birth, status and name, as to make further examination of our worth unnecessary. So Jesus having at Calvary expunged our inherited sin from the record, can now present us before God in the innermost sanctum, the 'Holy of Holies', as though we have not sinned. Every jeer and sneer, every lash of the whip, every cruel nail of his passion, wiped away more and more of our sin: 'By his bruises we are healed' (Isa. 53:5). In Christ's blood, therefore, is our hope: not in the blood of innocent animals; not in the tragedy of the scapegoat driven into the wilderness on the Day of Atonement (Yom Kippur); not in the once-a-year penetration of the Holy of Holies by a high priest of the old order; but in the sacrificial blood vicariously shed for us by Christ, our high priest of the new order.

## Melchizedek the mysterious

Yet linking the two orders is the mysterious, shadowy form of Melchizedek (whose name literally means 'King of Righteousness'). Even Abraham gave tithes to this strange figure, who came out of the mists of the unknown, and vanished back the way he had come. Melchizedek has been seen as a symbol of the ideal king-priest; he cannot be traced by human ancestry; yet he forms a unique link between the old and new orders, emphasizing the constancy of God, the ongoing creation process, and the efficacy of our Lord's declaration: 'I have come not to abolish, but to fulfil' (Matt. 5:17).

## Unchanging purpose

It is in this unchanging purpose of God – that what has been is a preparation for what is, and for what is to come – that our hope in Jesus lies. He came to give us the hope of eternal life, and, without this hope, Paul says, 'we are of all people most to be pitied' (1 Cor. 15:19). We have hope, because our sins have been borne by Christ, expiated by Christ. The high priests of the old order no longer need to wait 364 days for each Yom Kippur; because Jesus has been victorious over death and sin, he has made possible unlimited access to the Holy of Holies – and not just for himself, but also for us.

What does this mean in practice? Simply (but magnificently) that we can now 'approach the throne of grace with boldness, so that we may receive mercy and find grace to help in time of need' (Heb. 4:16). For the Christian, God-in-Christ has made possible an accessibility that was not operative before the rending of the temple-veil at Calvary. Satan is as active as ever – and even more vicious since losing the Calvary battle – but God is always accessible, always available to help in our times of need.

## Divine continuity

We have the same Almighty God that Abraham, Jacob, Isaiah and Malachi knew, for the order of the priesthood is unchanged: it is still that of Melchizedek. It always will be. There is surely great comfort in the magnificent continuity of God. We can rely on him and his promises absolutely.

*We rest on thee, our Shield and our Defender!*
*We go not forth alone against the foe.*
*Strong in thy strength, safe in thy keeping tender,*
*We rest on thee, and in thy name we go.*
(Edith Gilling Cherry, d.1897)

## Suggested Hymns

Be still and know that I am God; Jesu, our hope, our heart's desire; Lord, enthroned in heavenly splendour; There is a Redeemer.

# Third Sunday of Epiphany   22 January
*Principal Service*   **Glory Revealed** Gen. 14:17–20; Ps. 128; Rev. 19:6–10; John 2:1–11

> *'Jesus did this, the first of his signs, in Cana of Galilee, and revealed his glory; and his disciples believed in him.' John 2:11*

## Divine provision

John interprets the power that Jesus showed at Cana's wedding-breakfast, as revealed glory. A need had been answered, a provision made, a want supplied – and with a generosity that took people utterly by surprise. But that's the way God works (John is saying): we ask him for our need to be met; and he gives us not just the cake, but the icing on the top as well. That's glory: bigger, better, brighter than that on which we have set our sights. God deals in quality. If we could only focus on this beautiful truth more often, life would be bigger, better and brighter here, even before we tasted the glory of Hereafter.

> *My God is so big, so strong, and so mighty,*
> *There's nothing that he cannot do.*
> (Phil Bert)

The children's hymn focuses on the power of God in creation. But at Cana, Jesus showed that this power is available also in the smallest matters: even a local marriage-celebration. God is a master of the unusual. One might have thought that the first miracle (or sign) of the Saviour of the world would have been one of healing,

41

raising the dead, or stilling a storm. Well, those were all in the pipeline, but Mary, who had been pondering her Son's uniqueness for 30 years, was inspired to encourage him to 'come out of his shell' at a domestic party.

## On our level

In a way, it could not have been more appropriate: for hadn't he come to experience life on our level, at every point? Hadn't he come to show us that following him to God was not a duty but a joy? Why not, therefore, infuse a joyful occasion (and, indeed, one of fulfilling the marriage-union of a man and wife, in accordance with God's law) with even more joy!

Jesus was to go through three years of ministry repeatedly encouraging the disciples – and others within earshot – to be of good cheer and not to be afraid of anyone or anything. His was a positive, upbeat message; a life that fostered joy and never killed it; an openness of spirit that could enjoy a party, could accept the hospitality of folk far beneath the pharisees' dignity, and a freedom that could reinterpret the hardline sabbath rules invented by the religious grandees. On all counts, Jesus was a beautiful person with whom to be in company. Why do some folk today believe the Christian life is dull, boring and restrictive? Could it be that 'pharisees' of a later age have meddled with the simple, uncompromising gospel of our Lord?

## The glory of Jesus

This is the 'glory' of Jesus, as understood in the present life. Our understanding of it in the Hereafter will almost certainly be bigger, better and brighter. But for now his glory is his power, love and joy operating in us and through us. If other people haven't seen it, then it's time for us to get serious with God and discover why. People in first-century Palestine were drawn to Jesus by his glory. Many of them would not have been able to explain its attraction: but to them, it just felt good to be with Jesus.

Is it so with his people today?

He showed his glory also in calmly riding through each new circumstance and situation, whether it was due to natural causes, or to human sin and animosity.

Is it so with his people today?

He would enter (or be invited to enter) a situation, and would always improve it – whether by healing, teaching, raising the dead, bringing calm out of chaos or joy out of anguish – always making life better and brighter for those whom he met.

Is it so with his people today?

If it is, we are helping to show nothing less than the glory of Jesus to the world of today.

### Family Service Input

Encourage the young folk to discover from current newspapers and periodicals items that show the glory of Jesus being revealed today.

### Suggested Hymns

Deck thyself, my soul, with gladness; Forth in the peace of Christ we go; I come with joy to meet my Lord; Songs of thankfulness and praise.

## Third Sunday of Epiphany

*Second Service*   **Waiting in Hope** Ps. 33; Jer. 3:21—4:2; Titus 2:1–8, 11–14 [Matt. 4:12–23]

> *'We wait for the blessed hope and the manifestation of the glory of our great God and Saviour Jesus Christ. He it is who gave himself for us that he might redeem us from all iniquity and purify for himself a people of his own who are zealous for good deeds.'*
> *Titus 2:13–14*

### Waiting for hope

In hope, in sheer confidence and trust, we wait for hope, when the hope of the nations will come to call his own to eternity. To Paul, this may have seemed not far distant. To us, since it has delayed for 2,000 years, it probably impacts less on our day-to-day living. But it will come – and, maybe, in our lifetime.

Meanwhile, Paul tells Titus, we must be up and doing, 'zealous for good deeds'. We can surely translate that as packing as much good as we can into each day. 'Zealous' isn't often heard in common parlance, yet doesn't it ring sweetly? Full of energy for God, alive and alert to what he is telling us, keen to serve him in all the opportunities he gives, taking seriously the great truth that our zeal for Christ can make a vital difference in others' lives (and do our own lives a power of good into the bargain) – all this is wrapped up in Paul's teaching here. And we have only to read what he did for Jesus, after the dramatic Damascus Road experience, to see that Paul had zeal for Christ in abundance.

## Today's biggest killer?

Today's biggest killer is not the bomb or the bullet. It's apathy: mental, physical and spiritual apathy. Millions can't be bothered to take up the cross; they are the spiritual apathetics (and what a dreadful sound that word has!). Millions more won't take the trouble to read the Bible and to search out the true meaning of life and death; they are the mental apathetics. And yet more millions choose to pursue leisure and pleasure of one sort or another, rather than come to church and show the world they are Christ's; they are the physical apathetics.

'Be zealous!' Paul thunders today, to the apathetics of 2006.

'Be more zealous!' he tells the practising Christians of 2006, just in case we were toying with the idea of apatheticism.

Remember how the Holy Spirit threatened to deal with the apathetic church of Laodicea (Rev. 3:16). It wouldn't make good reading to the folk gathered there, in the city where fortune and fame came so easily they'd developed a laid-back attitude to everything.

## Keeping the flame of hope alight

Wouldn't it be tragic if we were physically, mentally or spiritually asleep, when God was trying to tell us something, to point us somewhere, to show us a situation where we could do some good? We mustn't let go our zealous hope just because the Lord's coming seems to have been delayed. If he is true to form, he'll come in such a surprising and unusual way, that unless we're zealously alert and seriously hopeful, we may miss the divine point.

> Let all who look hasten that coming joyful day,
> By earnest consecration to walk the narrow way;
> By gathering in the lost ones, for whom our Lord did die,
> For the crowning day is coming by and by!
>
> (El Nathan)

## 'So that . . .'

'Jesus gave himself for us, SO THAT he might redeem us', Paul tells Titus. By the same token, we became Christians, SO THAT with zeal we might make Christ known to others. Surely we needhelp to misunderstand either of these great truths.

### Suggested Hymns

Christ is the King! O friend, rejoice; Jesus, Lord, we look to thee; One shall tell another; When I needed a neighbour.

## Fourth Sunday of Epiphany (or, Presentation of Christ in the Temple (Candlemas), q.v.) 29 January
*Principal Service* **Master of the Situation**
Deut. 18:15–20; Ps. 111; Rev. 12:1–5a; Mark 1:21–28

> *'They went to Capernaum, and when the sabbath came, he entered the synagogue and taught. They were astonished at his teaching, for he taught them as one having authority, and not as the scribes . . . They were all amazed, and they kept on asking one another, "What is this? A new teaching – with authority!"'*
> Mark 1:21–22, 27

### Authoritative teaching

The second time they marvelled (v. 27), Jesus had healed a man with an unclean spirit (we'd probably say today, 'mentally ill'). But their initial amazement had stemmed from the way Jesus taught, and what he taught. They were hearing a 'new teaching', because it was being given with an authority that no one else could claim. He, the world's Saviour, was uniquely and powerfully authorized to preach the gospel of salvation, the taking up of the cross, justification by faith, and good works. There would not be too much in this new, authoritative preaching about the man-made laws and regulations tacked on to the Mosaic covenant by generations of pharisees; nor would the message of Jesus be overloaded with ritual purification, animal sacrifices, sabbath observance and the like.

And, in between this new, authoritative teaching, the strange young rabbi whom folk said came from a carpenter's shop in Nazareth, could calmly perform healings that took people's breath away even more convincingly.

## In fulfilment

Yet Jesus was not there to demolish the old covenant, but to fulfil it: to show people a newer, better way of life: a way that embraced the world, and a life that would last eternally. Stretch your minds, folks, this is for you! No wonder they were astonished and amazed! No wonder news of the new preacher ran out from the Capernaum synagogue in all directions (v. 28)!

## The love of Jesus

Our Lord loved them so much (hadn't he given up so much just to bring them the new gospel?), he gave it them straight. As was later reported (e.g. by Matthew 5:21, 27, 33), he and he alone had the authority to say: 'You have heard that it was said to those of ancient times . . . BUT I SAY TO YOU . . .' The sheer power of such authority, the 'updating' of scriptures that had been even more sacrosanct and unalterable than the laws of the Medes and Persians, truly was amazing and astonishing. And as the disciples themselves marvelled, Jesus taught them: 'As I have loved, so you must now love. This is my new commandment.'

## The new law

Loving people as Jesus loved them means sharing the gospel, preaching, teaching and healing, as he did: loving and teaching in the name of Jesus – that is, entrusted with his authority. When they were given the world mission to start, the disciples could have worried themselves into such a state with the responsibility, that the mission would not have got off the Jerusalem soil. Instead, they were so energized with the love and joy of the authority that Jesus had invested in them, they simply obeyed . . .

## Obeying Jesus

. . . which is simply what our Lord requires of us today: obedience in publishing his new commandment, speaking with his authority, secure in his resurrection power that will see us through this life

# New Testament Early Christians Word-Search

| K | A | L | B | M | S | I | L | V | A | N | U | S | T | P |
|---|---|---|---|---|---|---|---|---|---|---|---|---|---|---|
| O | N | C | E | H | C | Y | T | N | Y | S | W | L | A | H |
| D | P | E | Q | F | R | G | S | H | E | I | C | J | B | O |
| R | A | Q | U | I | L | A | N | F | M | D | R | C | K | E |
| K | Q | J | P | I | O | G | J | U | N | I | A | H | L | B |
| A | N | D | R | O | N | I | C | U | S | N | S | M | T | E |
| S | J | S | C | T | R | W | Q | A | I | B | T | O | I | P |
| S | I | M | A | R | K | T | C | W | L | A | U | B | M | D |
| I | G | T | R | Y | P | H | E | N | A | C | S | S | O | D |
| L | J | H | P | H | G | I | F | F | S | E | A | A | T | E |
| A | K | L | U | O | A | N | R | A | K | I | H | N | H | B |
| S | P | M | S | I | Q | M | I | L | D | G | C | E | Y | I |
| Q | L | R | D | S | E | D | C | O | J | I | J | Z | F | A |
| N | O | Y | B | P | T | D | U | H | S | G | T | E | W | D |
| L | L | O | W | A | F | E | T | R | Y | P | H | O | S | A |

| | |
|---|---|
| ANDRONICUS | ERASTUS |
| TRYPHENA | SILVANUS |
| QUARTUS | TIMOTHY |
| STEPHANAS | TRYPHOSA |
| PHOEBE | LYDIA |
| SYNTYCHE | AQUILA |
| EUODIAS | JUNIA |
| ZENAS | MARK |
| CARPUS | SILAS |

and into the next. Folk may ask who we think we are, and who gave us the authority; they may try to 'ground' us, as they tried to ground Jesus, to the carpenter's shop.

Of course they'll try – because today, no less than 2,000 years ago, very many people refuse to be surprised by God.

### Family Service Input

Encourage the young folk (a) to solve the Word-Search, and/or (b) to compile one of their own, using words from the Titus reading.

### Suggested Hymns

Christ is our cornerstone; How sweet the name of Jesus sounds; King of glory, King of peace; O, for a thousand tongues to sing.


## Fourth Sunday of Epiphany
*Second Service*   **Each for All** Ps. 34; 1 Sam. 3:1–20; 1 Cor. 14:12–20 [Matt. 13:10–17]

*'So with yourselves; since you are eager for spiritual gifts, strive to excel in them in building up the church.' 1 Cor. 14:12*


### The fiery apostle

No one reading any letter of St Paul can fail to be struck by the fiery enthusiasm of the apostle. We can believe that what he tells others to do, he does himself. He has been eager for 'spiritual gifts', and he has certainly striven to excel in them in building up the Church. And he goes on to talk about glossolalia, the gift of speaking in tongues: a beautiful gift, but one that is difficult for those who don't have it to understand. Therefore, Paul cautions, it is better for this to be kept for private use, between the Christian and God. This is the well-travelled missionary talking; the apostle who is all too well aware of the danger of new or enquiring believers being put off by the unusual or hard-to-understand. Are we as sensitive today, or do we assume that because we understand everyone else will, or should? Because we like a particular liturgy or practice, others will, or should accept it? Do we ever stop to consider how strange something familiar to us may seem to another hearing or seeing it for the first time? This teaching of Paul on spiritual gifts – so precious that we long after them and prize them so highly – is a lesson in sensitivity. Are we really using the gifts God has given us in the best way – for the good of the Church, or merely for ourselves? Are we attracting others to God by these gifts? They've been bestowed on us to further the gospel and the kingdom of God, because that is God's purpose in keeping us alive.

## Paul's energy

Paul had always had an abundance of energy; in the days before his conversion, it had been zealously directed towards hunting down Christians (though the earliest followers of Jesus had not then received that title), arresting them and getting them imprisoned, tortured or killed. So great had been his energy, he was recognized as the arch-persecutor of the Church. God chose a man with drive (energy that, channelled away from persecution to preaching, would take the gospel of Jesus far beyond the walls of Jerusalem); a man with sufficient zeal and stamina who would ride out physical, mental and spiritual vicissitudes. Pointed by God in the right direction, Paul just went from strength to strength; but he never forgot what he had been, and the misdirected energy from which God had delivered him; 'I am the least of the apostles,' he told these same Corinthians, 'unfit to be called an apostle, because I persecuted the church of God. But by the grace of God I am what I am, and his grace towards me has not been in vain. On the contrary, I worked harder than any of them – though it was not I, but the grace of God that is with me.' (1 Cor. 15:9–10)

'Striving to excel', he knew (he wasn't boasting, but being absolutely honest) that in the exercising of the gifts God had given him, he had worked harder than the other apostles. Yet, honest as ever, he gave all the credit to God. The more we use our spiritual gifts, the harder it can be to remember to give credit where credit is due.

## Knocking down/building up

The Church is not short of knockers-down in the world of today; but among the ranks of builders-up there is often more elbow-room. Let us strive to be zealous in our building-up of the Family of God. As a prerequisite, we can do no better than to take a little time to consider – on the local front, at least – where the church is heading, what it is saying to the parish at large, what expectations it has of itself (and what outsiders expect of it) . . . and what God may be telling us to do about it.

If we decide the gifts we need are greater than what we presently have, we can be sure that God will take care of that problem.

### Suggested Hymns

A safe stronghold our God is still; Jesus Christ is waiting; Spirit Divine, our wants relieve; Thy Kingdom come, O God.

## Fourth Sunday before Lent (Proper 1)   5 February
*Principal Service*   **Demons of Today** Isa. 40:21–31; Ps. 147:1–12 [21c]; 1 Cor. 9:16–23; Mark 1:29–39

> '[Jesus] answered, "Let us go to the neighbouring towns, so that I may proclaim the message there also, for that is what I came out to do." And he went throughout Galilee, proclaiming the message in their synagogues and casting out demons.' Mark 1:38–39

### Holistic mission

Jesus operated a holistic ministry: he was preacher, teacher, doctor, exorcist, all rolled into one; and it was this pattern that the apostles of the early Church followed, partly because they wanted to do as Jesus had done, and partly because it WORKED. But somewhere in history the Church either chose to divide these aspects of ministry, or tacitly allowed them to be hived off, until today we tend to concentrate on the preaching (and a bit of teaching and exorcism, and still less healing). Instead of everyone going to church as the place to get healed as well as preached to, we divide our time between services, hospitals and half-a-dozen or so other places; and then wonder why folk treat the Church as peripheral.

### How brave can we be?

Are we brave enough to ask God how we can return to the pattern set by Jesus? Do we believe it's possible? We may not feel it is in line with the world of today; but shouldn't the Church, rather than the world, take the lead?

There is surely a place for established parochial structure, and for mission outreach; the two have coexisted with much success for a very long time. But for both to foster holistic ministry, would mean many changes, changes involving the secular world and its structures. 'This would be well-nigh impossible, now we are a multi-faith society!' would be the cry, if it hasn't already surfaced.

Yet the first-century world of the early apostles was a multi-faith society – in some ways much more akin to the world of 2006 than, say, the heyday of monasticism, or the late-Victorian period.

The Jesus pattern of ministry is a question that will not go away; and in parishes throughout Christendom it will need to be addressed before the Church becomes truly peripheral: before the power of God is limited by those already chosen as its purveyors; before we become too worldly-wise for our own good.

## Going about

Let us reflect on that watershed in Acts, where Peter, sent by God to Cornelius, comes to terms (a little against his will) with the truth that God wants his Church to admit Gentiles as well as Jews – Gentiles on a par with Jews. As Peter explains the gospel to Cornelius, he tells how 'God anointed Jesus of Nazareth with the Holy Spirit and with power, how he WENT ABOUT doing good and healing all who were oppressed by the devil, for God was with him' (Acts 10:38). Why? Because he'd been anointed with Spirit and power to do good and to heal. And so he used the anointing, to the full. In parts of the Church today, don't Christians carry on as though they've not received God's power (or as though that power has become so diluted, it isn't there to be given)? We need to pray earnestly for a renewing of the awakening of the Spirit and his gifts in us. We need to pray for a realization of what, by the grace of God, we can be as light and salt for the world. It's grand to meet with fellow-Christians, but EVERY night of EVERY WEEK? Perhaps we should reflect more often on today's text, where the disciples come to Jesus and tell him everyone in the area is looking for him. Does he call a local meeting and give them another preaching and teaching session? No, he tells the disciples: 'Let us go on to the neighbouring towns, so that I may proclaim the message there also, for that is what I came out to do.'

## Family Service Input

Encourage the young people to discuss/illustrate how very busy Jesus was, as recorded in Mark 1:29–39 – and how this is/could be mirrored in the Church today.

## Suggested Hymns

Forth in thy name, O Lord, I go; I, the Lord of sea and sky; O Jesus, I have promised; Thine arm, O Lord, in days of old.

# Fourth Sunday before Lent
*Second Service* **Keeping Faith** Ps. 5; Num. 13:1–2, 27–33; Phil. 2:12–28 [Luke 5:1–11]

> *'It is by your holding fast to the word of life that I can boast on the day of Christ that I did not run in vain or labour in vain . . . I have no one like [Timothy] who will be genuinely concerned for your welfare. All of them are seeking their own interests, not those of Jesus Christ.' Philippians 2:16, 20–21*

## Honest assessor

This is Paul, hard-pressed in his mission, urging the young church in Philippi to stand firm, and sending them Timothy as an encouragement. Only Timothy because, in an honest assessment of his fellow-workers, Paul has to admit that the rest have fallen by the way: self-interest has smothered the interests of Jesus. Sensitive to the core, Paul takes their defection personally: he hasn't run hard enough, he hasn't worked as well as he might: we can infer this self-flagellation from his hint in verse 16 as to how he would feel if the Philippians also let their faith slip. We may consider Paul is being too hard on himself; yet surely every minister worth his salt has felt the same: 'What, Lord, have I done, that I shouldn't have done? And what have I failed to do?' Yet whether or not any fault lay with Paul, he had to carry on – with or without the backsliders. The work of God must continue: we may pray for the recalcitrants, and leave their future with God.

## Paul's care

Meanwhile, Paul cared enough for the struggling Christians at Philippi, not only to write them a letter of encouragement, but also to send not merely anyone as a back-up, but his tried and trusted protégé, Timothy. Here was someone who could explain the faith and thus encourage and help the Philippians even more. It's a beautiful example of Christian care and concern, in a man near the end of a long and taxing life, under house-arrest in far-off Rome, but who would know exactly the dangers his little congregation at Philippi were facing.

## Follow-up

It was said of the great evangelistic crusades of the nineteenth and twentieth centuries in America and England, that three out of every four people who 'decided for Christ' at those events, would subsequently fail to continue in the faith. So it had been with the seed in Jesus' parable of the sower: three out of the four types of seed didn't make it. Is it so today? Probably God alone knows. Was it so in Philippi? Paul at least did his best to see that the success rate was higher. A 75 per cent rate is enough to give the devil a sore head. May we take a leaf out of Paul's book, and nurture our young Christians (young in the faith, if not in years), for Satan is ever on the prowl to deflect faith into fear.

## The interests of Christ

If we open the door to fear, the interests of Jesus have taken flight. Only faith promotes them; and where fear is, faith is not. Holding on to faith (to the 'words of life', in Paul's words), means giving God the green light to show us how we can promote the interests of our Lord: how we can meet someone's need in his name; how we can bring his light into someone's life; how we can enrich people with his word, heal them with his power, encourage them with his joy, and calm their fear with his love. And while we're doing this, that person called our 'self' will be nicely hidden behind the shining light of Christ. Simple? No; it's so hard to put into practice, we mess it up time and again. But let's remember Paul, and how he continued to care for his distant church in Philippi, when he was hard-pressed and nearly abandoned by his fellow-ministers.

Waiting for our situation to improve may be a non-starter; God is encouraging us to do something about it improving.

Brother, sister, let me serve you; Dear Lord and Father of mankind; Help us to help each other, Lord; Inspired by love and anger.

## Third Sunday before Lent (Proper 2)   12 February
*Principal Service*   **On God's Terms** 2 Kings 5:1–14; Ps. 30; 1 Cor. 9:24–27; Mark 1:40–45

> *'If you choose, you can make me clean . . . He went out and began to proclaim it freely, and to spread the word, so that Jesus could no longer go into a town openly, but stayed out in the country; and people came to him from every quarter.' Mark 1:40, 45*

### The Lord's cleansing

Whether it is of physical or spiritual impurity and defection, Jesus has the power to cleanse; but the cleansing is on his terms, which may or may not be in synch with ours. We wonder why some people receive cleansing or healing and others do not. There is a reason known to God, but as yet hidden to us. And it's of little use for us to say: 'It's not fair!' Our idea of fairness and God's don't invariably run in tandem. Nor is cleansing an arbitrary matter: God is in control, but he can change his mind; his word shows that on occasion (for instance, when Abraham interceded for the Sodomites) God is willing to be persuaded, if we come boldly to him and present our case (cf. Isa. 1:18). But he will still reserve the right of the final decision.

Jesus 'chose', on this occasion, to cleanse the leper, and for his own reasons counselled the man to keep quiet about his cure. Why? We don't know. We are not privy to all the local factors involved. In the event, the leper disregarded the injunction, and probably we should have done the same. But in so doing, he disobeyed Jesus, and the consequence was that Jesus' ministry moved away to another area: local folk who might have received healing on their own doorsteps, had to trek out into the country to where Jesus was operating.

### That little voice

There are times when the little voice sounds a warning, a piece of advice, or an insistent command. And we probably don't understand the reason (don't we all like to find a 'reason' for everything!), so we decide to use our own judgement, to please ourselves. And then we may wonder why things don't turn out the way we wanted them to. Instead of introducing his friends and neighbours to Jesus, and having joy in watching them being healed and ministered to in their home town, the cured leper may have been left standing while the townsfolk hurried out of town in search of Jesus. Did he go, too? Very probably; but things were not turning out as he had envisaged. With probably the best of intentions, he had disobeyed Jesus. His cure was not reversed – God does not stoop to petty dealings – but who knows what other blessings might have come his way, had he done as Jesus commanded and left the talking to God? 'Tell no one.' Those were the terms of his healing, and he did not keep to them.

## The right time = God's time

There is a time and a place for everything. In the will of God, the time of the leper's cleansing was not appropriate for immediate publication of the event. The time for publishing the work of Jesus would come in different places at various times. But the leper either thought he knew better than Jesus, or, in sheer ecstatic joy at being healed, either didn't even hear or disregarded Jesus' words.

Today, if we are alert to Jesus, he will tell us when to speak and when to be silent. Being human, we shall not get it right every time, but if we have tried our best, he will understand. He would understand when the cured leper couldn't keep quiet about his healing, because he had chosen as his foremost disciple a man who time and again impulsively spoke out of turn. Yet he forgave Peter, and patiently disciplined him until the lesson had been learned.

Like Peter, we are usually keen to say something about everything. And, as in Peter's case, the Lord will patiently go to work on us until we are what he wants us to be, and what he knows we were created to be.

And the end result may surprise us!

## *Family Service Input*

Encourage the young folk to plan a Lenten project, if possible in conjunction with another church/parish in either this country or a mission field abroad.

## Suggested Hymns

Be thou my vision; My times are in thy hand; Not for our sins alone; Take my life, and let it be.


# Third Sunday before Lent

*Second Service*   **The Power of Jesus** Ps. 6: Num. 20:2–13; Phil. 3:7–21 [Luke 6:17–26]

> *'But our citizenship is in heaven, and it is from there that we are expecting a Saviour, the Lord Jesus Christ. He will transform the body of our humiliation so that it may be conformed to the body of his glory, by the power that also enables him to make all things subject to himself.' Philippians 3:20–21*


## Full authority

'All authority in heaven and on earth has been given to me,' Jesus had told his disciples, when he was leaving them to return to glory (Matt. 28:18). In his resurrection power, he is responsible for heaven and earth and all that they contain. Such power is infinite, and as Christians we are a part of it. Rather than getting overwhelmed by wonder at this tremendous truth, we are simply to keep on keeping on sharing the gospel. Jesus will do his part: in no one else could we have more confidence. We need to concentrate on our part of the powerful bargain.


## Transformation

We know that Paul was well aware of his non-inclusion in the Twelve; how he regretted not having been a part of the three-year ministry of Jesus. But he had been royally, divinely compensated. Jesus had given him personal revelations, and, since Paul tells us so much about the Hereafter, we may surely reverently believe that he received this teaching from the Lord. In the 'resurrection chapter' (1 Cor. 15), as well as in today's reading, his teaching appears to be in response to questions actually posed, or expected: questions that continue to be asked; such as 'with what body shall we rise?' Paul tells the Philippians that the resurrection power of Jesus will transform our physical body into a 'resurrection body' such as Jesus had himself. We know that this body could appear and disappear at will, yet it could consume food; it could be touched; and it was also recognizable as belonging to the pre-resurrected Jesus; it carried forward the wounds that he had received at Calvary. We shall be 'conformed' from 'humiliation' to 'glory', though quite how is still a mystery. What is more immediate, is that the power of Jesus is working miracles in and through us already. We may not recognize it. We may in fact give the credit to someone other than Jesus, but that doesn't negate the power.

## Geared up

The more we are, spiritually speaking, geared up to recognize this power, the more we shall use it. To a Lord who gave up so much to die for us, save us and rise for us, it must seem singularly ungrateful if we career through our days giving him only the occasional acknowledgement. If we deliberately, determinedly involve him in all our doings, how he must warm to us! How he must take delight in affording us power upon power, grace upon grace! We are not required to crawl into his presence like the most abject of slaves: do we approach our physical brothers in such a way? No, Christ invites us – as friends, and family members – to come boldly to him and find grace to help in time of need. Being the frail, fallible people that we are, practically any time is our time of need.

## Present transformation

We look ahead to the transformation to glory, but Christ's power is presently transforming situations for us – and already transforming us into what God wants us to be: energized sons and daughters of the Almighty. Roll those words around in your mind, and pray Christ's transforming power to work a miracle of understanding. If more of us realized more of the power that our Lord has invested in us, more people would be aware of what our Lord is doing in the world today.

Let's not get so hung up on the future that we fail to make the most of the present.

## *Suggested Hymns*

Blessed assurance, Jesus is mine; Lord, for tomorrow and its needs; Today thy mercy calls us; Will you come and follow me?

# Second Sunday before Lent   19 February
*Principal Service*   **An Only Son** Prov. 8:1, 22–31;
Ps. 104:26–35; Col. 1:15–20; John 1:1–14

> 'And the word became flesh and lived among us, and we have
> seen his glory, the glory as of a father's only son, full of grace
> and truth.' John 1:14

## Heir presumptive

The only son of a king is the heir presumptive: all his father's
power, authority and influence is his by right. All the riches of the
kingdom are his by inheritance. The main difference between an
earthly crown prince and Jesus, is that Jesus inherited his kingdom
from the beginning while his Father was still alive, for both he and
his Father live in perpetuity. By this same divine alchemy, at baptism
we were made inheritors of a kingdom; we don't have to wait for
anyone to die, before we come into our inheritance: we are living
beneficiaries of a living Lord. In our human culture where everything else comes to an end and dies, and beneficiaries need to wait
for the death of the testator to inherit, the concept of infinite life
and inheritance after a death that itself swallowed up death and
went on living, is hard to understand. But we must try, because we
are an integral part of this process. We're not outsiders looking in
as a court case of inheritance unfolds in someone else's family. We
are especially privileged, prime inheritors and beneficiaries, of this
all-important, ongoing, infinite family of God.

## Jesus has come

Jesus has come, 'and we have seen his glory,' says John. We have
seen it in the witness of the New Testament writers, in the fulfilment
of the Old Testament promises and prophecies. We have seen it in
the 2,000 years of Christian history, as the world is slowly changed
by the message and gospel of Christ. And we are seeing it in our
own lives and in the lives of those around us. Christ's 'glory' is not
only something wonderful to anticipate in eternity: it has walked
the earth and is still around today in every one of his followers. It
is 'full of grace and truth'; as brimful as is only possible in the
Crown Prince of the King Almighty.

And that's a lot of grace, and a lot of truth.

## A father's only son

Jesus came, not 'in terror, as the King of kings' (H. F. Lyte), but as a FATHER'S only son. He showed the touching, human love of God that until then had been masked in majesty, divinity and magnificence. 'Pray to "our Father"', he told his disciples. Don't worry about what you'll eat, drink or wear: your heavenly FATHER knows all about these needs already. His recurrent message was, that God is not only mindful of us as a creator, but as a father – more than that, as our 'Dad' (Abba). We are so close, so precious to him. Well, we might have cottoned-on to the truth that no earthly dad could ever love us more than our heavenly Dad loves, but Jesus came to underline the truth most convincingly. God does love us more, and he wants to love us so much, he'll even accept us for the rest of eternity.

And that's a long, long time to love anybody.

## God's deep love

He loved us so much, as to be hurt to the core when the Crown Prince died at Calvary. And the Father heart of God still weeps when folk don't believe, when apathy takes the strength out of faith, and when compromise is made with the gospel of Christ. But still he offers the fullness of his grace – his unmerited favour – to give us one chance after another to make good. Still he offers us the Truth, not walking in the flesh among us, but invested on a non-negotiable basis in our hearts: for growing and sharing, witnessing and worshipping.

And that's a lot of investment.

And our Dad's expecting a good return on it.

## *Family Service Input*

When the young folk have completed this week's Word-Search, 'Prophets', encourage them to find biblical references for the prophets involved, and if time permits to discuss their lives. [For Word-Search, see next page.]

## *Suggested Hymns*

A Man there lived in Galilee; God of glory, God of grace; Meekness and Majesty; Jesus, stand among us.

## Prophets Word-Search

| P | C | O | A | N | L | E | I | N | A | D | Q | D | R | E |
|---|---|---|---|---|---|---|---|---|---|---|---|---|---|---|
| B | Z | E | P | H | A | N | I | A | H | T | G | S | F | W |
| J | C | M | B | J | I | I | H | C | A | L | A | M | H | A |
| D | O | E | F | K | L | G | H | A | G | G | A | I | H | E |
| I | O | N | P | Z | E | C | H | A | R | I | A | H | I | L |
| N | S | Q | A | R | M | A | S | L | T | K | H | O | J | I |
| J | I | A | G | H | I | L | E | N | C | A | P | S | W | S |
| Q | K | H | I | M | F | L | M | D | I | O | B | E | A | H |
| M | R | J | E | A | E | W | I | D | A | S | B | A | C | A |
| S | L | R | K | I | H | H | A | Q | G | J | A | M | O | S |
| N | E | T | K | O | W | B | P | F | R | E | O | T | D | M |
| J | B | E | O | A | O | Q | N | R | M | K | S | E | L | I |
| P | Z | C | H | A | B | A | K | K | U | K | T | J | L | C |
| E | F | D | G | E | D | F | H | G | B | H | W | I | A | A |
| E | C | N | A | H | U | M | I | H | A | J | I | L | E | H |

| | |
|---|---|
| ZECHARIAH | MALACHI |
| EZEKIEL | HOSEA |
| JOEL | NAHUM |
| OBADIAH | JEREMIAH |
| ISAIAH | MICAH |
| DANIEL | AMOS |
| JONAH | ZEPHANIAH |
| HABAKKUK | HAGGAI |
| ELIJAH | ELISHA |

# Second Sunday before Lent
*Second Service*   **Partners with Jesus** Ps. 65; Gen. 2:4b–25;
Luke 8:22–35

> *'Then the Lord God said; "It is not good that the man should be alone; I will make him a helper as his partner."' Genesis 2:19*

## Bride and groom

So the first bride and groom came to live in Eden, in mutual help and partnership – until the bride made compromise with Satan. Centuries later, another groom was to come, but the bride this time was to be the Church, the millions of Christians who would look to Christ as their Partner, Helper and Groom. Would this second bride be as fickle as the first? Well, on this side of glory she wouldn't be perfect; in fact, at times, far from perfect. But she would have a Groom who, unlike Adam, would not only refuse to go Satan's way, but who at Calvary would prove to be the Master over Satan.

## To love, cherish and obey

Adam's and Eve's was not the perfect union; but Christ is looking for more in the partners he takes on. At baptism, we enter into our partnership with him. The words of the rite vary from the marriage service, but it's a virtual commitment to 'love, cherish and obey' our Lord: not 'until death us do part', because this is an infinite union. The more we love our Lord, the more we shall cherish him, and the greater will be our commitment to obey his commands. The ongoing union is founded on love. We know we can trust him, and when he chooses and calls us, he is showing that he wants to trust us to be committed partners: partners in mission, preaching, teaching and across the whole range of ways in which the Church shows her Bridegroom to the world.

## How long?

How long is the first stage of this marriage to last? Christians have been called into partnership for two millennia, and still there are millions of people who are waiting to learn of the gospel. Still there are millions who are dying without knowledge of Christ. Still Jesus is choosing and calling new people into partnership in the Church.

61

How long will that go on? Until heaven's banqueting tables are all full? Probably, if this coincides with the completion of worldwide mission.

## Out of Eden

The first Adam had to leave the Garden of Eden with his partner because they had both sinned. The Second Adam – Christ, our Bridegroom – suffered at Calvary so that in time we can leave earth for a brighter Eden: an existence beyond time. What Adam had learned to do in Eden would help towards his survival after expulsion. What we can learn to do here may also be used by God in the next stage of our life.

## Putting our Partner first

In a successful marriage, each partner puts the other first, looking to preserve the other's honour and dignity. Christ is forever lovingly treating his partners so. Are we reciprocating? Do we point others to him, or try to take some of the credit for ourselves? Are we loyal to him when others vilify or deny him? Christ wrote our marriage contract in the waters of Galilee, the sands of the Jordan Valley, the blood spilled at Calvary; wherever we look in the Gospels, he was setting out his part of the agreement. The final signature came on Easter morning.

That was the point of no return

Have we signed our part of the contract? Have we given ourselves to Jesus, and promised to follow him?

Then we, too, have passed the point of no return.

## *Suggested Hymns*

Jesus, I my cross have taken; My times are in thy hands; O Jesus, I have promised; The Church's one foundation.

## Sunday next before Lent   26 February
*Principal Service*   **Terror on the Mountain**
2 Kings 2:1–12; Ps. 50:1–6; 2 Cor. 4:3–6; Mark 9:2–9

> '[Peter] did not know what to say, for they were terrified. Then a
> cloud overshadowed them, and from the cloud there came a
> voice: "This is my Son, the Beloved; listen to him!"' Mark 9:6–7

### Not the time to fear

Fear is not good at any time, but certainly not when Jesus is giving
his best friends a glimpse of glory. Luke follows Mark in noting
the disciples' terror (Luke 9:34), and also the absence of recognition of their fear by Jesus. But Matthew says they 'were overcome
by fear', and that Jesus said: 'Get up and do not be afraid'
(Matt. 17:6–7). The disciples were left wondering, in any case:
wondering what had happened, why it had happened, why it had
been so frightening; and, not least, why, every time they were scared
(because wasn't it natural to be afraid now and then?), Jesus either
ignored their fear or told them to snap out of it. Today, we may
reflect on how often when God has moved in our lives, the very
strangeness and unexpectedness of his operating has caused us to
be fearful. Perhaps we've become so conditioned to fear, we don't
notice it any more, much less regard it as a sin. But if, with hindsight, we can see that being afraid – of someone or something –
didn't materially affect the outcome of a situation (or detrimentally
affected it), can't we learn the lesson that God is telling us fear is
bad news, unproductive, and not Christian?

### Things we fear the most

Quite often, we become fearful of a change in our life's work: perhaps a new job, in new surroundings, among strangers. Today is a
good time to reflect on how Jesus reacted to this very same situation,
as Lent approaches. His 'Nazareth years' are practically a closed
book, but it's safe to say that the carpenter's shop would be relatively quiet. Now, having been baptized by John, Jesus has had the
green light for a new job, in new surroundings, among strangers.
What does he do? Retreat into the desert for 40 days, to think
things through with God, starving his body so that God can feed
his spirit.

63

## Fasting for the right reasons

Fasting merely to starve oneself is singularly unproductive, apart from whittling away useless and possibly dangerous fat. But fasting as Jesus did it, away from observers so that the praise of people is not an issue, fasting to pray more, worship more and to fellowship more with God, is to follow in our Lord's footsteps. Who knows? We, like the disciples, may be treated to glimpses of glory. If so, can we remember not to be afraid? Probably not, because God has a habit of taking us by surprise!

## The Lord expects

But, according to the scriptures, the Lord expects us not to fear. So when we do, we're somehow messing up our created components and our divinely formed anatomy: mental, physical and spiritual. In plain language, we've allowed Satan, the arch-dealer in fear, access to our nature; and, given an opening, the devil will do his best to capitalize on it. He was on the Mount of the Transfiguration, where he had no right to be. But he couldn't resist the opportunity to instil terror into the astonished disciples.

## Again and again

Jesus in the Gospels would not have issued the command not to fear so often, if it had not been such a serious matter. But he knew – even better than do we – how quickly fear can grow until it distorts every situation and circumstance. 'With the Lord on my side I do not fear', sang the psalmist (Ps. 118:6). Surely we, knowing Jesus as Saviour, can sing likewise!

## *Family Service Input*

Encourage (and, where necessary, help) the young people with the crossword (pp. 66–7), letting the very young illustrate (some of) the clues as they are solved.

## *Suggested Hymns*

Christ is the world's true light; Christ whose glory fills the skies; In days of old on Sinai; 'Tis good, Lord, to be here.

# The Sunday next before Lent

*Second Service*  **Lights that Shine** Ps. 2 [99];
1 Kings 19:1–16; 2 Peter 1:16–21 [Mark 9:[2–8] 9–13]

> *'We ourselves heard this voice come from heaven, while we were
> with him on the holy mountain. So we have the prophetic mes-
> sage more fully confirmed. You will do well to be attentive to this
> as to a lamp shining in a dark place, until the day dawns and the
> morning sun rises in your hearts.' 2 Peter 1:18–19*

## We were there

Let's not be too clever and decide after much semantic argument
that Peter the Galilean fisherman, and the author of this letter, were
not one and the same. The writer says he was a witness of the
transfiguration, and why should we seek to disprove him? He has
concluded that the vision came, 'so (that) we have the prophetic
message more fully confirmed'. In other words, this vision is 'spiritual
proof' that Jesus is the one to whom the old scriptures pointed; he is
who he says he is, and who they said would come. It's as though God
has decided that we need this extra affirmation, this 'icing on the
cake' of faith, in order to accept the truth of Jesus, the veracity of his
promise of ongoing life in glory, and his teaching that God is God 'not
of the dead, but of the living' (Matt. 22:33; Mark 12:27; Luke 20:38).
Look (God appears to be saying), you don't need to take just my
word for it, here is visible and aural proof!

## Today's fuller confirmation

Is God still operating like this today? Has belief slipped so far that
visible and aural proof is needed as fuller confirmation of the truth
of our faith? There has been the Turin Shroud. Many tests seem to
show that it is not from the first century; but, suppose it was? There
were other crucifixion and flagellation victims besides Jesus. No
one would know that the shroud was actually his. Or the ossuary
that came to light in Jerusalem in 2002, inscribed: 'James, son of
Joseph and brother of Jesus', which some authorities believe dates
from the time of Jesus. Yet these three names were so common, it
has been calculated that there could have been 20 or more Josephs
with sons called James and Jesus in Jerusalem at that time. Surely
of more veracity are the miracles of healings, the dead being raised

## Sunday next before Lent Crossword

to life, and the survival and growth of God's word in some of the most seriously war-torn and poverty-stricken areas of the world. They may not make more than local headlines, but, if we will, we can do something about that, so that each lamp shines brighter over a larger area. This world has still far too many dark places.

### Lighting up

Since it takes a very little light to dispel even quite a lot of darkness, the more we shine the light of God's word, God's love, joy, peace and the rest of the fruit of his Spirit, into the darkness of apathy, indifference, animosity and unbelief, the more darkness will be dispelled. And once the light of God has shone in a place, that place

## Clues Across

1. Brother of John. (5, 3, 5)
8. Boy's name. (4)
9. Intended. (5)
10. Jesus did this on the cross. (4)
11. Lords of the manor? (8)
12. Heathen god. (6)
13. The game begins. (4, 6)
16. Falsehoods. (4)
17. Short for Christmas. (4)
18. Good Samaritans. (10)
20. Resolution. (6)
22. Trace lines? (4, 4)
24. Our thinking part. (4)
25. Tribe of ancient Britons. (5)
26. Red meat. (4)
27. Times of summer harvest. (9, 4)

## Clues Down

1. The heavenly city. (9, 2, 4)
2. ...... Picchu of the Incas. (5)
3. Good man in Jesus' parable. (9)
4. Croakier. (7)
5. Natural insulator. (5)
6. A plot. (9)
7. The men of revelation. (3, 4, 8)
14. The day before today. (9)
15. Austrian currency. (9)
19. Modern Israelite. (7)
21. Russian forest land. (5)
23. Snake. (5)

*See page 69 for solution*

can never revert to being as dark as it was before. God's light, even for a season, has shone: a difference has been made.

## The morning sun

*The light of the morning is breaking,*
*The shadows are passing away;*
*The nations of earth are awaking,*
*New peoples are learning to pray.*
*Let wrong, O Redeemer, be righted,*
*In knowing and doing thy will;*
*And gather as brothers united*
*All men to thy cross on the hill.*

Does God's sunlight rise in our hearts with each new day? Yes, as the natural sun rises. But, as the sun is hidden by clouds on some days, so we also allow Satan to roll along clouds of doubt, fear and anxiety, to mask our God-given light. 'You are the light of the world,' Jesus is still saying to us (Matt. 5:14).

He's speaking the truth.

### Suggested Hymns

Lead, kindly light; Light's abode, celestial Salem; Shine, Jesus, shine!; Thee we adore.

## Ash Wednesday   1 March
*Principal Service*   **Lenten Ambassadors** Joel 2:1–2, 12–17 or Isa. 58:1–12; Ps. 51:1–18; 2 Cor. 5:20b—6:10; Matt. 6:1–6, 16–21 or John 8:1–11

> *'So we are ambassadors for Christ, since God is making his appeal through us; we entreat you on behalf of Christ, be reconciled to God.' 2 Corinthians 5:20*

### A larger helping!

Let's take verse 20 as a whole, for on this first day of Lent it seems most appropriate to realize afresh our ambassadorial status for Christ. Lent needs Christ's ambassadors ever as much as does the rest of the year – probably even more – for, like it or not, the non-believing world has to acknowledge this season of the Church's year – with its introduction of ashes, and Easter as its grand finale. We are ambassadors for Christ this Lent, and as such we can make a difference, if we choose. Today, as we leave worship with the visible mark of Lent, what will the smudgy black ashy cross on our forehead say to those whom we meet? Will they stare? Will they ask questions? Or, will they be too embarrassed to admit they have noticed? Our gospel reading tells us not to parade our religion, so we have a real challenge to use today's ashy opportunity for witness, without flaunting the cross in virtuous proof that we have been to church.

## Day of fasting and abstinence

Today we can fast – either from all food or some – and abstain from overt pleasure and whatever we consider is at variance with the observance. But witnessing for Christ as his ambassadors should be on our daily schedule at all times.

We may have decided to give up something for Lent, such as sugar, chocolate, outings or a particular hobby. The absence of these may focus our minds on the season, or narrow our waistlines somewhat. But unless we use the time and money saved by these deprivations in a positive way for God, they are rather futile. The purpose of Lent is not to make us feel miserable or virtuous, but closer to God and therefore better able to fight the devil. It also provides a time for reflection on the direction our life may be taking.

## The example of Jesus

Jesus went into the wilderness to do all these things; and the Gospels tell us very convincingly how well everything worked out for him: this in itself is surely a great encouragement for us to do likewise. Few may be able to withdraw from the world as thoroughly as Jesus, and in any case we have less, if any, justification for doing so. Jesus left the hustle and bustle to prepare for his saving mission: once, and for all. We are not told he went into the 40-day seclusion each year. But we have our mission already lined up for us by Jesus. We can hone it by more prayer, more reflection, more Bible study in Lent, but the world needs Christians to be where the action is.

## Reconciliation

God in Christ came to reconcile the world to himself, and we have this work to continue in Lent. As we show Christ to others, the

---

**Solution**

**Across:** 1. James the Great. 8. Eric. 9. Meant. 10. Bled. 11. Esquires. 12. Adonis. 13. Play starts. 16. Lies. 17. Xmas. 18. Neighbours. 20. Intent. 22. Rule copy. 24. Mind. 25. Iceni. 26. Beef. 27. Haymaking days.

**Down:** 1. Jerusalem on high. 2. Machu. 3. Samaritan. 4. Hoarser. 5. Gutta. 6. Embroglio. 7. The wise prophets. 14. Yesterday. 15. Schilling. 19. Israeli. 21. Taiga. 23. Cobra.

invitation is there for them to be reconciled (brought into at-one-ment) with God. The groundwork, literally, has already been laid. All authority in heaven and on earth has been given to Jesus (Matt. 28:18), which means that even the most reprobate sinner is standing on Christ's land. For the Christian, it means that wherever we go, by land, air or sea, we are on our 'home ground', and any soldier will tell you he fights better on home territory. In Lent, as at any other time, we are not the aliens struggling for possession of another's land; we are already 'at home', in possession. With the advantage of rightful ownership, we can repel all boarders, and that includes Satan.

He'll try to con us into believing it's his territory.

But who in his right mind would believe anything the devil says?

### Suggested Hymns

Be thou my vision; Dear Lord and Father of mankind; Father of heaven, whose love profound; Jesu, lover of my soul.

## Ash Wednesday
*Evening Prayer* **We Have Sinned** Ps. 51 or Ps. 102; Isa. 1:10–18; Luke 15:11–32

> '*I will get up and go to my father, and I will say to him, "Father, I have sinned against heaven and before you."*' Luke 15:18

### What sort of sacrifice?

The Old Testament reading from Isaiah has God enumerating the various ways in which Israel tried to keep herself right with God; ways that had acquired the respectable aura of tradition, and whose origins could actually be traced to the laws of Moses. Admittedly, they had been supplemented with various extra observances and regulations over the years; but the nation had become so accustomed to relying on the ritual that the main point of the exercise had been lost: so long as the outward, visible practice was carried out, the need for true heart repentance could drop down the priority table unnoticed: hearts that should be as white as snow with the purity that comes from true repentance for sins committed, were scarlet with unconfessed, unrepented sins.

The prodigal son, by contrast, was conscious of his sins, and prepared to give up his position as a son of the house, and to become a lowly servant. Starvation and loneliness had brought about contrition and remorse. And he had a father who could see the genuine article when it came struggling home to ask forgiveness. We have a similarly generous, loving and forgiving Father. It may not take a starvation diet to bring us to our senses, but wherever, whenever we come to God, not on hands and knees, but boldly to the throne of grace for grace to help in time of need, he meets us more than halfway. If, by the father in the parable, Jesus meant us to understand 'God', then God is already on the lookout for us in love, even before we get to him with our pleas for forgiveness, our requests for help.

## What others may think

The prodigal's brother isn't hard to find today – critical, ungenerous and sulky; envious of another's good fortune, and quick to remember the earlier faults of those who have since seen the light and are trying to amend their lives. But what profit is there in having a good memory for others' sin, when their present lives are a vibrant witness to the glorious truth that God has forgiven them? Unless we cultivate a good 'forgettery' for others' shortcomings, they are likely to remind us of our own. If God can forget confessed sins, and can put them out of mind as far as the east is from the west, why can't we be generous?

## Taking the initiative

'I will get up and go . . . and say . . .' It's called 'taking the initiative'. His father (and still less his brother) was not (on this occasion, at any rate) going to come many miles to find him among the pigs. The prodigal needed to take the initiative himself. Once that step had been taken, good things would begin to happen. This Lent, and seriously for the rest of our lives, may we also resolve to be quick to take the initiative in this business of repentance and confession. God is waiting, on the lookout, for us, wanting us, willing us to dump our pride and to come boldly – yet in humility and contrition – to ask for forgiveness.

How long will he wait?

Dare we really try his patience any longer?

*Today thy mercy calls us,*
*To wash away our sin,*
*However great our trespass,*
*Whatever we have been.*
*However long from mercy*
*We may have strayed away,*
*Thy precious blood can cleanse us*
*And make us thine today.*
                    (Oswald Allen, 1816–78)

## Suggested Hymns

Forty days and forty nights; Lord, in this thy mercy's day; Rock of ages; Soldiers of Christ, arise.

# First Sunday of Lent  5 March
*Principal Service*  **The Spirit Moves** Gen. 9:8–17;
Ps. 25:1–9; 1 Peter 3:18–22; Mark 1:9–15

> *'And just as [Jesus] was coming up out of the water, he saw the heavens torn apart and the Spirit descending like a dove on him . . . and the Spirit immediately drove him out into the wilderness.'*
> *Mark 1:10, 12*

### On the divine scale

This is magnificence on the divine scale. Whether we focus on the two men – Jesus and John – standing in the Jordan, or on 'something' like a dove coming down, or on the heavens torn apart, or on Jesus heading, Spirit-driven, into the wilderness, we are seeing God's power. Can you imagine what the astral tearing-apart would be? No, because our vision is daily limited to clouds and blue 'sky', and to the darkness behind the stars at night. Even the most recent astronomical photographs of what we call 'outer space' don't answer the question of what happened that day over the Jordan.

It's exciting stuff, but then Jesus (not necessarily of his own volition, if we take Mark's account at face value) leaves all the excitement for quite the opposite situation: the eerie silence and desolation of the wilderness.

No one followed him. For the next six weeks or so, were he and his Father to be alone? No. Two would have been company, but they virtually had a crowd: the third member of the party was the devil, ever hopeful of nipping our Lord's ministry and mission in the bud. And in Lent we observe not only the trial, the temptations, the privations of Jesus' wilderness retreat, but even more importantly his victory over Satan's best efforts.

## Our own battle

That's why, if we go around in Lent like streaks of misery, getting imperceptibly thinner with our various token fasts, and making a virtue out of a few bars of uneaten chocolate, we are missing the reason for the season. Lent is for building up spiritual stamina, not weakening our already fairly frail physical strength. It's for following the example of Jesus, in meeting and defeating Satan by the word of God, which means, for everyone (even the best-qualified theologians) more study of the Bible, more memorizing of the verses that God brings to our attention (for these, in his wisdom, are the texts he knows we are going to need, sooner or later), more sharing of his word with others, more praying for the translation, printing and delivery of Bibles and Christian literature to communities and cultures which as yet don't have his word . . .

That's quite an agenda for Lent. It doesn't leave too much time to fret over the lack or otherwise of sugar and chocolate.

## Mission preparation

And that's not all. Remember that Jesus was using his wilderness experience as a preparation for mission. Most of us are already some way into our mission and ministry, but Lent is a time for getting close to God and discussing with him how he wants us to move forward in our work for him. He may show us the way through his word, or through prayer, or through an experience this Lent, if only we are open and alert for what he may be wanting to make known to us.

Don't we all love to be busy! With all this, we shall find Lent speeds by on the Holy Spirit's wings!

## Made alive by the Spirit

Peter, in today's epistle, is referring to the resurrection, when he says that Christ was 'made alive in the Spirit' (1 Peter 3:18). Yet, because Christ has risen, we Christians can accept this vivifying power of the Spirit in great measure this Lent. If we are open to God, and accept that we have been given yet another Lent for a purpose, to advance in grace and in the knowledge of Jesus (2 Peter 3:18), the Spirit is ready and waiting to revitalize, re-energize and reinvigorate us.

If we are open to God.

### Family Service Input

The young people can be encouraged to prepare designs and texts for the parish's Holy Week and/or Easter cards, for distribution with details of the services to be held.

### Suggested Hymns

Christian, dost thou see them; Forty days and forty nights; O, for a closer walk with God; Shepherd Divine, our wants relieve.

## First Sunday of Lent
*Second Service*   **Killing Death** Ps. 119:17–32;
Gen. 2:15–17; 3:1–7; Rom. 5:12–19 or Luke 13:31–35

> *'Just as sin came into the world by one man, and death came through sin, and so death spread to all because all have sinned . . . death exercised dominion from Adam to Moses, even over those whose sins were not like the transgressions of Adam, who is a type of the one who was to come.' Romans 5:12, 14*

### Long established

It was a massive proposition, by any standards. Jesus had come to overthrow the inevitability of death, the power of death, which since Adam all those centuries before had been an integral part of the human existence. He came to abolish the finality of death, and to open a door beyond death; a door so 'permanent', so solidly constructed, that it would need supernatural, divine, resurrection power to accomplish the demolition of the barrier.

All that was at stake, as he faced down Satan in the wilderness. Our Lenten struggles pale in comparison, yet even the smallest of them has significance for us, for God and for others they might affect.

## The victory of Jesus

The victory of Jesus over Satan in the wilderness, and even more conclusively at Calvary, encourages us to believe that in the strength of our Lord we, too, can move mountains. Nothing is impossible with God. Someone very clever with language has said: 'Success comes in cans, not can'ts.' But there is a way that 'cannot' can be made to act positively, for the Christian can say: 'In the strength of Christ I cannot fail!' God-in-me will win!

> *He cannot fail, for he is God;*
> *He cannot fail, he pledged his word;*
> *He cannot fail, he'll see you through;*
> *He cannot fail, he'll answer you.*
> (C. E. Mason, Jr)

## Big problems

Yet, human nature being as perverse as it is, we sometimes persuade ourselves (or allow the devil to persuade us), that we've come up with a problem too big for God to solve. Can we, at such times, remember this victory of Jesus, conquering death so well established and apparently unchangeable? In every cross, every word of scripture, every miracle and blessing we receive, he is saying: 'I did it! I killed death for you! Just remember this!' Focus on this – and now, does your own problem still seem as large as before?

## Bereavement

The immensity of Christ's victory over death, gives the Christian courage and confidence when physical death occurs and we are asked: 'Is it for ever?' We can point to the empty cross (and even more to the empty tomb), and say, 'No': and surely that's the most positive negative ever affirmed! No, the death we see has had its sting removed, and is harmless and impermanent; the Life we cannot see is there and waiting, and each morning brings us closer to it. 'But no one has come back to prove it!' protest the sceptics. One person did, very convincingly appearing to Mary Magdalene, to the disciples, to more than 500 others, to James and to Paul

(1 Cor. 15:5ff.). If the protesters could demolish this weight of evidence, their case may be a little stronger. But think of all that Jesus has continued to do, since then, to the present day! That is not for demolition!

> *I serve a risen Saviour,*
> *He's in the world today.*
> *I know that he is living,*
> *Whatever men may say.*
> *I see his hands of mercy,*
> *I hear his voice of cheer;*
> *And just the time I need him,*
> *He's always near.*
> *He lives! He lives!*
> *Christ Jesus lives for aye.*
> *He walks with me, he talks with me,*
> *Along life's narrow way.*
> *He lives! He lives!*
> *Salvation to impart.*
> *You ask me how I know he lives?*
> *He lives within my heart.*
> (Alfred H. Ackley)

### Suggested Hymns

Living Lord; Lord, the light of your love is shining; O, the love of my Lord is the essence; Spirit of the living God.

## Second Sunday of Lent   12 March
### Principal Service   Challenge of the Cross Gen. 17:1–7, 15–16; Ps. 22:23–31; Rom. 4:13–25; Mark 8:31–38

> '[Jesus] called the crowd with his disciples, and said to them, "If any want to become my followers, let them deny themselves and take up their cross and follow me."' Mark 8:34

### The invitation

This is Christ's invitation to accept and bear the burden of life –

not to duck it, nor to leave it for someone else to cope with, but to be willing to carry it ourselves.

## For the whole of our life?

No, for as we accept the cross and follow Jesus, we find that he will lift it from our shoulders and bear the heavy end of it for us. Our way of escaping the weight, is in those three words 'and follow me'. The Stoic would bear the whole of his cross virtuously, and make himself and those around him miserable in his self-inflicted anguish. But Jesus has a loving heart, not an unfeeling heart of stone. Yet he requires us to make those first two moves – the lifting of the burden, and then the following – together, they open the door of faith for him to move into our lives.

## The royal way?

On the face of it, the invitation to take up their cross, wouldn't seem at all a royal way to the disciples. For one thing, crucifixion was the most shameful form of death at the time; and for another, it was an alien method of torture. And what self-respecting Jew wanted to be reminded of the hated Roman army of occupation?

Jesus knew their immediate reaction and reservations. Are you ashamed of such an exercise? was his unspoken question behind this teaching: 'Those who are ashamed of me and of my words . . . of them the Son of Man will also be ashamed when he comes in the glory of his Father with the holy angels' (Mark 8:38). So, it IS the royal way to which he is calling! A way that ends in glory! Who therefore would baulk at carrying the cross for a while, to enter eternal glory?

Millions would, and have baulked at it. But millions more have accepted Christ's terms.

*I'm not ashamed to own my Lord,*
*Or to defend his cause;*
*Maintain the glory of his cross,*
*And honour all his laws.*

*Jesus my Lord! I know his name,*
*His name is all my boast;*
*Nor will he put my soul to shame,*
*Nor let my hope be lost.*

*I know that safe with him remains,*
*Protected by his power,*
*What I've committed to his trust,*
*Till the decisive hour.*

*Then will he own his servant's name*
*Before his Father's face,*
*And in the New Jerusalem*
*Appoint my soul a place.*

(Isaac Watts)

## A hard calling?

If our calling today seems difficult, we have the assurance that Calvary took the shame from the 'cross'; that Jesus emerged convincingly as Victor; that – as in the days of pre-Calvary, when he called his first disciples – he asks us to face nothing that he knows we cannot win with him; and that still for us, as for Peter and the others, glory waits. Our end of the cross may still at times seem heavy, but at the front end, he is still taking much more of the load. Let's remember this, when we seem unable to take any more pain or anguish: Jesus is still in front, at the business end of the problem.

If he isn't, we're not following him, and we'd better improve our navigation, fast.

## Calvary was not the end

It's a measure of the infinite love of God that Calvary was not the end of Christ's cross-bearing. It would have been so much simpler – and cheaper – for God to have limited glory to those who, say, 'made it' in the first, second or even third century.

Thank God, that he doesn't settle for the cheapest option.

## Family Service Input

Encourage the young people to illustrate what they understand by 'the cross' in the life of Jesus and/or themselves. Combine these into a collage or presentation for display in the church.

## Suggested Hymns

Cross of Jesus, cross of sorrow; In the cross of Christ I glory; Take up thy cross, the Saviour said; Thou didst leave thy throne and thy kingly crown.

# Second Sunday of Lent
*Second Service* **God's Preparation** Ps. 135; Gen. 12:1–9; Heb. 11:1–3, 8–16; [John 8:51–59]

> *'By faith we understand that the worlds were prepared by the word of God, so that what is seen was made from things that are not visible.' Hebrews 11:3*

### Abraham, a shining faith example

Abraham is a shining example of the assurance that can believe in faith (for) things that are not yet visible (vv. 18ff.). Old, and by natural laws incapable of procreation, he nevertheless believed when God promised him a worldful of descendants! And he stuck to this belief for 25 years! How often have we believed in one of God's promises for so long? We usually ask in prayer today, and expect the answer tomorrow, if not sooner. 'Dear Lord, give me patience, but make it quick, because . . .'

God had told Abraham to contemplate the night sky (Gen. 15:5), where the stars created by God's word were shining in their millions. If all of these (and we can only see a few of them!) could be so made, couldn't the Lord also move powerfully in the life of one little man called Abraham (or Abram, as he then was)? Well, we know that Abraham's faith embraced all that God could give. Doesn't it make our little petitions seem possible of being answered, too?

## Cause – and effect

We're so used to looking for cause and effect in the making of things: even the smallest plant grows from a seed that is visible. It's therefore difficult to understand *creatio ex nihilo*. But that is how God brought – and brings – everything into being. His word is creative. On a smaller scale, we 'bring to birth' ideas that grow into visible projects, but this isn't quite the same, since it is God that has brought to birth that idea in the first place. His word (whom John identifies as Jesus, John 1:1–14) echoed out from him into the vacuous ether, and called (literally) things into being. In the account of creation, God spoke before anything was made. We have an echo of the importance of the spoken word, in the teaching of Jesus: 'by your words you will be justified, and by your words you will be condemned' (Matt. 12:37), and also in the Letter of James: 'With [the tongue] we bless the Lord and Father, and with it we curse those who are made in the likeness of God' (James 3:9, but see vv. 1 through to 12, also).

## Valuing the word

We place supreme value on the word of God, understood as Jesus; but also on God's word understood as scripture; and on the words of blessing whereby we share the gospel with others. With Abraham, we can gaze into the night sky, and reflect on the power that called such wonders into being, and also that holds them in ordered motion. We can resolve – a wonderful resolution for Lent! – to keep a closer watch on the millions of words we let our tongues form and release into the atmosphere every day. Are they helping others to a better understanding of God? Are they promoting Jesus and not anyone else (for instance, ourselves)? Are they true words that will pass muster on the parade-ground of heaven, or hold up in the throne room of God? Are they words that we should not be ashamed to have played back to us, just in case God sets the cine-film of our lives running, over there in glory?

## Other words

Let's remember, too, that God is not the only one who can bring words to our minds, although he is the one and only Creator. The devil has no real creativity, but within the parameters allowed him by God till the End of Time, he can manipulate words and thoughts created by God, and can make life difficult for us. So far, and no further (see, e.g., Job 2:6). Praise the Lord, that God has ultimate power; but may we be mindful that the words escaping our lips are God's, and his alone.

## Suggested Hymns

Breathe on me, Breath of God; Firmly I believe and truly; Lord, speak to me, that I may speak; Sing them over again to me.

# Third Sunday of Lent   19 March
*Principal Service*   **The New Way** Ex. 20:1–17; Ps. 19; 1 Cor. 1:18–25; John 2:13–22

> '[Jesus] told those who were selling the doves, "Take these things out of here! Stop making my Father's house a market-place!"'
> John 2:16

## Looking ahead

This was the preliminary to Calvary, where Jesus' death would usher in the new covenant. Yet in effect the new covenant had begun with his coming: already the need for animal sacrifices had been done away: the new offering had come to Israel, but as yet the temple authorities had taken no notice. And they didn't understand why their traditional marketing of sacrifice material had been so abruptly and convincingly attacked. For so long it had been much easier for people to purchase the animals and birds needed for sacrifice in the temple precincts. Each sheep, cow and dove had been certified as conforming to the ritual standard, so this was an additional saving of time and convenience: those bringing their own stock, or that purchased outside the temple, needed to wait in a queue for a priest to become available to examine the animal: and waiting for a long time with a restive heifer could be uncomfortable. Then the money-changers were there in order to convert (for a fee) the normal currency to that demanded by tradition for the temple taxes and offerings. All in all, the whole entrepreneurial enterprise was well established, well organized, and benefited a lot of people.

And Jesus demolished it, virtually at a stroke. Of course, it would fairly quickly be resumed, but the seed had been sown. The writing, for animal sacrifice, was on the wall.

## Show a sign!

The grandees asked for a sign. They were spiritually so blind, they could not recognize that a sign had been given. And they had compromised with financial expediency for so long, it didn't appear to them an infringement of the true purpose of the temple.

It is still possible to allow time to invest practices and developments with the patina of respectability, before realizing that they conflict with the original laws of God. If we take the teaching of Jesus in this gospel reading at face-value, how does it square with our bookstalls, cafes, halls and conference rooms – all included under the church roof? All on consecrated ground? Does Jesus frown on these? Their aims may be laudable, but are they in the right place? No doubt the priests would defend their 'marketplace' as contributing to the worship or upkeep of the temple.

## In spirit and truth

But 'God', as Jesus was to tell the Samaritan woman at the well, 'is spirit, and those who worship him must worship in spirit and truth' (John 4:24). The worship of God is so important, and we need to take especial care that it is not adulterated in any way. The abolition of animal sacrifices with the new covenant, brought about a new awareness of what it means to worship God. It was not a new concept: the prophet Hosea had ventilated it: 'I desire steadfast love, and not sacrifice,' God had said: 'the knowledge of God, rather than burnt-offerings' (Hos. 6:6). Not an outward ritual to make those offering the sacrifice feel good; not a convoluted financial set-up to enrich a few at the expense of the many; but deep-down, genuine, personal heart repentance and commitment.

## Was it too much to ask?

Yes, on the day when Jesus whipped the temple market into mayhem, the authorities could see only a tradition assailed, rather than the adulteration that had crept in over the years.

Perhaps today we can reflect on how we are caring not only for the material house of God, but for the worship that is its *raison d'être*.

*Family Service Input*

Encourage the young people (a) to begin a project on their parish church, (b) to compile an illustrated guide to it, or (c) to discuss what parts of the church mean most to them, and why.


*Suggested Hymns*

O worship the King; The Church of God a Kingdom is; The Church's one foundation; We love the place, O God.


## Third Sunday of Lent
*Second Service* **Through Faith in Christ** Ps. 11, 12; Ex. 5:1–6:1; Phil. 3:4b–14 or Matt. 10:16–22

> '. . . I regard everything as loss because of the surpassing value of knowing Christ Jesus my Lord. For his sake I have suffered the loss of all things, and I regard them as rubbish, in order that I may gain Christ and be found in him, not having a righteousness of my own . . . but one that comes through faith in Christ . . .'
> Philippians 3:8–9


### Our faith, his righteousness

The old monks believed that the more they contemplated an icon, the more of the likeness of Christ they would take on. But we have already been made in the image of God (Gen. 1:26–27). It is the inner righteousness of Christ we need: the mirror-image of his 'love, joy, peace, patience, kindness, generosity, faithfulness, gentleness and self-control' (Gal. 5:22–23). And we gain this, not by looking at a portrait of Jesus, but by purifying ourselves of sin by the atoning power of his blood, and our lives by ridding them of the secular impedimenta that has been accumulated in the mistaken belief of necessity. The world is very good at telling us what it thinks we need; but our Lord would surely not subscribe to most of what today's media calls 'absolutely essential'.


### Profit and loss

Money, possessions, prestige and material safety: none of these will accompany us to the eternal life ahead. In moderation, they cer-

83

tainly help to make this life pleasant, but is that the reason for our existence? To know Jesus and to share that knowledge as much as we can, is surely on the 'profit' side of life's scales. And on the 'loss' side, comes practically everything else. Didn't Jesus say: 'Go and proclaim the kingdom of God . . . No one who puts a hand to the plough and looks back is fit for the kingdom of God' (Luke 9:60, 62)? With one's hand on the plough, there's not too much extra baggage one can carry.

> Money, in truth, is one of the most unsatisfying of possessions. It takes away some cares, no doubt; but it brings with it quite as many cares as it takes away. There is trouble in the getting of it. There is anxiety in the keeping of it. There are temptations in the use of it. There is guilt in the abuse of it. There is sorrow in the losing of it. There is perplexity in the disposing of it. Two-thirds of all the strifes, quarrels and lawsuits in the world, arise from one simple cause – money! (J. C. Ryle, *Practical Religion*)

And what applies to money, applies to most other items that Jesus – and Paul, in our epistle today – would call 'non-essentials'. Isn't it therefore preferable to jettison these, in favour of gaining 'Christ, and being found in him'?

## Both . . . and, or, either . . . or . . . ?

'But possessions and prosperity can surely be used for God!' is the cry heard, when wealth and goods are threatened. Yes, they can be used for God. Jesus told us to sell them and give the money to the poor (e.g. Matt. 19:21; Mark 10:21; Luke 12:33; 18:22); he kept on repeating the message. Riches and goods are not evil per se (though they can be put to evil use); but if they reduce our zest for Christian witness, and the time available for God, they are standing between us and righteousness.

## Faith in Christ

Faith in Christ means exactly what it says. Faith stands alone. If we have fear, we don't have faith (Mark 4:40). If we have material impedimenta that rob God of our time and talents, we don't have the faith we should. Faith in Christ means trust in Christ, enthusiasm for Christ, attention for Christ.

84

Have we, therefore, absolute faith in Christ?
Or is someone or something else vying with him for our attention?

## Suggested Hymns

All for Jesus, all for Jesus; How sweet the name of Jesus sounds; Jesus, the name high over all; To the name of our salvation.

# Fourth Sunday of Lent (Mothering Sunday)
## 26 March
*Principal Service*   **Mother Love** Ex. 2:1–10 or
1 Sam. 1:20–28; Ps. 34:11–20 or Ps. 127:1–4; 2 Cor. 1:3–7 or
Col. 3:12–17; Luke 2:33–35 or John 19:25b–27

> *'As God's chosen ones, holy and beloved, clothe yourselves with compassion, kindness, humility, meekness and patience.'* Colossians 3:12

## Be a mother

In short, be a mother, act like a mother, feel like a mother. Love as Mary loved her Son. Show the virtues of Mary, Mother Church, and the mother heart of God. That is a full-time job description for true Christians. Its very thoroughness can leave us gasping, so God in Christ Jesus gives us extra strength to meet the challenge and to see it through.

The Blessed Virgin Mary shows us what it means to say 'Yes' to God in faith. Everything the Lord calls us to do is, in the natural, impossible. It was sheerly impossible for a young virgin to conceive: Mary had no idea what God was about, or what he was going to do in her to bring his words to pass. But she said 'Yes'. Do we always ask to know the means and the end, before we accept any of God's commands? If we do, we're going to miss out on an awful lot.

## Mother Church

'You are Peter, and on this rock I will build my church,' our Lord told his number one disciple (Matt. 16:18). It took Peter a little time to get his will and his ways in line with this tremendous challenge, but he got there. On the face of it, a rough-hewn Galilean fisherman who often said and did the wrong thing, would not be our example of a motherly sort; yet Peter learned to show the care and love that were to characterize the ideal Christian. Mother Church through the centuries has suffered a lot, cared a lot, loved a lot; and has welcomed millions into her fold. We may not agree with all that goes on in this fold, but she is still mothering us, this side of the grave. Our expectations of her mothering may vary, as do those of a child. We may even believe that Jesus did not envisage the convoluted establishment systems, synods and ecclesiastical bureaucracy that is part and parcel of the Church today; perhaps, in fact, God is calling us to re-evaluate these, and to strip away what is not essential. Yet how does a mother show her love? Not by clinical examination and evaluation, but spontaneously, extravagantly, and without counting the cost. Perhaps, after all, this is a fairer description of how Mother Church is presently operating!

## The mother heart of God

A wise person has said: 'God couldn't be everywhere, so he made mothers!' But to make mothers, God must surely have had their components within himself. He is our 'Dad' (Abba), but he also loves us, cares for us, caresses us, trains and instils gentle qualities in us, like a mother. And who but a mother could have the patience with us that God shows? And who but God could have included with such a high profile as he gave Mary, a mother's love in the life and mission of the Saviour of the world?

> In the sunshine or the shadow,
> In the tempest or the calm,
> Underneath and round about you
> Are those everlasting arms.
> (Revd Tom Jones)

Just like a mother's arms, ever there to enfold and support and uphold us, whether things are fraught or wonderful. The Irish folk song says much, but not all the story:

> A mother's love's a blessing,
> No matter where you roam;
> Keep her while she's living,
> For you'll miss her when she's gone.

*Love her, as in childhood,*
*When feeble, old and grey;*
*You'll never miss your mother's love*
*Till she's buried beneath the clay.*

Thank God, that the mother love he gives – to Mary, the Church and every other mother – does not end at the grave.

### Family Service Input

Have flowers and materials ready for the young folk to make up into posies and/or cards, to present to mothers and all cherished friends at the end of the service.

### Suggested Hymns

For Mary, mother of the Lord; For the beauty of the earth; Jesus, good above all other; Maiden, yet a mother.

## Fourth Sunday of Lent
*Second Service*   **By Grace** Num. 21:4–9; Ps. 107:1–3, 17–22; Eph. 2:1–10; John 3:14–21

*'For by grace you have been saved through faith, and this is not your own doing; it is the gift of God – not the result of works, so that no one may boast. For we are what he has made us, created in Christ Jesus for good works, which God prepared beforehand to be our way of life.' Ephesians 2:8–10*

### Divine antidote

This teaching, in Paul's letter to the Ephesians, is the divine antidote to egotism. God is saying, in effect: 'Just remember what you came from, and who made you what you are. You are living and breathing by my grace. You are surrounded by good things by my grace. You've been preserved from all sorts of evil and tragedy by my grace. And you have the potential to do more, work more, live more by my grace.'

## As children

We are, in God's eyes, children. As a mother sees her offspring as children for as long as she knows them, so – in a manner of speaking – in God's eyes we never grow up! As a mother knows her children so intimately that they cannot hide anything from her, so God knows us through and through, even to the thoughts and intentions that never make it to the folk around us. With the penetrating, yet loving, insight and intuition of a mother, God operates in grace. By its very qualities, grace is a feminine virtue; and therefore with God's grace we can see right through to the mother heart of God.

Isn't that wonderful? Yes, it is, for it surely calls forth from us in response the best and purest that is in us.

By grace, God has given us gentleness, meekness, kindness, patience and all the virtues that shine out of a mother and which make her the beautiful person she is.

All by grace.

## Gracious reflection

On this Mothering Sunday, when hearts reach out in love and gentleness, thoughts recall days of a mother's care . . . it is good to reflect on the gracious love of God: all that he has given us, to become what he knows we can be. We may consider we are well on the way to that goal; we certainly haven't yet reached it, or we shouldn't still be here. Or perhaps on reflection we have veered a bit off course; we've lost some of the graciousness we once had. Can we pray the Lord to show us how to regain this precious quality? Not for ourselves alone, but so that it may benefit others. It is redeemable. God made us with the necessary equipment; we don't have to wait until we get to glory. Our God-given graciousness in the here and now, may mean that more people will eventually get to glory with us.

## Not by might

It's 'not by might, nor by power, but by my spirit, says the Lord of hosts' (Zech. 4:6). We can't bribe our way into grace by good 'works', otherwise, says Paul, in this lesson today, we may be tempted to boast. The 'good works' are those that Jesus enables us BY GRACE to do: the credit is his, the glory is his; and the only part that we can 'boast' about is the fact that he has used us as his instruments BY GRACE, by God's unmerited favour.

As a mother does so much good that is either unobserved or taken for granted (until she's no longer around to do it), so Jesus tells us that we should be unobtrusive in our working; yes, even in our working for God: ESPECIALLY in our working for God, since we should (like John the Baptist) be living to show the grace of God.

That grace is his, after all, not ours.

### Suggested Hymns

God of mercy, God of grace; Great is thy faithfulness; I am thine, O Lord; Will you come and follow me.

## Fifth Sunday of Lent  2 April
*Principal Service*   **A Troubled Soul** Jer. 31:31–34; Ps. 51:1–13 or Ps. 119:9–16; Heb. 5:5–10; John 12:20–33

> *'Now my soul is troubled, and what should I say – "Father, save me from this hour"? No, it is for this reason that I have come to this hour. Father, glorify your name. Then a voice came from heaven: "I have glorified it, and will glorify it again."' John 12:27–28*

### Our feeling Lord

The impassivity of the pantheon of pagan gods is as far removed from our Lord Jesus as is possible to be. He cares, he loves, he weeps and he hurts for us. And here, in this poignant passage leading up to his passion, he says, very personally: 'My soul is troubled'. Yes, it's troubled for what he knows is ahead. We cannot begin to imagine the anguish he must have gone through, in the knowledge of the passion to come. At such a time, can we not thank God for mercifully keeping our future hidden from us? But he was also troubled for our sakes. If he did not go through 'his hour', we should not be saved. OUR future, as well as his own (dare we suggest, even MORE than his own) was at stake, that day, as Jesus prayed in trouble of soul to his Father.

It is wonderful for us to have a Saviour with such deep feelings of care and love for us; but here we get a glimpse of the cost of caring that he paid.

89

## God came through

But on the scene also was the Father who also cares: for the Saviour, and the saved. And God came through for his Son, with encouraging words. 'Oh, it's thundering!' cried some of the insensitive onlookers – and probably waited for the rain. 'No, wasn't that an angel?' asked the more enlightened. But Jesus knew even better than these.

It had been a very public prayer, and God had responded in a very public way. Why are we so often determined to whisper our communications to God? Why, also, are we often so unwilling to give him the credit when his answer comes in a way other than the 'still, small voice' we expect? Read the early chapters of Isaiah, and see just what a noisy, dramatic, exciting place heaven is, and pray for grace not to limit the Lord to whispers!

## The right time

With the passion approaching, it was not the time for whispers. The great saving act of the world was going to be noisy, public and dramatic, with attendant earthquakes, thick darkness, and resurrections (Matt. 27:45, 51–53). This was the right time to 'go public', even though Jesus knew that, come Easter morning, despite all the forecasting, he was going to have a hard time convincing even his nearest and dearest that he had won through. This was 'his hour', and the most important work was to see the Father's name glorified, or, in popular understanding, to make God's power known. Nothing like it had happened before. People were going to be slow to comprehend. But God was at work, and eventually truth would 'out'.

Even in acknowledging that the Father had power to save Jesus from the passion, our Lord was glorifying God. And today, 'God is able' are three words that need to undergird all we do, and say, and pray. 'God is able': we thus acknowledge his supreme authority. However he answers our prayers, however he works in our lives, he is operating fully on his terms. Satan works within God-ordained limits; always it has been so, and until the End of Time it will continue to be so. After that, it's God's business how he deals with the devil. God is able to take care of eternity.

He is able. After the voice from the heavens, the Saviour knew that the passion would go forward. The Father, through the Son, would save the world.

He remains faithful to that promise.

### Family Service Input

Encourage the young folk to design a 'Passion Cross', including as much detail as possible (the whip, nails, bag of silver, dice, etc.). If the cross is made as large as possible, it can be set up in the church, and the various parts coloured, as the passion unfolds.

### Suggested Hymns

Father, we love you (Glorify your name); God's glory fills the universe; Man of sorrows; O sacred head.

# Fifth Sunday of Lent
*Second Service*   **Good Over Evil** Ps. 34; Ex. 7:8–24; Rom. 5:12–21 [Luke 22:1–13]

> *'But law came in, with the result that the trespass multiplied; but where sin increased, grace abounded all the more; so that, just as sin exercised dominion in death, so grace might also exercise dominion through justification leading to eternal life through Jesus Christ our Lord.' Romans 5:20–21*

## So much more

The victory of Jesus is so much greater than the fall of Adam. The first man had introduced evil into God's good earth; the second Man cleansed us from the inside, so that the effects of Adam's sin were annulled. Many souls had been lost as a result of Adam's compromise with Satan; many more would be saved because of what Jesus accomplished. Adam's sin was pre-eminently selfish; Jesus' victory was vicarious and magnanimous. The first man's fall led to the adulteration of the earth; the second Man's victory opened the door to eternal perfection. Good was shown in the life, death and resurrection of Jesus, to be stronger – infinitely stronger – than evil, on all counts.

## Through justification

Jesus did not come to justify himself; he had no need to. He came, on our behalf, to justify us. We couldn't have done it on our own,

Adam's sin had gone so deep. But Jesus at Calvary went down as deep, and deeper still. He got under the sin of Adam, in order to reverse it completely; and out of the deepest darkness he brought once again the undimmed light and resurrection power of God, as it had been in the days before the Fall.

Yet not absolutely as it had been. There is now a big difference, to remind us (in case we stood in danger of forgetting) of the tremendous cost of the love involved: our Lord forevermore carries the scars of sacrifice. Each of those wounds is a mute yet powerful reminder, of saving grace.

## The dominion of grace

Some of the sheer dominion of this grace is surely seen in the ongoing power of Jesus, to bring us to glory; for still, after Calvary, mankind has the tendency to sin, the freedom of choice to choose another way than God's, the ability to dance to Satan's tune. Where would be the challenge of the gospel, if Satan had not been toppled to earth after losing the war with Michael and his angels (Rev. 12:7–9)? But, tap into the grace of God, take up the cross and follow Christ, and this grace grows and continues to abound. We go, in the strength of Christ, from grace to more grace.

## Passion Sunday

Passion Sunday prepares us to go with our Lord again through the commemoration of his passion, to reflect in gratitude and not a little wonder, on his love for us that made it possible. There will never need to be another passion. Satan, despite his strongest efforts, cannot eradicate the growing influence of Jesus in the world. But the devil will continue to try, for he's the most stubborn creature alive, and refuses to give up while there are still Christians to attack. And every time we see haunting despair in the eyes of the starving, the homeless, the pain-wracked and crippled, we see again something of what Christ suffered to give hope to our world.

Every time we see it, doesn't it move us to do something about it, in the name of Jesus?

### Suggested Hymns

A debtor to mercy alone; Lift high the cross; Sing, my tongue, the glorious battle; With joy we meditate the grace.

## Palm Sunday 9 April
*Principal Service* **God Does Not Deal in Waste**
Isa. 50:4–9a; Ps. 31:9–16 [17–18]; Phil. 2:5–11;
Mark 14:1—15:47 or Mark 15:1–39 [40–47]

> *'But some were there who said to one another in anger, "Why was this ointment wasted in this way? For this ointment could have been sold for more than three hundred denarii, and the money given to the poor." And they scolded her.' Mark 14:4–5*

### Such a waste?

... And the time spent in cheering Jesus as he rode into Jerusalem, could have been channelled into ministering to the poor ... And the poor would no doubt have been grateful if the cloaks strewn for the donkey to walk on had been thrown their way ... And, what about the donkey? Couldn't it have been given to a poor man, too?

'But Jesus said, "Let her alone. She has performed a good service for me. For you always have the poor with you ... but you will not always have me"' (Mark 14:6–7).

Matthew 26:8 identifies 'the disciples' as the Holy Joes; John tells us it was Judas (John 12:4–5). It seems to sit better on Judas than on Peter and the others. Still today there are those who carp and criticize when service is given to God: 'What is the point? What a waste!' they sneer, and often leave the poor to fend for themselves anyway.

### Divine generosity

God is an abundant giver, showering us with far more than 'the bare essentials', and how it must warm him when we respond generously. Yet there are many who find it hard to come to terms with this reference of Jesus to the poor. He came to heal the sick, to raise the dead, thus showing his concern for the physically handicapped. But how about the financially deprived? His answer to the disciples of John was simply: 'The poor have good news [the gospel, AV] brought to them' (Matt. 11:5). Would that put food on their table, wine in their stomachs, clothes on their back? Not directly: it didn't aim to be a social security hand-out. But it would show them how to live. God knows we need food, drink and clothing: 'strive first for the kingdom of God and his righteousness,' Jesus taught, 'and all these things will be given to you as well' (Matt. 6:33).

## Answer to poverty

That is our Lord's answer to financial, mental, physical and spiritual poverty. He neither put material poverty up in lights, nor disregarded it. Instead, he preached the good news that was the answer right across the board: the gospel that everyone needs, whether rich or poor, black or white, Jew or Gentile. There is a glorious irrespectiveness in Christ's good news. The gospel knows no bounds: the poor need to take the step of belief, the rich the step of selling what they have. We have a glimpse of how faithfully the early Church put the gospel of Jesus into practice in Acts: 'All who believed were together and had all things in common; they would sell their possessions and goods and distribute the proceeds to all, as any need . . .' (Acts 2:44–45, and read on to v. 48). A waste? By no means!

## The best

Mary (or whoever the woman was) gave the best ointment she could afford, and its aroma would delight others present, as well as Jesus. When we offer our best to God – in time, talents or finance – we shall certainly benefit others as well as ourselves; but most importantly, we shall please the Lord. Do we deprive ourselves of anything in the process? Are we giving 'till it hurts'? That's not the issue: so long as we delight God, our implied or perceived deprivation is not only irrelevant, but at worst short-lived.

> Be still, my soul; thy Jesus can repay,
> From his own fulness, all he takes away.
> (Katharina von Schlegel, b. 1697; tr.
> J. L. Borthwick, 1819–97)

What is true of dying, is also true of living; there again, God is no respecter.

### Family Service Input

Encourage the young people to illustrate the love shown to Jesus, from the ointment up to his passion.

## Suggested Hymns

All glory, laud and honour; Oh, the love of my Lord is the essence;
Ride on! ride on, in majesty; Said Judas to Mary.


# Palm Sunday
*Second Service*   **Devastation Foretold** Ps. 69:1–20;
Isa. 5:1–7; Mark 12:1–12

> *'And now I will tell you what I will do to my vineyard. I will remove
> its hedge and it shall be devoured. I will break down its wall, and
> it shall be trampled down.' Isaiah 5:5*


## God had been patient

Through the centuries since Adam, God had been so patient, urging,
commanding, cajoling, encouraging humankind to reverse the trend
and to return to his way, his will, his goodness. For generations
through the prophets, he had warned of devastation as the outcome
of Israel's backsliding; and at length he sent his Son to give the
people one last chance. So deep was his feeling, so great his love
for folk who had done nothing to merit it, that our Lord wept as
he looked at Jerusalem (Luke 19:41). There she lay, like a tawny
lion basking in the sun. The great walls were to fall in AD 70, under
the Roman onslaught, and the magnificent temple – the third on
that site – was to be taken over by enemies.


## What more could God have done?

What more could the Lord have done (Isa. 5:4)? And what more
can we do today, that we are not already doing, to bring non-
believers to Jesus? If a resurrection from the dead leaves them
unmoved (Luke 16:31), what can we do? Are they doomed for
ever? There is a dreadful finality about God's promise: 'I will command the clouds, that they rain no rain upon it' (Isa. 5:6b). Without
sustenance, there can be no life: it will not be snuffed out abruptly,
but will die a lingering death. And it will have deserved its fate.

## For the right reason

But Jesus came, not only to warn people away from disaster. He wants us to believe in him for the right reason: not out of fear, but love. That is why God never compels anyone to believe. Our faith, to be a true living faith, needs to be spontaneous, joyful, unconditional and therefore full of love. We can come to Jesus with a sense of obligation, giving him our loyalty and service in some return for our debt that he settled in full at Calvary. That is acceptable, so long as love overrides as well as undergirds our obligation; but if we follow him merely from a sense of duty, or from a mistaken idea that by taking up with him we can set the record straight, it's a pretty useless exercise. The Father heart of God asks for mercy (= love) and not sacrifice (= duty).

## God's fairness

God is magnificently unfair in his fairness! He gave ample warning of what would happen if people did not (and do not) believe in his Son. And he is still giving people 'time for amendment of life, and the grace and comfort' of his Holy Spirit, if they will only accept his invitation.

> *The Palm Sunday crowds on the roadside that morning*
> *Knew little by knowledge, yet hailed you in faith;*
> *Their shouts now we echo, as knowing you better:*
> *Our King – yet the carpenter's Son of the lathe.*

It does not do, to be too wise in our dealings with God. The stronger is our faith, the less proof, logic, commonsense or reason we shall either demand or miss. We either come to God on his terms, or not at all. We have a fairly short time in which to make up our minds, but an awfully long eternity to regret making the wrong decision.

## *Suggested Hymns*

A charge to keep I have; Christ is made the sure foundation; I will enter his gates; My song is love unknown.

# Monday of Holy Week   10 April
**Purified by Blood** Isa. 42:1–9; Ps. 36:5–11; Heb. 9:11–15;
John 12:1–11

*'For if the blood of goats and bulls, with the sprinkling of the
ashes of a heifer, sanctifies those who have been defiled so that
their flesh is purified, how much more will the blood of Christ,
who through the eternal Spirit offered himself without blemish
to God, purify our consciences from dead works to worship the
living God.' Hebrews 9:13–14*

## Through the Spirit

We get a glimpse here of the writer's understanding of Jesus' motiv-
ation. At the beginning of Lent, we shared Mark's version of how
the Spirit 'drove' Jesus into the wilderness (Mark 1:12). Now we
see the Spirit again as the moving force at Calvary. Recall how
active this same Spirit was in the earliest days of the world, when
'the Spirit of God' swept over the waters (NRSV mg, AV). The
energizing force, which makes visible the work of God the Father
and God the Son, is this dynamic Spirit, the third Person/Partner/
Emanation – call him what one will – of the Deity. Therefore, it
was natural for Jesus to make clear to his disciples, that when he
had visibly returned to glory, his Spirit would be given to them, so
that they could see the effects of what God was continuing to do
in the world. Today, the Holy Spirit is more active than ever before:
but he is nowhere near the limit of his capability ... for he is
limitless. Were everyone in the world to be converted to Christianity, the Spirit would still have reserves of power. This thought
should add an extra dimension and vitality to our prayers. Are we
asking God for big things? Are we seeking mega-miracles? If not,
we are seriously undervaluing and underusing the spiritual power
on offer.

## Holy Week

Holy Week is an appropriate time to think along these lines, for it
is in the passion of Jesus that we see God so powerfully at work.
A Roman procurator was baffled; an Idumaean puppet king was
perplexed; the whole of the Jerusalem ecclesiastical hierarchy was
wrong-footed; and a new order was born. The world (or at least

that part of the world that was up in Jerusalem for the Passover) saw one man crucified. God saw his Holy Spirit at work. On Easter Day, a few people saw an empty tomb. God saw Satan defeated and the Underworld smashed open. Today, if we'll only open our spiritual eyes, there is a feast of activity to be seen, an array of messages to be read – activity and messages that non-believers either misinterpret or miss altogether.

There will never be another Calvary, but there are plenty of lesser calvaries to concentrate our minds:

> *Still stands his cross, from that dread hour to this,*
> *Like some bright star above the dark abyss;*
> *Still, through the veil, the Victor's pitying eyes*
> *Look down to bless our lesser calvaries.*
> (Sir John S. Arkwright)

## Pleading the blood

'Pleading the blood' is a phrase not too often used these days, but this is where the heartbeat of the Holy Spirit is: rooted in the blood shed at Calvary, that washed away man's inherited sin; visible in the wine at every Eucharist, that keeps the great sacrifice in remembrance. We who drink this blood are re-energized with the resurrection power of God, fired up by the Spirit to live free from the weight of sin's load. So lightened, we can do and dare for Jesus what in the natural seems impossible. All because of that precious fountain that flowed from the Saviour's veins: it was his lifeblood pouring from him into us, with vivifying strength. From that day on, his veins wouldn't need it: resurrection power works on a higher energy than blood; but it makes the difference between spiritually living and dying for us.

> *There is a fountain filled with blood*
> *Drawn from Immanuel's veins;*
> *And sinners plunged beneath this flood*
> *Lose all their guilty stains.*
> (William Cowper, 1731–1800)

Beneath the cross of Jesus; In the cross of Christ I glory; Lord, through this Holy Week of our salvation; When we walk with the Lord.

# Tuesday of Holy Week  11 April
**The Power of God** Isa. 49:1–7; Ps. 71:1–14; 1 Cor. 1:18–31; John 12:20–36

> *'For the message about the cross is foolishness to those who are perishing, but to us who are being saved it is the power of God.'*
> *1 Corinthians 1:18*

## Seeing by sight

The events of Holy Week and the passion itself are a contradiction in terms to many who see in the natural. They 'see' what is visible: Jesus becoming weaker and weaker as the net closes in around him, until he dies on a cross between two thieves. It is God visibly vulnerable, while man gets the upper hand. Promises and prophecies are fulfilled, certainly: the King comes riding on a donkey; the temple-court is cleared; the Son of God is betrayed, and the betrayer dies at his own hand; the arrest, trial, scourging and crucifixion – all have been foretold. But to what end? Absolute darkness on Good Friday afternoon.

That is 'seeing by sight'. And, so far as it goes, it appears the whole story ... Except that appearances can be misleading ...

## Seeing by faith

When the same events are 'seen by faith', they tell a very different story. Jesus became stronger, not weaker. By Friday afternoon, he was strong enough to power down into hell; and that led to Satan being shown very convincingly who was the Master, come Sunday morning. Prophecy had been fulfilled, because this was God honouring his promises made long before. That Jesus died in the most shameful way was a part of that fulfilment that had to be: the power of God had to be seen to triumph over the worst that could happen.

## The two ways

The cross stands as an uncompromising choice between the two ways: the one, of believing and following Jesus; the other, at right angles and cutting straight across the first in completely the opposite direction, of believing in the foolishness of it, and rejecting Jesus. The two ways meet only once, when the upright meets the horizontal at Calvary. Calvary's sacrifice is the meeting-point of decision: we make that our time of either commitment or negation. Nowhere else, ever again, does the cross come together. If we reject Calvary, we are on a road that is forever running away from Jesus; and the only way back is, literally, back: back to Calvary, and the time of decision.

'Do you doubt whether you are saved, or whether you shall hold out to the end? Then I counsel you to go back to the Cross, and begin again as a penitent sinner to put your trust in a pardoning Saviour. Full many a time I have to do that' (C. H. Spurgeon). Praise God, the road to – and from – Calvary is kept open by the power that still offers salvation on a worldwide scale!

### Suggested Hymns

Cross of Jesus, cross of sorrow; Lord, through this Holy Week of our salvation; Thou art the Way, by thee alone; When I survey the wondrous cross.


## Wednesday of Holy Week   12 April
### Divine Endurance Isa. 50:4–9a; Ps. 70; Heb. 12:1–3; John 13:21–32

> *'looking to Jesus the pioneer and perfecter of our faith, who for the sake of the joy that was set before him endured the cross, disregarding the shame, and has taken his seat at the right hand of the throne of God.' Hebrews 12:2–3*


## At its most loving

This is divine endurance (= patience) at its most loving, for Jesus had the power to back out of his contract at any time. Did he ever wonder if he was leaving his 'little children' (John 13:33) too soon? Did he have doubts about their readiness to take the gospel out from Jerusalem? No, for he was fully in the will of his Father, and knew that the disciples were going to be so empowered with the Holy Spirit that they would accomplish the work. He had pioneered their faith, and (except for the betrayer, whose wickedness had been foretold), he would see them through to a perfect end. It is the same today, for the Lord never changes. If only we could take this truth into our hearts, we should surely not worry like we do. We shall 'make it', because Jesus is the perfecter as well as the pioneer of our faith.

## Divine disregard

The AV says Jesus 'despised' the shame of the cross, which is pretty strong language. He treated it as though it wasn't there. His mind was so concentrated on his mission of salvation, he focused on all those who could look forward to sharing eternity with him, once he had accomplished his saving act. The means just didn't count with him; it was the end that mattered. Are we so single-minded in the sharing of the gospel? Do we take note of difficulties, ridicule, animosity, apathy? Or do we just forge calmly on, letting Satan get more and more frustrated in his efforts to stop us? Remember that in those efforts the devil is not merely coming against us, but against the all-powerful Spirit of Jesus in us. If we believe that Satan can do us serious harm, we are in effect negating Christ's Calvary sacrifice; saying that it may work for some, but not for us.

None of us is smart enough to come up with a difficulty that the Holy Spirit cannot handle.

## Lord, increase our faith

He will, because he has already expended so much energy and love on us, we'll never know how much. Yet the investment he made in us at Calvary did not bankrupt him, but gave him so much joy he is determined still to do all he can for us to reach the goal set before us. To have such an Advocate means that he takes the strain (unless we're so dumb, we want to try to do his job for him), and all we need to do is to stand firm, walk in truth, and let Jesus' worth carry its considerable weight with the Judge. Just go on increasing our faith, Lord, because we're still human, and there are times when we forget you're gunning for us.

How often, for instance, do we focus on our Lord seated at the right hand of God's throne? Not too often, for it's a glory that as yet we haven't experienced. A glimpse of it came, with the death of the first Christian martyr. Stephen, before he had actually died, shared his vision with all within earshot: 'Filled with the Holy Spirit, he gazed into heaven and saw the glory of God and Jesus standing at the right hand of God. "Look," he said [as though his human companions could see what he was looking on], "I see the heavens opened, and the Son of Man standing at the right hand of God!"' (Acts 7:55–56).

As we move further into Holy Week, what a wonderful vision this is, on which to reflect!

### Suggested Hymns

Around the throne of God a band; Lord, through this Holy Week of our salvation; Round the Lord in glory seated; Ye holy angels bright.

## Maundy Thursday   13 April
### Setting an Example Ex. 12:1–4 [5–10] 11–14; Ps. 116:1, 10–end (or 9–end); 1 Cor. 11:23–26; John 13:1–17, 31b–35

> '[Jesus said], "For I have set you an example, that you also should do as I have done to you. Very truly I tell you, servants are not greater than their master, nor are messengers greater than the one who sent them."' John 13:15–16

### How to do it

What an example! How a Jewish Passover meal could form the eucharistic sacrment of the Christian Church; and how God could show such loving humility as to perform the lowliest act a man could do for another! Our Lord knew that the apostles could be feted as gods, but they must remember who had commissioned them, and give the glory and credit to God. He knew the delight that healing, exorcism and preaching could – and would – bring; but again, they must not allow pride and self-satisfaction to blind them to the fact that to Jesus rightfully belonged the power, to God the glory.

## And what has happened?

And what has happened? In many parts of the world the Church has become known for magnificence, pomp and circumstance; the simple meal in fairly humble surroundings is at times overlaid with liturgy and grandiose architecture. The purveyors of the gospel are often decked out in gold and scarlet thread, and their message camouflaged with ceremonial. And, when challenged, don't we hear the defence: 'Only the best is good enough for God!'

So it is. But only so long as our best is God's best. Only so long as what we do and say shows Jesus and nobody else to the world. Ego-trips are not the stuff of which a Christian worthy of the name is made.

## Night of the institution

'Do this, in my memory', Jesus commanded. And the words, albeit gentle, were certainly a command. And the Christian Church, in the way it has perceived, has obeyed the command. Every Eucharist is a revisiting of Jerusalem, a re-enactment of the meal when so much was done, so much left undone; so much was said, and so much left unsaid. The remembrance is at our Eucharist, too; the love, concern and service. But less obvious is the perplexity of that first Eucharist, when the disciples didn't know what was happening, still less, what was going to happen. The night had fallen, the betrayer had left.

And they didn't know what it was all about.

Knowledge makes our Eucharists different; just how different, depends on the extent of our knowledge, the depth of our faith, and the grace that God gives us to see beyond our modern surroundings and pomp and circumstance, to the heart of the memorial. Jesus has come visibly again, in the bread and wine, to meet up with his Spirit in us, and to continue making and developing us into the people he wants us to be.

Can we, on this Maundy Thursday, use Horatius Bonar's hymn as a prayer:

> *Here, O my Lord, I see thee face to face;*
> *Here faith would touch and handle things unseen;*
> *Here grasp with firmer hand the eternal grace,*
> *And all my weariness upon thee lean.*

*Here would I feed upon the Bread of God,*
*Here drink with thee the royal Wine of heaven;*
*Here would I lay aside each earthly load,*
*Here taste afresh the calm of sin forgiven.*

*I have no help but thine, nor do I need*
*Another arm save thine to lean upon.*
*It is enough, my Lord, enough indeed,*
*My strength is in thy might, thy might alone.*

## Suggested Hymns

Bread of heaven, on thee we feed; I hunger and I thirst; O thou, who at thy Eucharist did pray; We pray thee, heavenly Father.

## Good Friday   14 April
*Principal Service*   **Unaccepted Challenge**
Isa. 52:13—53:12; Ps. 22; Heb. 10:16–25 or Heb. 10:14–16; 5:7–9; John 18:1—19:42

> *'Jesus answered, "I have spoken openly to the world; I have always taught in synagogues and in the temple, where all the Jews come together. I have said nothing in secret. Why do you ask me? Ask those who heard what I said to them; they know what I said."' John 18:20–21*

### 'They know'

Well, they did, but where were they? Peter was out in the courtyard hall, warming himself at the fire and wishing he was somewhere else. The other disciples? They were missing links. The crowds who had cheered Jesus into Jerusalem? They'd be asleep in their homes. Only a few priestly supporters (who almost certainly had been bribed) were around, and they said exactly what the high priest wanted to hear.

Peter and the others who did not accept the challenge to speak in Christ's defence, were in for a dreadful weekend, for as yet they did not know that it would end in triumph. Today, we, too, fail to accept challenge after challenge to speak up and out for Jesus: the talk we could have given, but 'something else cropped up'. The meeting we could have addressed, but it was a bad night. The young man who seemed to want to ask a question, but we were running late. The news item on the telly – we were going to 'write-in' about it – and then forgot . . .

Little, little things, but what a lot of unaccepted challenges they add up to!

## God is able

Yes, God is able, and Peter, warming himself at the high priest's fire, probably thought that Jesus was well able to extricate himself from the situation. Of course he was – more than able. But he had already told Peter that he must suffer, and Peter had already been reprimanded for protesting (Matt. 16:21–23). What Peter had not accepted, was that Jesus WAS ABLE to suffer, and yet to win through. May we today not fall into Peter's trap of being overly protective of God: God is still able to meet and defeat, whatever it takes, to get a soul to eternity. Some of us, years after we've graduated from nursery-school, still try to impact every situation with the 'Once upon a time . . . happy ever after' formula. God is not so restricted.

## All that work

The tragedy was, Jesus had worked so hard teaching, preaching and healing, for the past three years, yet no one who had been blessed by his ministry could find the courage to speak out in his defence. Not that their witness would have affected the outcome, but it would have been an encouragement for our Lord, as well as being a tribute, however small, to his endeavours.

Jesus had been open in his ministry, yet no one could come forward at this critical time to vouch for him. Throughout the 2,000 years since, millions have 'lain low', rather than speak out for Christ; millions more have simply walked away when the 'hour of decision' arrived. Yet still he is saying, to all who will hear: 'Ask those who [have] heard what I said to them; they know what I [have said].' Of course we know, because the Holy Spirit has grafted the words of Jesus into our hearts.

God is waiting.

Are we going to accept the opportunity while it's still on offer?

## Suggested Hymns

Forgive them, O my Father; His are the thousand sparkling rills; O, come and mourn with me awhile; We sing the praise of him who died.

# Good Friday

*Morning Prayer* **Telling the Truth** Ps. 69; Gen. 22:1–18; John 18—19 (any part, if not used at the Principal Service); or Heb. 10:1–10

> 'Pilate asked [Jesus], "What is truth?" . . . One of the soldiers pierced [Jesus'] side with a spear, and at once blood and water came out. (He who saw this has testified so that you also may believe. His testimony is true; and he knows that he tells the truth.)' John 18:38; 19:34–35

## At a premium

Truth and her sister justice were at a premium on Good Friday morning, as the religious grandees incited the crowd to call for a crucifixion verdict. In his way, Pilate tried to grasp the elusive truth. But, though Truth Incarnate stood before him, he could not hold on to it, and chose instead the easier option of going with the crowd.

John, as a witness of it all, goes to some lengths to promote the veracity of his reportage. He saw what he says he saw, and we must believe what he says. By the time he writes his account, there will have been many false stories circulating, many so-called 'testimonies' that conflict. 'You can believe THIS testimony,' John assures his readers.

## Integrity

Our own integrity in preaching, teaching and sharing the gospel, needs to be of an equally high standard. The world, in any case, has enough inaccuracies, without our adding to them. 'I'm telling you,' John is saying, with poignant sincerity, 'THIS is show it happened.'

## Where are we?

And what are our thoughts, as another Good Friday draws towards its close? With Pilate, in his well-meant, but unsuccessful, search for truth? With John, as he took on the care of Mary (John 19:25–27)? Was he already thinking: 'I must remember everything I can, to tell those who are not here'? Or are we suffering with our Lord, as so many of those he had come to save, are shouting for his death? We know the outcome; perhaps we cannot therefore feel as much of the agony and anguish as we otherwise would. But the cruelty, the pain, the blood – we cannot blot them out of today's thoughts. Nor should we, for unless we truthfully enter into our Lord's passion, how truthfully shall we be able to share it with others? How much will Sunday's joy impact on us, if Friday's sorrow has passed us by?

## What is truth?

What is truth, but the simple telling of what has been? Not elaborated, altered or adulterated in any way; not dramatized, to 'appeal to the modern world', but telling it as it is. And then God works a miracle, for the truth emerges as to what it means to us; we find we are sharing OUR Saviour with others, OUR Lord who stood before Pilate, and who then went to the cross bearing OUR sins, and died for love of US.

And when this truth hits us, so does the reality of John's words: '(S)he who saw this has testified so that you also may believe. This testimony is true, and I know that I tell the truth.'

Then the trauma of today, even at a 2,000-year remove, will not have been in vain.

### Suggested Hymns

Glory be to Jesus; It is finished! Blessed Jesus; My Lord, my Master, at thy feet adoring; We sing the praise of him who died.

# Easter Eve   15 April

## (not the Easter Vigil)   **Good Joseph** Job 14:1–14 or
Lam. 3:1–9, 19–24; Ps. 31:1–4, 15–16; 1 Pet. 4:1–8;
Matt. 27:57–66 or John 19:38–42

*'When it was evening, there came a rich man from Arimathea, named Joseph, who was also a disciple of Jesus.' Matthew 27:57*

## Into the open

We have heard nothing of Joseph until now, but the trauma of Good Friday has brought him very convincingly into the open. When did he first meet Jesus? Where is Arimathea? Surely, being a rich man, he would have a high profile? How has he managed to keep his discipleship secret until today? He comes into the open, is influential enough to seek out Pilate for official permission to take the body of Jesus ... This is no downtown convert, but a man of the world, a landowner, a person of substance and stature.

There is just the inkling here, is there not, of a ministry of Jesus that has escaped the evangelists. Perhaps our Lord went much further with his gospel than Matthew, Mark, Luke and John would suggest from the written record. Nicodemus is no stranger: his introduction to Jesus has been documented (John 3:1ff.). But Joseph (rather like Melchizedek) comes out of the miasma of unknowing, yet just at the right time.

## The unexpected

It is the unexpectedness of his coming that makes an impact on us, even now. The disciples whom one would normally expect to be 'up-front', are conspicuous by their absence (except for John). And yet it's surely significant that two rich men – who, on normal grounds, may have found their riches, power and prestige a hindrance to reaching the kingdom of God – come forward with generous gifts of embalming oils and a brand-new tomb, to give our Lord 'decent burial' in every sense.

Is the Lord telling us here, that wealth need not be an impediment to the Christian life? This would surely encourage many today, for whom the otherwise stark message to 'sell all' seems too high a price to ask. Perhaps this question has not impacted on too many Easter Eves, yet we may indeed reflect on it with no feeling of impropriety. The event of Easter Day would have gone ahead, if Jesus' body had not been given such loving, lavish care, but in the fact that it was given – and by two previously secret disciples – is surely importance.

## Declaring openly

Not that we should emulate Joseph and Nicodemus in keeping our faith hidden until a 'big opportunity' for disclosure rolls along; it would be a tragedy if God called us home before anyone else had an inkling of our commitment. But let's, by all means, follow the example of these two good men, in giving of our best unstintingly to the Lord. Neither of them knew that Jesus would rise on the Sunday; they treated his body as though 'once dead, forever dead'. But this was a measure of their love: extravagance for God. May we also not count the cost of what we do for God; we can rest assured he will keep an accurate record.

### *Suggested Hymns*

Good Joseph had a garden; Low in the grave he lay; Resting from his work today; There is a green hill far away.


# Easter Vigil   15–16 April
**Where God Has Been** Ex. 14:10–31; 15:20–21; Isa. 55:1–11; Ezek. 37:1–14; Ps. 114; Rom. 6:3–11; Mark 16:1–8

> *'And very early on the first day of the week, when the sun had risen, [the women] went to the tomb . . . When they looked up, they saw that the stone, which was very large, had already been rolled back.' Mark 16:2, 4*


## In God's footsteps

These women were treading hallowed ground, where God had walked that morning. Love had prompted them to come, but Love had been before them, moving the heavy stone and preparing the tomb to tell its own story. For them not to have come, not to have cared enough to bring spices for Jesus, would have been to delay learning of the good news. It's the same today, for the Lord doesn't change. Love will prompt us to set out on a kindly mission, and we find as we progress, that God has already trodden the way before us; and we end up not merely blessing someone but receiving an even greater blessing ourselves.

## Through Lent

We've come through Lent and Holy Week, keeping as close as possible to our Lord out of love for him. But today, he's waiting to give us far more than we've given him: an Easter blessing big enough for the whole world . . . except, not all the world knows of him yet; and much of the part that does, still rejects him. We, with our Easter joy, can make a difference in some of these lives, if we pray God to show us how. To keep the joy of Easter to ourselves is to run counter to the Great Commission.

We are Easter people. We know we are, but how can we tell the folk next door?

## God's provision

Resurrection power capable of raising a body after several days, could surely have replaced the great stone, probably not needing to move it in the first place. In that case, these women would have hung around until someone came who was strong enough to roll it back; or they would have returned to Jerusalem for reinforcements; or they would have abandoned their mission. God was not willing for any such alternatives, so he did the necessary work himself. He was so eager for the Easter truth to be told, and so keen to show his gratitude for their love in caring for the Lord.

What are we bringing for Jesus, this Eastertime? Love that we don't quite know how to offer or express? We can sympathize with the women here; and can surely also believe that, as God facilitated their way, he will do no less for us.

Christ has risen! It's not in God's interests for him to put any barriers in the way of our celebration and sharing.

## With Jesus

We are with Jesus in our Easter joy. We don't have to wait to be united with him in a resurrection like his, as St Paul tells the Romans in our epistle (Rom. 6:5). His Spirit is here. He is with us. When he left his disciples to enter glory, he promised them he'd always be with them (Matt. 28:19). And his Spirit, whom he promised would remind us of all that he said, is today filling us with the Easter miracle of new life, new birth, new hope, new power, new joy.

### Is that all?

No; there's the newness we can bring to him: a new resolve, a new intention, to 'love him more dearly, follow him more nearly and know him more clearly, day by day' (based on the prayer of St Richard of Chichester).

### *Suggested Hymns*

All in an Easter garden; Christ the Lord is risen today; Now the green blade rises; The day of resurrection.

## Easter Day   16 April

*Principal Service*   **The Miracle** Acts 10:34–43 or Isa. 25:6–9; Ps. 118:1–2, 14–24; 1 Cor. 15:1–11 or Acts 10:34–43; John 20:1–18 or Mark 16:1–8

> *'Jesus said to [Mary], "Do not hold on to me, because I have not yet ascended to the Father. But go to my brothers and say to them, 'I am ascending to my Father, and your Father; to my God, and your God.'"' John 20:13*

### Would they believe?

Would they believe a woman, and an ex-prostitute into the bargain? The miracle had been foretold, yet apparently nobody expected it to happen. How often do we pray for a miracle, without really believing that God will grant us one? And how often, when it comes, do we forget to thank him for it?

Mary ran to tell the others, with no other 'proof' than the empty tomb, and not even the evidence that she had touched the Lord – only his command forbidding such contact.

It was really not a lot on which to build the 'case' for the resurrection. Until anything further happened, the disciples would need to believe in faith.

## 'Hard' evidence

The hard evidence came before they had had to wait much longer: evidence that St Paul was to enjoy citing later on (1 Cor. 15:5–8): Peter, the disciples, over 500 men and women, James and all the apostles, Paul himself ... It's an impressive list of witnesses. We either believe that all these people agreed to fabricate the evidence or that the resurrection actually happened ... that millions of people since then have been deluded or that Jesus is really alive ... that martyrs have died for a lie or that Jesus is Lord. If we can believe, the risen Jesus has promised to be everything to us; if we can trust, Jesus will prove to be all we need. The first step of faith is the biggest; we need to remember this when we take the gospel to non-believers. We may be 'cradle-Christians', not able to pin-point our 'day of conversion', or we may have had a dramatic meeting with Jesus that changed us from unbelief to faith. Into whichever category we fall, let us remember that the more established in unbelief a person is, the greater will be that initial step on to the straight and narrow road. Let us pray that we may be as gentle with them as Jesus was with Mary on that first Easter morning (while we remember how forthright he was, come the evening, with two of his disciples on the Emmaus Road, Luke 24:25 – a lesson to us that we, who believe, must not waterdown our faith, nor hide behind an ignorance we should not have)!

## 'Tell my brothers'

'Tell my brothers.' Jesus was at pains to prove to Mary that the risen Lord was the same as the recently crucified Lord. Hadn't he taught the disciples in his ministry years to pray: 'OUR Father ...'? Then, Mary, remind the disciples that I am still their brother – we still share the same Father: 'My Father, and your Father.'

This is no reincarnation as understood by non-Christians today. Jesus has not come back to life as someone else, but as the Lord and Master whom they have followed for the past three years or so. This – together with the appearance of the long-dead Moses and Elijah on the Mount of the Transfiguration – adds to our Easter joy; for it tells us that neither we nor our loved ones in glory will be anything other than the people we are or have known. God is not so strapped for ingenuity, enterprise, inventiveness and creativity, that he can't continue bringing 'one-offs' into being, and giving us an eternity where we continue OUR life in him.

### Our spiritual sight

At times, our spiritual sight lags behind what we see in the natural. It was so at first with the disciples, on that Easter Day so long ago. What they wanted most to happen came to pass; the person whom they longed above all to see, stood in front of them. They saw him with their physical sight, but spiritually it took them practically the whole day for belief to catch up with sight.

Can we pray the risen Easter Jesus to show us anything we might be missing today?

### Family Service Input

Have ready the relevant materials for the young people to make into Easter cards for families, hospital patients, those in prison, etc.

### Suggested Hymns

Alleluia, alleluia, hearts to heaven; Jesus Christ is risen today; Jesus lives! thy terrors now; Ye choirs of new Jerusalem.

## Easter Day
*Evening Prayer*   **Out by the Spirit** Ps. 105 or Ps. 66; Ezek. 37:1–14; Luke 24:13–35

> 'The hand of the Lord was upon me, and he brought me out by the spirit of the Lord and set me down in the middle of a valley; it was full of bones . . . "Can these bones live?"' Ezekiel. 37:1, 3

### Can you see?

Can you see Jesus in Ezekiel's place, and the 'valley' as Jerusalem? On this Easter Day, we can try. It is the Spirit of God who has 'brought [Jesus] out' – out of the tomb, into a place, not quite of dry bones, but of people going about their business in a spiritually lifeless way. And we have the Spirit asking Jesus if they can be brought to life – spiritual life – with a knowledge of and love for our Lord. And here we come to a point of divergence, because Ezekiel wasn't prepared to commit himself to a declaration that those scattered bones could live. Yet, in his cagey reply to God there

113

is an inkling that he knows God can do anything: 'O Lord God, you know' (v. 3). Jesus, on the other hand, rose powerfully from the dead, in the sure certainty that what he had done made possible many other resurrections in the future, and spiritual revival in the short term.

## The mighty Spirit

It was the outworking of the indwelling Spirit of God, at his most mighty; and it took everyone by surprise, although those familiar with the old scriptures had been given ample proof that God could do the impossible. Throughout history, something in the human nature has tacitly assumed that each miracle wrought by God will be the last. Why don't we in our generation, by God's grace, do what we can to reverse this soul-restricting pessimism? God's power cannot diminish: it's a lie of the devil if we believe (or act as though we believe) it could.

## 'I am going to open your graves'

'I am going to open your graves,' God had promised Ezekiel (v. 12), and so it came to pass (Matt. 27:52), and nowhere more convincingly than on Easter morning. God was doing impossible things with life and death, throwing normal laws out of order, and extending the boundaries of hope. He's still at the work, though now the field of operations has extended beyond our valley of dry bones, to a world where millions of Christians have accepted the challenge of Jesus.

> New life, new hope, awakes,
> Where'er men own his sway;
> Freedom her bondage breaks,
> And night is turned to day.
> (G. W. Briggs)

## God's opening power

The message of Easter is God's power opening what has been closed: opening the tomb, to free it from the power to hold death; opening up a new hope to new life here and now, and more wonderfully Hereafter; and opening up our hearts to accept that the parameters we have put in place over the years, must be pushed back.

This is a message not accepted overnight; it had taken the disciples three years of concentrated teaching by Jesus, and still they were wrong-footed on Easter morning. Time after time, he had commanded them: 'Don't be afraid!' Yet the next time something unusual happened, they went into virtual paroxysms of fear, because that's how they'd accustomed themselves to living. Time after time, he foretold his suffering, dying and resurrection, and it seemed to go in at one ear and out at the other. We're exactly the same a lot of the time. And to reverse the trend, we need to take today's joy into the rest of our lives, expecting our Lord to capitalize on it, as we trust him more and doubt him less.

## Suggested Hymns

Good Christian men, rejoice and sing; He is Lord, he is Lord; The Lord is risen indeed; The strife is o'er.

# Second Sunday of Easter   23 April
*Principal Service   Pax Vobiscum* Acts 4:32–35; Ps. 133; 1 John. 1:1—2:2; John 20:19–31

> *'When it was evening on that day, the first day of the week, and the doors of the house where the disciples had met were locked for fear of the Jews, Jesus came and stood among them and said, "Peace be with you".' John 20:19*
> *'God is light, and in him there is no darkness at all.' 1 John 1:5*

## Without fear

> *We will walk through the valley, in the shadow of death,*
> *We will walk through the darkness without fear;*
> *Though the night may be long, the dark enclosing,*
> *We know Jesus, our Morning Light, is near.*
>
> *He has walked through the valley of the shadow of death,*
> *He has walked through the night of fear alone.*
> *Though the darkness had gathered to destroy him,*
> *He was there at the rising of the sun.*

*We will walk in the glory of the bright morning sun,*
*We will walk in the light that guides our way.*
*For with Jesus the Lord of light beside us,*
*We will walk in the glory of the day.*

(Michael Cockett)

With the resurrection of Jesus, new light came to replace darkness, new faith to replace fear. This is the last time in the New Testament that we hear of the disciples being afraid. The very last time. Yet somewhere between that first Easter and today, we allowed Satan to reintroduce fear into our hearts, so much so that 'I'm afraid . . .' has become part and parcel of daily life. We shouldn't be afraid, of anyone or anything. Were we asked, we'd quickly deny wanting to give the devil saitsfaction; yet that's exactly what we're doing when we give way to fear, whether it's fear of losing our job, fear of sickness, fear of a stock market slump, fear of terrorism, or just a depression that makes living a drudge instead of a pleasure. Does our Lord at such times sigh in sadness that all his work has had so little impact? Does our misery set the heavens ringing with joy? Come on, Christians! We bear Christ's name, and he's commissioned us to be the light of the world (Matt. 5:14)!

## Jesus knows

Jesus knows about our propensity to fear. While he may not approve, that doesn't stop him coming into the situation and endeavouring to turn us from fearful into faithful folk. He came through locked doors to get the disciples over from fear into faith: however we have barricaded ourselves in with our phobias, he can come and get us and save us. We can hide from anything and everyone but Christ. And that's a comfort, not a threat!

## A new, big life

It was a new, big life that God gave us, starting with Easter: a life that need not admit fear, a life that looks to the light not the darkness, a life that expands instead of limits. God is bigger than we are, but are we getting bigger for him? Are we using this new life he has given us, to grow? Or, spiritually speaking, have we wrapped it up and put it carefully away, for our 'coming out'; our 'graduation'; even our 'retirement'? This great, new, big life is not given us to be stashed away where 'moth and rust consume and where thieves break in and steal' (Matt. 6:19), but to be kept active and in use, for our sakes and for others'.

Let's resolve, this Eastertide, to use God's new life to the full, rather than mothball it for a time that may not come.

### Family Service Input

Encourage the young folk to solve the Word-Search (p. 118) – and, if time permits, illustrate it.

### Suggested Hymns

Christ is the world's true light; Fight the good fight; The light of the morning is breaking; To the name of our salvation.

## Second Sunday of Easter
*Second Service*   **Value of Trust** Ps. 143:1–11; Isa. 26:1–9, 19; Luke 24:1–12

> *'Trust in the Lord for ever, for in the Lord God you have an everlasting rock . . . Your dead shall live, their corpses shall rise . . . and the earth will give birth to those long dead.' Isaiah 26:4, 19*

### We shall be who we have been

Do you believe in reincarnation?

The question has been around for a long time. Reincarnation (the reappearance of the spirits of the dead in other living persons) has no foundation in the Bible, and certainly not in today's reading from Isaiah. In the resurrection, we shall be the people we have been on earth; just as Moses and Elijah were at the Transfiguration; and as Jesus was on Easter Day. We shall be known, and shall know Hereafter, as here. God has made us unique, and we shall be so while ever our Creator lives. And that's a long time. Read the Gospels and see, for example, how Jesus valued his friends for their individuality, their weaknesses as well as their strengths. Only a moron would want to see an eternity of uniformity – boring uniformity – or one where identities had been lost in chaos. God has endowed us with the valuable gift of individuality here; would he settle for something less in eternity? We can surely trust him better than to imagine that.

## Easter Word-Search

| S | U | S | E | H | P | E | A | R | B | E | J | O | E | L |
|---|---|---|---|---|---|---|---|---|---|---|---|---|---|---|
| G | C | A | F | E | K | L | E | M | T | C | N | D | O | D |
| H | G | O | X | W | T | D | S | E | R | P | Q | E | L | P |
| I | A | S | M | J | I | G | L | I | B | S | L | M | E | N |
| B | B | O | E | M | E | L | H | A | N | J | K | E | P | O |
| C | R | M | F | L | A | P | G | A | R | N | M | T | S | I |
| M | I | T | D | R | T | N | I | E | O | A | S | R | O | T |
| A | E | A | A | Q | R | S | D | S | L | T | A | I | G | C |
| G | L | P | C | B | S | E | O | M | A | W | M | U | O | E |
| D | E | G | D | O | E | F | I | P | E | M | O | S | N | R |
| A | H | I | L | M | J | G | K | L | A | N | H | P | Q | R |
| L | T | O | E | W | H | A | E | G | D | C | T | S | R | U |
| E | C | R | A | T | H | E | N | S | F | B | H | I | K | S |
| N | O | R | Y | P | L | D | R | E | H | P | E | H | S | E |
| E | T | M | S | Q | N | G | A | L | I | L | E | E | J | R |

RESURRECTION  
COMMANDMENT  
ALMIGHTY  
REDEEMER  
PARACLETE  
GOSPEL  
COLOSSIANS  
JOEL  
APOSTLE  

PATMOS  
ATHENS  
EPHESUS  
DEMETRIUS  
GALILEE  
SHEPHERD  
GABRIEL  
MAGDALENE  
THOMAS

## Unending trust

God asks for unending trust: trust that whatever he says, he will do; whatever he does, will be the best; whatever he promises outside and beyond our understanding, is still set to happen on the divine agenda. Has he called you to believe the impossible? Just trust him to accomplish it. God deals in positives, not negatives. Is your life an unholy muddle right now? Trust in God to straighten it out, and to bless you (and probably others) in the process. Trusting when we can't see the future, is a prerequisite of the Christian's life. Trusting when everything in the natural tells us there isn't a future, is scaling that mountain of trust that brings us right into focus with our Holy Spirit. Thus enabled, he can go to work, and invest our trust with the Holy and Undivided Trinity, which pays a princely rate of interest that makes our secular financial world look pedestrian by comparison.

## When we've run out of options

Too many Christians (never mind non-believers) fray their nerves and exhaust their energy in trying all the 'sensible' options first: the options that the world praises as ingenuity, self-reliance, competence and smart dealing. The spiritual, as well as the physical, cost of these is high. Why won't we take our problems, in trust, to God first? Is it pride? Intellectual oneupmanship? 'Trust in the Lord with ALL your heart, and do not rely on your own insight' (Prov. 3:5): a verse we could profitably carry around with us. We may tell ourselves that financial and commercial understanding is our province: don't we give God his 'slot' on a Sunday? But that's a long way from giving him ALL our heart, all of the time. If it was not for the grace of God, we shouldn't have any time; we'd be in a place where time had passed us by.

## Letting go

Letting go of our egocentric inclination to 'be in charge', means turning over the responsibility to God. In case this sounds a cop-out, we call it simply 'trusting God'. And it's not a soft option, unless we've made a complete success of it already.

### Suggested Hymns

Abide with me; Forever with the Lord; Just as I am; Put thou thy trust in God.

# Third Sunday of Easter  30 April

*Principal Service*  **Gospel of Love** Acts 3:12–19; Ps. 4;
1 John. 3:1–7; Luke 24:36b–48

> *'[Jesus said], "Thus it is written, that the Messiah is to suffer and to rise from the dead on the third day, and that repentance and forgiveness of sins is to be proclaimed in his name to all nations, beginning from Jerusalem."' Luke 24:46–47*
>
> *'Everyone who does what is right is righteous, just as he is righteous.' 1 John 3:7*

## Reaching out

Reaching out in love with the gospel of repentance and forgiveness of sins, is the Christian's mission. There are no half-measures; we're either locked-on to our work in zealous determination, enthusiasm and joy, or we're not. We're either putting the gospel of Christ first place in our lives, or we're not. We're either in communion with our Lord, or with someone, or something, else. This is the 'uncomfortable' truth of the gospel: the 'putting one's hand to the plough' truth. The truth that follows on from our dedication and commitment is the blessed, 'comfortable' truth that Christ is here, in Spirit, with us, giving us all it takes, all we need (and quite a lot more), to get the work done with joy. NOT to get everyone whom we meet converted, but to share the gospel of repentance and forgiveness of sins with them, so that they have the choice of accepting it.

## The whole gospel

'Well, if I lead a good life, surely that shows Christ to others, without my actually having to preach to them?' Well, a good life, lived overtly as a Christian, does show Christ to others, but the full gospel consists of more than 'a good life'. We may not all stand in a pulpit of a Sunday morning, but to fulfil Christ's commission we do need to share with people the repentance necessary for God to forgive their sins. There has to be that turning away from sin, in full contrition, and an intention to lead a new life in Christ, otherwise the sins just stay with us, to make our way to God unnecessarily difficult at best, and at worst impossible.

# Easter Word-Search, People and Places

| A | N | H | W | G | T | M | E | H | E | L | H | T | E | B |
|---|---|---|---|---|---|---|---|---|---|---|---|---|---|---|
| I | B | A | R | N | A | B | A | S | U | I | D | V | F | A |
| J | C | B | Z | V | R | A | B | Q | J | C | J | E | B | G |
| Z | O | X | C | A | I | A | P | H | A | S | E | P | E | S |
| D | S | S | H | U | R | E | S | D | E | D | R | A | T | G |
| E | Y | F | E | C | G | E | C | S | H | O | U | U | W | A |
| M | A | R | Y | P | M | K | T | F | P | E | S | L | H | L |
| U | A | T | T | A | H | B | J | H | D | B | A | A | I | L |
| A | D | S | J | R | K | L | E | C | F | P | L | H | G | I |
| N | C | B | E | O | A | T | I | X | J | G | E | F | S | C |
| R | D | T | R | M | N | I | C | O | D | E | M | U | S | S |
| E | E | E | H | A | N | D | R | E | W | U | N | E | I | I |
| P | A | Z | G | N | Y | L | N | S | M | D | T | O | M | R |
| A | C | F | B | S | O | P | A | T | N | S | O | F | O | P |
| C | Q | B | N | O | I | T | A | L | E | V | E | R | N | G |

| | |
|---|---|
| PROPHET | PETER |
| NAZARETH | BETHLEHEM |
| JERUSALEM | PAUL |
| NICODEMUS | REVELATION |
| CAIAPHAS | ROMANS |
| CAPERNAUM | JAMES |
| SIMON | PRISCILLA |
| ANDREW | MARY |
| JOSEPH | BARNABAS |

## Conviction

'Conviction of sin' is a phrase that many associate with the 'hell-fire' sermons of an earlier age. Yet not only did those sermons produce revivals, they were biblical, in line with our Lord's commission, and vital to the growth of the Church. We can waterdown the gospel of repentance and forgiveness of sins, until people miss the point. That is not Christian, and, moreover, it can be spiritually dangerous, for we are tangling here with matters of life and death.

## Preach the word

'Preach the word' (AV), 'proclaim the message', Paul commanded Timothy. 'Be persistent, whether the time is favourable or unfavourable' (2 Tim. 4:2): 'convince, rebuke and encourage, with the utmost patience in teaching.' It's excellent advice and, according to tradition, Timothy made good, becoming the first Bishop of Ephesus. But how closely do we follow this command? How much do we yearn to share the gospel? How much effort and care do we expend in telling others of 'repentance and the forgiveness of sins'? This is the foundation of the gospel; the 'love your neighbour' part and 'take up the cross' will follow. Do we build our gospel-sharing from the ground up, or try to construct the upper storeys before seeing to the foundation? Whether the perceived time is 'favourable or unfavourable', the climate right, the 'vibes' good, Paul says we are just to go ahead and share. God has brought us into a situation, whether a 'one-to-one' or in a crowd – and we may not have that particular chance replicated again. 'Woe betide me if I do not proclaim the gospel!' cried Paul (1 Cor. 9:16). And how did this No.1 missionary preach it? 'Not with plausible [AV, 'enticing'] words of wisdom' (1 Cor. 2:4), but the plain, unvarnished truth as had been revealed to him by Christ. And Paul, with his Damascus Road experience coming after a time of hard persecution of Christians, knew better than anyone what 'repentance and forgiveness of sins' meant.

## *Family Service Input*

Encourage the young folk to solve and then illustrate with relevant texts, the Word-Search of New Testament people and places.

## Suggested Hymns

Go, tell it on the mountain; In Christ there is no east or west; Let the song go round the earth; Tell out, my soul.

## Third Sunday of Easter

*Second Service*   **To Everyone Who Conquers** Ps. 142; Deut. 7:7–13; Rev. 2:1–11 [Luke 16:19–31]

*'To everyone who conquers I will give permission to eat from the tree of life that is in the paradise of God.' Revelation 2:7b*

### God's lovely garden

This is virtually saying that those who win through will enjoy Paradise (God's lovely garden) with their Lord, in everlasting life. The Spirit ends each one of these letters to the seven churches of Asia with the similar expression: 'To everyone who conquers . . .' It's a measure of the seriousness of the enterprise: following Jesus is entering his service on a wartime footing. Unless we prove true soldiers, we shall not 'conquer'. The fact that he has promised to be with us always (Matt. 28:19), doesn't absolve us from making an effort. The fact that we can tap into his strength (Phil. 4:13), and his grace (1 Cor. 15:10), doesn't mean that we can settle for being 'sleeping partners'. We are partners with Christ, but he is looking for us to show eagerness, enthusiasm, commitment and dedication, for him to increase more than either we desire or deserve. He's looking to surprise us by his love, joy, peace and the rest, until we surprise ourselves (and others), and Christ is thus shown to be at work. If we look at the saints of Christian history, we cannot doubt that Christ has been working in and through them, with a power and a love beyond the natural. They, with this power and love, have conquered in Christ; and we can surely believe that by now they know exactly what it is to be eating from the tree of life in the lovely garden of God.

### A modern problem

Ephesus, Smyrna and the other churches to whom the Spirit wrote, were not light-years removed from the twenty-first century; their problems are in various ways to be seen today. Ephesus, for instance, was heavily into idol-worship. We may not be called to share the gospel in a situation where the dominating cult is that of Artemis (Diana), but substitute porn, drugs, satanism or witchcraft for Artemis and the problem is the same: getting the truth of Jesus into a hornet's nest of falsehood and depravity. It takes ever as much commitment to conquer in this environment, as in the centre of the Artemis cult in the sophisticated Ephesus of 2,000 years ago.

## The modern answer

So, if that is the problem today, what is the modern answer? Precisely the same as it was then: to share the true, uncompromised word of God, the gospel of 'repentance and forgiveness of sins' (Luke 24:47). If we adulterate it to 'conform' to modern thinking, we are playing with fire (Rev. 22:18, 19). People have not changed, deep down; they still want to know about the key issues of life, death and Hereafter, as they have always wanted. They still want to know God; if only whether he is, or is not. They are still fascinated (whether or not they admit it) by Christians and what we believe, and how it makes us what we are. Deep down, they are still thrashing about in a spiritual search for something that has so far eluded them. We can come to them, as Paul went to the centre of sophisticated Athens; we can point to their focus of the moment, and tell them, as Paul told the Athenians: 'What therefore you worship as unknown, that I proclaim to you . . .' (Acts 17:23).

If we don't, someone may take our place, and lead them into even murkier, darker waters than those in which they are paddling now.

### Suggested Hymns

Father God, I wonder how I managed; I love to tell the story; Lord, speak to me, that I may speak; Tell me the old, old story.

## Fourth Sunday of Easter   7 May
*Principal Service*   **One Flock, One Shepherd** Acts 4:5–12; Ps. 23; 1 John 3:16–24; John 10:11–18

> *[Jesus said], "I have other sheep that do not belong to this fold. I must bring them also, and they will listen to my voice. So there*

*will be one, flock, one shepherd. For this reason the Father loves*
*me, because I lay down my life in order to take it up again."'*
*John 10:16–17*

## God's love

For the whole of Christian history, these verses have been linked together; and who are we to suggest that they were not together in the mind of Jesus, and that God loves him no less for opening his arms to sheep of other folds, as for laying down his life? On the grandest scale of all, Jesus was doing what his sheep are called to do as their 'lesser calvaries': to blend his will with that of his Father, and to take up the cross. Whether it is traversing the Via Dolorosa, or forsaking other creeds for that of Christ, we are in a sense martyrs for Jesus, but it is a glorious martyrdom, hard fought, hard won, for eternity with him.

## One flock

Naturally, the immediate recipients of this teaching would understand this 'one flock' to mean of Jewish identity. Just how much or how easily they took on board the coming worldwide mission, is questionable. For centuries, the generality of Jews had heard this wider mission foretold in the old scriptures, but had largely ignored it. Now it was knocking on their door. I MUST bring these other sheep, Jesus calmly says. He would not bring them in the personal mission currently in operation, but his Holy Spirit, working in and through his followers, would take the next two millennia (or longer) to accomplish the work.

And because he was laying his life on the line to this end, the Father loved him. He was in God's will. There would be one flock, one shepherd: it had been ordained by the Almighty. Next time we get hard-pressed, and even a bit despondent, may we reflect on this encouraging teaching of Jesus. Our Lord did not despair – ever – because he knew that what God has willed will come, not to pass, but to stay. God's shots hit their mark.

## In our work

In our work for God, there is this same encouragement, that whatever we do in his name and in his will, is assured of success. We may not stay around to see the success, but others will – and God will. And he will not forget those who have done the work. It has been done in the strength of one who so magnificently has said: 'I have power to lay [my life] down, and I have power to take it up again' (John 10:18). No one but Jesus can say this. And it surely gives us the strength to go on until we can go on no longer, for there at the end, at the meeting of the ways, is the power to pick us up and make us into something more glorious, to do more, for all eternity.

## This 'exclusive' flock?

So, what is this flock, this single gathering of folk, for whom Jesus has surrendered and then redeemed his life? All nations, cultures, colours? Yes. All creeds and religions? No. Jesus says, categorically: 'No one comes to the Father, except through me' (John 14:6). If there are those who do not believe in Jesus, then whatever, whoever else they believe, on this premiss will not count. These are hard words, a hard teaching, but Jesus has just told us to believe them: 'Believe in God, believe also in me' (John 14:1). He could hardly be more emphatic. Those who have had the chance to believe in Jesus, but who have rejected him, are not of his flock. Those who as yet have not had the chance – those for whom the Bible is still an unknown book – are still dying without this kowledge that can save them for eternity.

But the gospel is on its way to these people's children and grand-children . . . They will hear it, because God is determined that the whole world will have its chance, or Calvary has been in vain (Matt. 24:14; Mark 13:10).

### Family Service Input

Encourage the young people to discuss a non-Christian religion, and how prayer and evangelism can help to bring a knowledge of Jesus to these other believers.

### Suggested Hymns

Brother, sister, let me serve you; Far round the world thy children sing their song; In Christ there is no east or west; I watch the sunrise lighting the sky.

# Fourth Sunday of Easter

*Second Service* **Double-edged** Ps. 81:8–16; Ex. 16:4–15;
Rev. 2:12–17 [John 6:30–40]

> *'And to the angel of the church in Pergamum write: "These are the words of him who has the sharp, two-edged sword . . . Repeat them. If not, I will come to you soon and make war . . . with the sword of my mouth."' Revelation 2:12, 17*

## Cutting words

This is the sword sharper than anything man can make, and it is none other than the 'word of God, living and active . . . piercing until it divides soul from spirit, joints from marrow; it is able to judge the thoughts and intentions of the heart' (Heb. 4:12). This shouldn't surprise us. We all know the tremendous power in a human tongue; God's word is even more tremendous, more powerful. And we, by his grace, are the purveyors of it. By his word, we can bring souls to him; and by his word, we can alienate them. It is a sobering thought, and one to encourage us to use the word with prayer and care. To duck the issue is to negate its privilege. We are Christians, with a solemn responsibility to handle God's word as he would have it used. It reaches the parts of the mind, body and spirit, that no other word can reach. Far stronger than X-rays, it penetrates into the deepest parts of the psyche, where thoughts and intentions are being brought to birth. If we pray the Lord to safeguard his word in us, then he will go to work on our as yet unconceived ideas, and not only save us a lot of heartache, but also bring blessings out of what we subsequently do and say. Far better to let the divine alchemist convert base metal to gold, than live to see the sharp, two-edged sword go into action on ill-conceived and unworthy or unfortunate intentions.

## How can it be?

How can it be, that God, with (at least) a world to oversee, can take such care over an individual's every fleeting thought? We cannot tell. It's almost as wonderful as a resurrection, and, since we believed that happened, we can believe the other. The struggling church at Pergamum was up against a barrage of heresies; she had given most of them a wide berth, but was compromising with one or two. You've made the grade with some temptations, see about overcoming the rest, the Spirit was telling her. It's still the way today; we're wonderfully successful in hitting the devil down over, say, pornography; well, then, says God, attack drugs (or alcohol, or crime . . . ) now, with all the power of the sword of my word. It's the way the Christian has fought for progress on the narrow road to God, since Christ first issued his call to 'follow'; we can only do it a step at a time, or we tie ourselves in spiritual knots. Life's journey is too short to waste time in struggling with tangles of our own making.

## The sword's purpose

The purpose of any sword is to kill. Yes, to annihilate. It was the sword (or spear) of the Roman on duty at Calvary, that caused the lifeblood of Christ, along with the water of life, to flow out of his body. That was destined not to go with the rest of him into the tomb, but to be poured out on the earth for the people of the earth. Similarly, the sword of the word of God will kill in us and others, our inclination to compromise with the devil. Piece by piece, if we'll only take in more and more of this divine weapon, it will attack our wayward thoughts, words and actions: not overnight (though many have been delivered almost immediately from dependency on one or another bad habits and sins), but more often gradually, with the patience and perseverance of a loving heavenly Father whose will it is that not one of his offspring should perish.

Are we showing to others the uncompromised word of God, or tailoring and manipulating it to conform to limitations of our making? Please God, if we are, he'll show us where.

## *Suggested Hymns*

A safe stronghold our God is still; Father of mercies, in thy word; Lord, thy word abideth; My faith, it is an oaken staff.

# Fifth Sunday of Easter   14 May
*Principal Service*   **Cleansing Word** Acts 8:26–40;
Ps. 22:25–31; 1 John 4:7–21; John 15:1–8

> '[Jesus said], "You have already been cleansed by the word that
> I have spoken to you. Abide in me, as I abide in you."'
> *John 15:3–4a*

## A two-way operation?

We can surely see this abiding as a two-way operation: the result
of our dialogue with God. As he gives us his word, cleansing us the
more we take it in, so our union, our abiding in him, grows as our
prayer life develops; and so we share his gospel: by our prayers and
our witness, we are establishing ourselves in the Father heart of
God, building on the foundation already laid there for us by Jesus
at Calvary. God-in-us, and we-in-God, made possible by our
indwelling Holy Spirit relating to and from us in God.

That's high thinking. One can't get much higher.

It's also positive thinking, for there is no negativity in God.

Jesus-in-us, by virtue of his Spirit, is operating a cleansing ministry, the more we focus on him and his word. As we take in more,
so shall we become more able from our (= Christ's) abundance, to
light up our corner and to cleanse others. Christ's light will shine
from us, in our eyes and on our lips, as well as in our actions.

## The war against darkness

Sometimes it helps to identify or quantify this light, by considering
(but not brooding upon) the enemy we are up against. Satan works
on a policy of darkening; initially, as Paul warns, he may disguise
himself as an 'angel of light' (2 Cor. 11:14), but he seeks to blacken
our characters, and those of the folk around us, in a host of ways.
God, on the other hand, is all light and no darkness at all
(1 John. 1:5). And God doesn't stoop to disguise or perjury, or any
of the low-down works of the devil. If we are taken in at first by
Satan, the devil hasn't the ability to maintain his act for long.

## Singleness of mind

The cleansing by God consists of showing us by his word, what is still dark (or pale-grey) in our lives. Do we, for instance, play at word games, saying one thing to one person and modifying it or even contradicting it to someone else? Would we accept some people for an evening meal, and not others? At church, do we distinguish between those who come with certain cars, fashions or company? Do we share the gospel with fellow-worshippers, or take it as well to those who never darken the church? Would we take time to listen to what a member of another religion believed, and to share with them the cleansing word of Jesus. Meeting with fellow-Christians is encouraging and strengthening; but if we concentrate on this, how are we putting into practice the Great Commission (e.g. Matt. 28:19, 20)? There's more than enough cleansing power in God's word for the world.

## Abiding in Jesus

There was a mid-twentieth-century song that ran:

> *Honey in the morning,*
> *Honey in the noontime,*
> *Honey at suppertime;*
> *Be my little honey,*
> *And love me all the time. (or words to that effect)*

The message was one of abiding in love. Lovers want to be in each other's company, doing the same things, talking and thinking about the same subjects, and, perhaps most importantly, simply telling (or showing by their actions) that they think the world of each other. We should be like this with Jesus; here he is, in his Spirit, abiding in us continually. Are we taking him for granted? Or trying to water down our togetherness by introducing other things, other interests? Is the Bible our number one reading priority? and not merely reading, but studying, sharing, memorizing?

Our Lord takes his abiding with us very seriously, and the more thought we give to our part of the contract, the cleaner and brighter we'll shine.

### Family Service Input

Perhaps with some more mature help, encourage the young folk to solve the crossword (p. 132), and the younger ones to illustrate the clues.

### Suggested Hymns

Abide with me; Light's abode, celestial Salem; The light of Christ has come into the world; Shine, Jesus, shine.

## Fifth Sunday of Easter
*Second Service*   **My God** Ps. 96; Isa. 60:1–14; Rev. 3:1–13
[Mark 16:9–16]

> *'If you conquer, I will make you a pillar in the temple of my God;*
> *you will never go out of it. I will write on you the name of my*
> *God, and the name of the city of my God, the new Jerusalem*
> *that comes down from my God out of heaven, and my own new*
> *name.' Revelation 3:12*

### Underlining the message

The Spirit underlines how close, how bound up he is to God: four times in this verse he affirms it: this is 'my God' we are talking about! Well, it is our God, too, isn't it? The Philadelphians are our brothers and sisters. They, like us, have kept the faith, often against severe odds – so we can all see ourselves as pillars in God's temple. Just how magnificent this temple is (and it's still growing), can be deduced from the sheer numbers of participants involved. And once a part of it, always a part. The name of our God will be written on us: quite how, is still a mystery. But God has promised. We shall be citizens of a new place, the new Jerusalem, which God has decked out as a bride adorned for her groom. And God is good at weddings: remember the trouble Jesus went to, to ensure not only sufficient wine, but the very best, that day at Cana.

### 'My own new name'

What is this 'new name'? Shall we not call God 'Father', or Jesus 'Saviour', or the Holy Spirit 'Comforter'? Jesus has told us that we

## Easter Crossword

shall be as the angels, in that we shall no longer marry in heaven. There will be no need to give birth to any future generations, so we may find that God wants to be known by a glorious name not yet divulged, perhaps a name to include the three operations of the Deity. But our new name will be God's, written on us. Perhaps we may reverently suppose that we shall be given work BEYOND the new Jerusalem, in which case our 'new name' would proclaim whose we were, and from where we came.

Can we not imagine the Philadelphians eagerly discussing such questions, as the Spirit's letter was read out in their church? And would God have caused John to receive such a vision, if he had not wanted its recipients to become enthusiastic about the time to come?

## Clues Across

1. Cute. (4)
4. Time of resurrection. (10)
9. Range of English hills. (6)
10. Without identity. (8)
11. Focus of Calvary. (3, 5, 2, 5)
12. Mode of transport. (5)
13. Protected. (9)
17. Eyewitness account. (9)
19. Most coloured part of a plant. (5)
22. Gives his life for the sheep. (3, 4, 8)
25. Midsummer clothing. (4, 4)
26. Little hen. (6).
27. Going back.(9)
28. . . . . and you shall find. (4)

## Clues Down

2. Providing? (7)
3. Human gland? (9)
4. Use. (6)
5. Drowns. (5)
6. Smother. (8)
7. Dress material. (5)
8. Quarrel. (7)
14. Mother of chick. (3)
15. Jumbos. (9)
16. A night at . . . . . . . . ? (3, 5)
18. Within the firm. (2, 5)
20. Land-measurement. (7)
21. Add to a cup for tea. (6)
22. More happy? (5)
24. Abram's wife's first name. (5)

*See page 135 for solution*

## Our Creator-God

In the beginning, God had created newness, *creatio ex nihilo*. He doesn't deal in secondhand goods. But for millennia he has been planning another world, another new creation. Since none of us knows everything about the earth we're on – although new things are being discovered every day – it's beyond our comprehension to picture what glory will be like. And the glimpses and hints that God gives us in the Bible only serve to heighten the mystery and anticipation. But before we become overwhelmed at the prospect, let's remember we presently have work to do: to see that as many people as possible besides ourselves and our nearest and dearest, are also given the chance of accepting all that Jesus made available by his sacrifice at Calvary. If we fall down on this, if we fail to give God 'job satisfaction', as well as a thankful heart, we can't blame him if our introduction to glory is not among friends. The more folk we love here in God's name, the more familiar the company will be there there. And the more folk will learn that God has loved us (Rev. 3:9).

## Mists of time

We see the mist rising from the valleys on an early autumn morning, and we know that before the day is out we shall be able to see the hills and God's blue sky. But a blind person seeing mist for the first time, does not know what's behind it. We are like that newly cured person: we see the 'mist' of death, and don't know what the departed can see when they've left us.

For them, everything is new.

One day, we'll be a part of that newness: recognizable, but new.

## Suggested Hymns

Angel-voices, ever singing; My God, my Father; New every morning is the love; Ye holy angels bright.

# Sixth Sunday of Easter (Rogation Sunday)    21 May
*Principal Service*    **So That . . .** Acts 10:44–48; Ps. 98; 1 John 5:1–6; John 15:9–17

> '[Jesus said], "You did not choose me, but I chose you. And I appointed you to go and bear fruit, fruit that will last, so that the Father will give you whatever you ask him in my name. I am giving you these commands so that you may love one another."'
> John 15:16–17

## A God of order

God is a God of order. In the beginning, he brought order out of chaos in the natural world, and he's been doing precisely the same in the human heart ever since. Jesus' teaching was not in a vacuum, nor random rules given in a scattershot manner; but deliberately formed with cause and effect: 'Go and bear fruit, SO THAT the

Father will give you what you ask ... I am giving you these commands, SO THAT you may love one another ...' Our Father's giving is consequent on our loving and working. Our combined operation sets in motion God's reciprocal loving and giving and working on our behalf. Both parties need each other, SO THAT the whole thing 'works'.

## Our great example

Jesus is our great example of this operation. Everything he did was for a purpose:

He came to earth, so that God's love could be made known.
He taught, so that we in turn could teach.
He healed, so that people could live and work in fullness of strength.
He suffered and died, so that we could be saved from our sins.
He rose, so that we could have the hope of a risen life in glory.

The 'SO THAT' system is still working, but many are operating it in the wrong way:

They work hard, so that they can have more free time.
They cram seven days into six, so that they can please themselves on Sundays.
They dabble in the occult, so that they can take a 'short cut' to the Hereafter.
They pack themselves with pills and potions, so that they feel independent of God's healing on offer.

The list could be extended a long, long way. But on the brighter side, we have millions of Christians (including ourselves) who try to follow the commands of Jesus, SO THAT we may claim his

---

Solution

Across: 1. Twee. 4. Eastertide. 9. Mendip. 10. Nameless. 11. The cross of Jesus. 12. Train. 13. Sheltered. 17. Firsthand. 19. Petal. 22. The Good Shepherd. 25. July wear. 26. Bantam. 27. Retreating. 28. Seek.

Down: 2. Whether. 3. Endocrine. 4. Employ. 5. Sinks. 6. Enmuffle. 7. Tulle. 8. Dispute. 14. Hen. 15. Elephants. 16. The opera. 18. In house. 20. Acreage. 21. Teabag. 23. Gayer. 24. Sarai.

promises, share his word, and grow in the grace and knowledge of him (2 Pet. 3:18).

## A hard task!

On the face of it, the command to love God AND our neighbour may seem a little strange – for we are more accustomed to being given negative commands, against sins such as murder, theft and their ilk. Why does God give us virtually an imposition to do something as beautiful and congenial as loving? It's the first of the old, Ten, commandments (and implicit in the rest), and so often on the lips of Jesus, we can't mistake its importance. The 'catch' lies, of course, in the sobering truth that loving (whether God, or our neighbour – often particularly our neighbour) is anything but congenial or beautiful. When things go awry, don't we rail against God? Don't we grumble when he doesn't answer every prayer as quickly as we think we need? And who wants to think of all the people who rub us up the wrong way, or 'do us down', or are in strife with us . . . ? We'd probably lose count, anyway.

Jesus' words cut right through these failings: 'I am giving you these commands, SO THAT you may love one another.' Our Lord has cut the ground from under us; we can't say we haven't heard. So, what are we going to do about it?

## Soldiers on duty

We're Christ's soldiers, on permanent duty. So we need to bring those parts of our lives (and the folk they involve) where there's strife of any kind, before our Lord; and if we can't bring love to bear on the problems, to pray CHRIST'S love in there. 'Lord, I really, really don't feel love to . . . but I know you love him/her. Please love for me, and through me, until . . . Until I feel like obeying your command?' Wow! That's the trouble about getting serious with God, he has a knack of getting his own way!

### *Family Service Input*

Involve the young people in making a map showing the parish boundaries, which used to be traversed with prayers on Rogation Sunday. If time permits, they could be encouraged to compose prayers for use in the Intercessions.

## Suggested Hymns

A new commandment I give unto you; Lord, in thy name thy servants plead; Love divine, all loves excelling; Love is his word.


# Sixth Sunday of Easter
*Second Service*   **Straddling the Fence** Ps. 45; S. of Sol. 4:16—5:2; 8:6–7; Rev. 3:14–22 [Luke 22:24–30]

> *'And to the angel of the church in Laodicea write: "The words of the Amen, the faithful and true witness, the origin of God's creation. I know your works; you are neither cold nor hot. I wish that you were either cold or hot."' Revelation 3:14–15*


### Creation-origin

The Amen, the Word calling creation into being, is saying to the lukewarm Laodicean Christians: I know. I know you through and through. I am all-seeing, all-knowing, all-powerful. Though you may mask your shortcomings with a veneer of enthusiasm and respectability, you cannot hide anything from me.

We have only to ponder on the power behind all creativity, to believe that God is more than able to see into the parts of us that neither man nor science can penetrate. From hot springs some distance away, Laodicea had her water channelled into the city; but by the time it reached her, the heat had cooled to tepidity. Her Christians, having started equally hot and fervent, had allowed their faith to go off the boil. It doesn't take much to simmer down today: an interruption of daily prayer, one or two Sunday services missed, a quick dash to the shops on Sunday ... The slide may start so imperceptibly that we are well down the slope to luke-warmness before we've even noticed.


### Reading the news

As realization dawns – and we can empathize with the Laodiceans as the Spirit's letter was read out – what do we do? Climb back to enthusiasm, or continue the downward slide? (The going becomes easier as we descend, for we become more proficient at it.) God knows that others beside himself are watching us: if we regain lost ground, we begin again to show Christ to the world; if we slide to the bottom, letting go of all our faith, at least others know we are no longer Christians, and the world accepts with equanimity our fall from grace. But if we straddle the fence, we send out mixed messages: an adulteration of Christianity. God hasn't our full attention, nor has the devil. And those looking on may be forgiven for deciding we are 'neither fish, fowl nor good red herring'. Who would settle for lukewarmness in anything, but particularly where faith is concerned.

## 'The Amen'

As if further to underline the solemnity of God's pronouncement against these tepid Laodiceans, Jesus the creative Word calls himself 'The Amen'. By his sacrifice and victory, he is justified in using this authoritative title. He is the Beginning – there before creation – but he is also the Ending; the Pioneer and the Perfecter; the Alpha and the Omega. He underwrites all that the Spirit says; and all that the Spirit says, the Amen has said himself. When Magnus Magnusson was the question-master of *Mastermind*, he became known for the saying: 'I've started, so I'll finish.' On the cosmic, universal, scale, Jesus could say the same. All that he has set in motion, he will bring to a conclusion; all the life he has brought to birth, he will see through death to eternity.

Isn't this exciting? How can anyone remain lukewarm about it? If Jesus had not put all his energy and enthusiasm into his incarnation, passion, crucifixion, resurrection and ascension, we today would have been heading down the road to oblivion – at best doing some good in this life, but with no prospect of glory.

That this is the route many have still chosen to take, despite Christ's efforts, is, tragically, beyond belief.

## *Suggested Hymns*

Forth in thy name, O Lord, I go; Give me oil in my lamp; Inspired by love and anger; Stand up, and bless the Lord.

## Ascension Day  25 May
**My Father's Promise** Acts 1:1–11 or Dan. 7:9–14; Ps. 47 or
Ps. 93; Eph. 1:15–23 or Acts 1:1–11; Luke 24:44–53

*'[Jesus said], "You are witnesses of these things. And see, I am
sending upon you what my Father promised, so stay here in the
city until you have been clothed with power from on high."'*
*Luke 24:48–49*

### On duty

Quite possibly, what the disciples wanted most to do, was to put
as good a distance between themselves and Jerusalem as they could.
It was certainly not a safe place for declared followers of Jesus at
that time. But God was not planning on sending his Spirit to downtown Galilee, but to Pentecost-celebrating Jerusalem, where the
event could not be missed. The disciples must stay on duty, ready
for 'being clothed with power'.

Sometimes we tell ourselves that a particular situation is too
fraught for comfort: surely God wouldn't want us to run the risk
of our ministry being prematurely curtailed? Wouldn't it be prudent
to take a back seat for a while? Wouldn't it give someone else a
chance . . . ? We become singularly proficient in the art of telling
God that we know best, when faith should tell us that the Lord can
outdistance us in any spiritual IQ test, by a very big margin.

### A beautiful compliment

In a way, the ascension of Jesus was a beautiful compliment. He was
saying to the disciples – and, by extension, to every Christian that
was to be – that he was relying on us to fulfil the mission that he had
initiated: not in our own power, lest we should become proud; but in
his, with the giving of his Spirit. But while the disciples had been given
the advantage of Christ's visible presence for three years, they – and
we – were henceforward going to have to operate without visible support. Christians were going to be vulnerable, and to look vulnerable. The divine power would still be here, but it would be hidden.

Does this seem like a handicap? By no means, for the local
Judaean ministry was to spread out across many countries; the
power and spiritual presence of Jesus was not to be concentrated
in a small part of the world, but across the globe.

## Recipe for success

God's recipe contains everything for success: unlimited power, unlimited resources, unlimited labour, unlimited opportunities, and eternity in glory to come. So, why is the world not yet evangelized, 2,000 years on? The answer is, that the enemy defeated but not annihilated in the heavenly war (Rev. 12:7–12) is still trying his utmost (and succeeding to some extent) to persuade people to believe in his lies: to convince them that hatred is better than love, darkness than light, hell than heaven . . . Of course, he doesn't put it as bluntly as this, but by the time his followers have awoken to his treachery, they're often beyond the point of no return. If Satan can persuade people that his power is greater than that of Jesus, he will; it's his only method of operation, since everything else but guile has been knocked out of him. Once he was a beautiful angel; now he's a fallen one, mortally wounded but still thrashing about. And when he happens on someone who is standing up for Jesus, he gets mad. We may grumble that we are suffering not only more than we think Christians should, but also more – significantly more – than non-believers. Better than grumbling, is praising God – and giving thanks (a) that we are accounted worthy to suffer for the name of Jesus, and (b) that we're giving Satan real trouble – for if we are making life hard for the devil, chances are we're doing something positive for Jesus!

As we reflect on our Lord's ascension, can we – even in the midst of our problems and attacks – hear him saying: 'In the world you face persecution. But take courage; I have conquered the world!' (John 16:33)?

## Suggested Hymns

Crown him with many crowns; Hail, the day that sees him rise; See, the Conqueror mounts in triumph; The head that once was crowned with thorns.

## Seventh Sunday of Easter (Sunday after Ascension Day)   28 May
*Principal Service*   **The Contract** Acts 1:15–17, 21–26; Ps. 1; 1 John 5:9–13; John 17:6–19

> *'[Jesus said], "I have made your name known to those whom you gave me from the world. They were yours, and you gave them to me, and they have kept your word."' John 17:6*

### A three-way process

God the Father, God the Son – and you and I – are in a three-way process that had its birth with the incarnation. Jesus is presently in us, as the Holy Spirit, rather than among us as the visible Rabbi; but everything else about this life-saving contract is the same. The Spirit is still making God's name known to those he chooses; and God is still giving their future development and progression to him; and we, like the disciples of two millennia ago, are still trying to fulfil the Great Commission.

But what of those who are outside the 'called and chosen'? Are they to be forever beyond the pale? Do we see in Christ's words, 'I have chosen you, you did not choose me', an exclusivity that human beings cannot alter? Surely not, for it's not the will of God that any should perish. The disciples had been chosen, called and cherished, yet one of them reneged on the challenge. Other disciples believed, and were cherished. Some of us today can pinpoint our calling, while others have 'grown into' Christ. Yet we can believe that these latter have been 'called', even as surely and convincingly as the others.

### 'The Spirit is on me'

This prophecy was being fulfilled in the person and incarnation of Jesus; it was natural that he chose it as his text for his first 'home-town' sermon. It was virtually a declaration of intent, setting the tone for his ministry. And the reaction of the crowd was also a precursor of the animosity and misunderstanding to operate throughout Christian history.

Jesus was 'filled with the Spirit', and this divine inspiration and guiding was to mystify many, right up to our own times. He did not measure up to people's expectations: not that he came with

141

lesser power, but in a different mode, with a different message, in a different style. And still today, Jesus does not fit the mould that many have decided to make.

'The Spirit is upon me.' In other words, this is God with whom we are tangling; and there is no way that God will be limited. Jesus has told us to 'ask, and we shall receive', but only so long as we don't try to tell God his business (oh, yes, though we may vehemently protest, this is exactly what we try to do, far too often; probably with the best of intentions, but yet very unwisely).

## Eminently strong

The Spirit of the Lord is the strongest power going. Jesus is good, meek, gentle, loving and so caring; but let us not lose sight of his great strength. We'd do well to do more, to meditate and reflect very often on it, simply because it's not only in Jesus. Since Pentecost (Acts 2), it's on all Christ's followers: in you, in me, in the person sitting next to us, in church, in the bus, in the tube, the supermarket check-out queue. This means, that whatever the situation, we have the means to overcome evil with good.

Every time.

If we fall down on the operation, it's not the fault of the Holy Spirit.

## Greatest power of all

Were we to walk around with sandwich-boards proclaiming: 'I AM INSPIRED, INDWELT AND MOTIVATED BY THE HOLY SPIRIT', how much attention would we attract? Dare we take the risk? It's nothing but the truth, yet how often do we proclaim it? How often, indeed, do we realize this greatest power of all, somewhere between our breastbone and backbone? Where is our holy boldness? The more we make the Spirit known, the more we are giving him the go-ahead to do more.

## Our 'Special Reserve'

It may help to visualize our Holy Spirit as the 'Special Reserve', an inexhaustible back-up waiting to be used. It's an unwise army that marches only on its skeleton force: it needs to calculate its operative success taking into account its Special Reserves. We can live without using our Spirit – millions of folk manage that – but we cannot bring others to God without it, nor can we take up the life that God offers, nor receive his forgiveness for our sins.

### Family Service Input

Encourage the young people to discover and discuss the variety of names for the Holy Spirit, and which names speak most to them.

### Suggested Hymns

Blessed by the Spirit's power; Holy Spirit, truth divine; Spirit of God, as strong as the wind; Spirit of the living God, fall afresh on me.

## Seventh Sunday of Easter
### Second Service    Divine Seed-Sowing Ps. 147:1–12; Isa. 61; Luke 4:14–21

> 'For as the earth brings forth its shoots, and as a garden causes what is sown in it to spring up, so the Lord God will cause righteousness and praise to spring up before all the nations.' Isaiah 61:11

### Inevitable growth

There is a comforting inevitability about the modus operandi of the earth's response to seed-sowing: not that there is 100 per cent germination, nor that growth is uniformly strong, weak or moderate; but growth there is, in line with the promise of God, that while the earth remains the seasons, climate and time will continue (Gen. 8:22). It is so with the word of God; not everyone will accept it; nor will those who do, make equal growth and advance. But growth there will be; God's word will not fall into oblivion, nor will it return to him with a negative rate of increase. We can have this assurance with all that we do for him: our efforts, our good deeds, our sharing of the gospel, our FAITH, lived out each day, even as an unconscious, unintended, witness, will find its mark (or A mark), and will count. Nothing done for God is ever wasted. God does not deal in waste.

## To what end?

It has been said, in one of our 'Wayside Pulpits', that 'If we stand for nothing, we shall surely fall over.' By the same token, if we grow aimlessly, we shall miss the mark. We grow, because that is the natural physical progression; but our faith determines HOW and WHY we grow. Even Satan's followers grow, but Christians are meant to grow positively, to make progress to God; to grow (as St Peter advocates) in grace, and in the knowledge of our Lord Jesus Christ (2 Pet. 3:18).

We are all different, but we take up our faith in the common knowledge that God is here, and God is alive. This means that we, in turn, are more 'alive' than non-believers; we cry more than non-believers, and we laugh more. In effect, our indwelling Holy Spirit converts us to 'God-in-action', the more we avail ourselves of his power. And the world has yet to see much more of 'God-in-action' before the Parousia comes.

## A safe environment?

Does the seed of God grow in a safe, congenial environment? By no means. We are standing on God's ground, our 'home-patch', if you like; but Satan invades wherever he can get a toe-hold, in the same way that he 'trespassed' into Eden. Yet in nature, very often plants grow best and strongest when conditions are not perfect; in fact, when plants feel threatened, that is the time they are activated by protective mechanisms to produce seed to perpetuate the species. Usually, it works in the opposite way with humans, at least, on the physical front. On the spiritual level, how does persecution, apathy, misrepresentation and the like, affect our faith? Positively, or negatively? If the latter, there is a danger that mediocrity may adulterate our faith.

## Going for growth

'Going for growth' is a buzz-phrase that has infiltrated many secular concerns. But can we – dare we – apply it seriously convincingly to our faith? 'Lord, increase our faith', should be our daily prayer, so long as we are prepared for God to take us at our word. Raising our level of faith, raises the morale of the Church. Going for growth in faith, is something that not only needs to be done right across the Church; it's imperative for the completion of world evangelization. The eagerness with which we go for spiritual growth, is a measure of the importance of our faith.

### Suggested Hymns

As the deer pants for the water; God of mercy, God of grace; Lord, teach us how to pray aright; Will you come and follow me if I but call your name?

## Day of Pentecost (Whit Sunday)   4 June
*Principal Service*   **Look, the Sight Is Glorious!** Acts 2:1–21 or Ezek. 37:1–14; Ps. 104:26–36, 37b; Rom. 8:22–27 or Acts 2:1–21; John 15:26–27; 16:4b–15

> *'Divided tongues, as of fire, appeared among them, and a tongue rested on each of them. All of them were filled with the Holy Spirit and began to speak in other languages, as the Spirit gave them ability.' Acts 2:3–4*

### Not to be missed

It was a glorious occasion, one not to be missed. God intended the coming of the Spirit to be, not an anticlimax to the resurrection, but an event that was both complementary and with a splendour and importance of its own. Pentecost (50 days) originally commemorated the fiftieth day after the harvest-consecration, sheaf-waving ceremony of 16 Nisan. It was held on 6/7 Sivan, and was also known as the 'Feast of Weeks' (Ex. 34:22; Deut. 16:10), the 'Feast of Harvest' (Ex. 23:16) and 'The Day of the First Fruits' (Num. 28:26). It virtually marked the end of the wheat and barley harvest, and opened the fruit harvest (though there could be quite a difference in these between the hot, semi-tropical Jordan Valley, and the Judaean hill-country areas).

### The Church's birthday

The Pentecost of Acts 2 marks the beginning of the Christian Church. The house shook as a strong wind hit it, the tongues of fire appeared, and then people started speaking 'in other languages'. Scholars are divided as to whether these 'languages' were (a) languages and dialects of the various nationalities gathered there, or (b) glossolalia, the special 'Spirit-languages', which can come when we are deeply in prayer or adoration, or suddenly surprised by God in joy, or even when we are in desperate trouble. Luke seems to favour the first; yet the fact that people describe the disciples as being drunk (v. 13) could suggest glossolalia, rather than sudden proficiency in foreign languages.

## Looking ahead

Yet the disciples were fairly soon to set out from Jerusalem, following the Great Commission of Christ, to other countries. Latin and Greek would get them a long way; but if other languages, and local dialects, were available, it would help considerably. Whichever is the answer to these 'languages', we do know that the gospel announced at this Pentecost was universal, and that in the assembly gathered there were representatives of many countries.

## Pentecost today

While the Pentecost of Acts would be seen as the begining of the harvesting of souls – the 'living fruit' of the Spirit (even as the natural fruit harvest was then just beginning) – the theme of harvest impacts less on the Church in the West, which on Whit Sunday is generally some months away from its cereal and fruit harvests. In fact, with the advent of the fixed spring bank holiday, Whit has less of an impact on the general public, particularly in those years when a bank holiday does not coincide with the religious festival. It is sad that the birthday of the Church can be overlooked in this way: sad that a 'holiday' can be divorced from the true 'holy-day'.

The Coming of the Spirit had been prophesied, promised by Jesus (see John 14—16). And so he came. It was God's spiritual empowering of the disciples for mission and ministry. Whatever they needed, the Spirit could, and would, supply: from strength in time of persecution, to reminding them of every word that Jesus had spoken (John 14:26). And we need to remember that this means ALL that Jesus had spoken, taught, prayed, preached and commanded, during his earthly ministry, which is undoubtedly a lot more than we can glean from the Gospels.

Isn't that thought exciting?

On this Whit Sunday, perhaps we can be bold enough to pray God to reveal to us more and more of these 'hidden' words of Jesus.

146

## Family Service Input

Encourage the young folk to illustrate Acts 2 as designs for (a) Whit-sun cards, (b) a collage, or (c) the start of an ecumenical initiative.

## Suggested Hymns

Come down, O Love divine; Come, Holy Ghost, our souls inspire; Come, thou holy Paraclete; O Holy Ghost, thy people bless.

# Day of Pentecost
*Evening Prayer*   **The Spirit's Power** Ps. 139:1–11 [13–18, 23–24]; Ezek. 36:22–28; Acts 2:22–38 [John 20:19–23]

> *'But God raised [Jesus] up, having freed him from death, because it was impossible for him to be held in its power.' Acts 2:24*

## The power of death

Death's power had for centuries operated as a virtual stranglehold on life here, and what was beyond. It was a hangman's noose, ever-present, ready to be tightened at any time. One could 'cheat' the hangman to an extent, by living years longer than the normal 'threescore and ten', but death was still waiting, still mocking, as the bodily functions grew weaker, and even the spirit of man pre-pared for the inevitable. Humanity had wandered off the straight way to God for so long that it was looking for an alternative, and it found it in an amalgam of prophecies that pointed to a Messiah who would be royal (i.e. would reclaim the earthly Jerusalem throne of David); a Messiah who would be holy (i.e. would assume the long-established place of high priest, after the order of Melchi-zedek); and a Messiah who would be glorious (i.e. who would show the glory of God to Israel).

If all this expectation dulled the visible power of death, wasn't that a good thing?

## The power of Jesus

So Messiah came. But he didn't fit the mould, and so many of the

Jews failed to see him, failed to reconcile the carpenter's son with their expectations. True, he had power – a power they couldn't explain – to heal, preach, cleanse and raise the dead. Thinking men like Nicodemus did believe, and were brave enough to speak out in the Council; trusting men, like Peter and the disciples, believed in faith, but were often ignored because they didn't have a degree in theology.

## The power of the Spirit

But things began to change when, in the space of six or seven weeks, the carpenter's son rose from being convincingly dead; ascended to glory; and sent his Spirit. So many more people were now believing that the authorities were forced to take the message seriously. God was showing a reversal in the situation that had pertained since Adam's sin in Eden: that death is not the end. Jesus had risen, to convince a few. The Spirit had now come, to convince the world.

And he's still at the job.

## The weight is lifted

An ex-prisoner convicted of murder revealed that for every day of his years of sentence, he had felt as though a heavy weight was on his shoulders: the weight of 'thirty seconds of madness'. He knew what Cain must have experienced for the rest of his life, after murdering his brother Abel. But then, on the morning of his release, the prison-door had opened to let in a gust of 'fresh, fresh air', and he walked out to greet it, with the weight no longer on his shoulders: forgiven on the inside, and free on the outside.

It's like that, when the Spirit enters a person who has repented and found God's forgiveness. The 'fresh, fresh air' of a great power that has broken the lesser power of death takes us over, and sometimes we say, in a sort of explanation: 'I feel ready for anything!'

And why not? God has given us the means to face anything. Let's make sure we give HIM the credit for it, though!

## *Suggested Hymns*

Filled with the Spirit's power; Gracious Spirit, Holy Ghost; Veni creator Spiritus; When God of old came down from heaven.

# Trinity Sunday  11 June
*Principal Service*  **God Loved So Much** Isa. 6:1–8; Ps. 29;
Rom. 8:12–17; John 3:1–17

*'[Jesus said], "For God so loved the world, that he gave his only Son, so that everyone who believes in him may not perish but may have eternal life."' John 3:16*

## Love of the Almighty

It's almost beyond belief that the power which called life into being loves us so much, though we do little enough to merit it, often nothing at all to merit it. Yet it is believable, because the Lord has gone to great lengths to convince us.

Nicodemus found it hard to take on board, and he was looking Jesus eyeball to eyeball. Sadly, truthfully, Jesus reproached him: 'We speak of what we know and testify to what we have seen; yet you do not receive our testimony ... you do not believe' (John 3:11–12). If one of the best intellects in Jewry had a problem, surely we can take heart. If the Divine Lord had trouble in getting his message across, let us not despair when folk turn away from us in disbelief.

## Embarrassed by good news

There has been a resurrection somewhere in Africa (as happens, when faith-filled folk unencumbered by sophisticated ideology, theology, or any other -ology simply believe that 'God is able'). You receive the news, and in a Holy-Spirit-surge of joy, run out to share it. Wow! What happens? Even friends – folk who won't bat an eyelid as the liturgy is sung every Sunday morning – raise eyebrows, smile politely, and walk away (inexplicably quickly). Why are we so often embarrassed by good news? It's just as though God has turned back the clock (or has let the shadow go back on the dial of Ahaz!) to the first Easter Day, when those who wanted most to hear the good news, didn't immediately receive it when it looked them in the eye.

But God loved the world so much, he went ahead with spiritually equipping it for mission and evangelism, anyway.

*God loved the world so much, he gave us Jesus,*
*To show us how to walk his Royal Way;*
*He came to teach us how to love each other,*
*To preach his word, baptize and heal and pray.*
*He came to save the world from dark destruction,*
*From compromise with Satan, prince of sin;*
*Through torture, passion, death and resurrection,*
*He paid the price of Calvary, our souls to win.*

## Divine encouragement

If there was no eternity with God to look forward to, what incentive would there be to make good for him in this life? We could follow Jesus out of gratitude for him dying for us, but could we love him as Saviour for saving us from our sins? Hardly. Could we love him for showing us that death is not final? Hardly. Could we enjoy his glimpses of glory, as a foretaste of our own eternity? Hardly.

His giving and loving, has given us a hope – THE hope – by which every part of our every day should be inspired. We don't know what we shall be doing Hereafter; but he is asking us to trust, and, meanwhile, to be doing all we can to show our love and trust.

*God loves the world today, and still is pleading*
*For us to take the news to every land;*
*To follow Love, wherever Love is leading,*
*To show his peace, where war's on every hand;*
*To share his joy, where sorrow strength is taking;*
*To speak his truth, where rules corruption's sway.*
*O, Holy Spirit, kindle an awakening*
*Of fervent zeal in all your Church on earth today!*

## *Family Service Input*

Encourage the young folk to solve the 'Saints' Word-Search (p. 151), and if time permits to illustrate their answers.

## *Suggested Hymns*

Have mercy on us, God most high; Holy, holy, holy, Lord God Almighty; Thou whose Almighty Word; Three in One, and One in Three.

## Saints Word-Search

| | | | | | | | | | | | | | | |
|---|---|---|---|---|---|---|---|---|---|---|---|---|---|---|
| E | R | O | D | I | S | I | F | B | E | R | N | A | R | D |
| C | T | G | D | H | G | Y | H | T | O | R | O | D | B | A |
| A | H | H | K | C | I | R | T | A | P | D | E | C | G | M |
| T | E | I | B | O | N | I | F | A | C | E | J | N | E | K |
| H | R | E | I | J | B | A | W | T | R | E | Q | P | O | O |
| E | E | F | C | F | K | L | D | U | S | M | R | N | R | L |
| R | S | X | P | G | N | E | T | O | O | N | P | H | G | S |
| I | E | Q | F | R | A | N | C | I | S | I | N | M | E | W |
| N | R | C | W | O | E | W | M | T | L | A | N | Q | J | I |
| E | S | P | T | V | A | L | S | K | B | P | C | K | D | T |
| H | F | I | A | C | R | E | J | L | G | B | R | F | D | H |
| A | I | N | L | B | I | S | A | N | I | U | Q | A | E | U |
| J | O | V | A | L | E | N | T | I | N | E | V | M | A | N |
| B | G | K | H | A | U | G | U | S | T | I | N | E | N | W |
| F | E | Q | U | R | D | G | A | N | D | R | E | W | T | B |

FRANCIS
AQUINAS
BONAVENTURE
THERESE
BERNARD
ALBAN
GEORGE
PATRICK
DAVID

ANDREW
VALENTINE
SWITHUN
AUGUSTINE
BONIFACE
DOROTHY
FIACRE
ISIDORE
CATHERINE

# Trinity Sunday

*Evening Prayer*   **Nothing Is Hidden** Ps. 104:1–10;
Ezek. 1:4–10, 22–28a; Rev. 4 [Mark 1:1–13]

> *'And the four living creatures, each of them with six wings, are full of eyes all around and inside. Day and night without ceasing they sing, "Holy, holy, holy, the Lord God the Almighty, who was and is and is to come."' Revelation 4:8*

## All shall be revealed

There is nothing hidden (now) that shall not be revealed (one day): this was an oft-repeated tenet of Jesus' teaching (e.g. Matt. 10:26; Mark 4:22; Luke 8:17; 12:2). And in the vision given to John, the 'living creatures' in permanent attention on God have all-round, inner and outer vision. However we understand this, the message is clear: we shall not be able to sweep anything under the carpet in heaven: all will be open to public, angelic, divine scrutiny (though many people conveniently choose to ignore this truth).

As we focus on the multi-operational Godhead, this Trinity Sunday, it's good to home in on the all-seeing power of God. Yes, our failings are all there, in technicolor vision; but so are the good points we have (and, let's have a bit of encouragement, most of us have and do so much good, we forget more than half ot it, more than half the time). On a bad day, the sheer grind may get us down. God knows. And in his time he'll do something about it. He'll either make it seem a blessing, or he'll replace it with a different blessing, or he'll call us to glory where we'll probably not even remember how we have suffered. But he knows. Let that realization cheer us, whatever the present circumstances.

He knows there's no justice in this world.

He knows Satan hassles us, the more we try to follow Jesus.

He knows: not only because, as God Incarnate, Jesus went the same route; but also because nothing on earth, or in heaven, or under the earth, escapes the Almighty's notice.

> *You know when I sit down, and when I rise up . . .*
> *Even before a word is on my tongue,*
> *O Lord, you know it completely . . .*
> *If I ascend to heaven, you are there;*
> *If I make my bed in Sheol, you are there.*

> *If I take the wings of the morning*
>     *and settle at the farthest limits of the sea,*
>     *even there your hand shall lead me . . .*
>
> (Ps. 139:2ff.)

There's no hiding from God! And how blessed a truth this is! Even in our tightest jams and stickiest situations, he's there: a breath, a prayer away; and always his attendants are also watchful: their alertness goes on unceasingly, unrestingly.

> *Unresting, unhasting, and silent as light,*
> *. . . Thine angels adore thee, all veiling their sight.*
>
> (W. Chalmers-Smith)

– yet not veiling their vision earthwards, but before the brilliance of God.

## The indwelling Eternal

As the creatures in glory worship the God 'who was and is and is to come', they mirror in a way what the Christian is doing already on earth. In our indwelling Spirit, we, too, have the God of the past, present and future. Now, the heavenly beings give constant worship, because that shows their relationship to the Almighty; they live to worship and praise and adore him.

How is our relationship with our Lord? Isn't it a combination of praise, petition, confession, repentance, intercession and thanksgiving? Shouldn't we, therefore, enjoy an even richer relationship than the all-seeing creatures? On this Trinity Sunday, may we reflect on our 'special relationship' with God.

> *There's a song which even angels*
> *Can never, never sing;*
> *They know not Christ as Saviour,*
> *But worship him as King.*
>
> (A. Midlane)

## *Suggested Hymns*

Around the throne of God a band; Jerusalem the golden; O, worship the King, all-glorious above; There is a land of pure delight.

# First Sunday after Trinity (Proper 6)  18 June
*Principal Service*  **This Long Green Road**
1 Sam. 15:34—16:13; Ps. 20; 2 Cor. 5:6–10 [11–13] 14–17;
Mark 4:26–34

> *'[Jesus] also said, "With what can we compare the kingdom of God, or what parable will we use for it? It is like a mustard seed, which, when sown upon the ground, is the smallest of all the seeds on earth; yet when it is sown it grows up and becomes the greatest of all shrubs, and puts forth large branches, so that the birds of the air can make nests in its shade."' Mark 4:30–32*

## Taking time

So often we want things done 'yesterday'. We hate waiting for time and effort to take its course. 'Lord, give it to me now, and make it quick!', usually. is the thought that underlies our more moderate verbal requests. But real, productive, positive and worthwhile growth does not necessarily, or often, happen overnight; and Jesus pointed up the example of a living, growing mustard tree, as illustrating the steady, unhurried growth of the kingdom of God. We in the West are used to cutting our sprouted mustard seed for salads and sandwiches when it is barely three inches tall; but in Palestine there is more than one species of mustard that grows tall enough to give a perch and shelter to the birds.

## Trinity

We have entered once again the 'long green road' of the Trinity season; and there is a definite change in our lections. Instead of being largely based on the various stages of Jesus' life – primarily his passion and what followed – we now take time to explore his teching in more detail. And much of that teaching was about the kingdom of God. It starts in a person's heart, as hidden or buried seed. But it cannot stay hidden: even as the green shoot breaks through the soil into full view, the working of the Holy Spirit in a person's life becomes visible to others. And if God's kingdom-Spirit has found a congenial environment (a life devoted to Jesus), it will grow and grow.

But it needs that seed-beginning: the first step to Jesus. Once that has been made, the Spirit can go to work.

## Living for others

We should note that the mustard tree does not grow only for its own benefit, but to provide a home and shelter for the birds. In the same way, people come to those whose Christian lives are making a positive impact: they come with their problems, their sickness, their grief. And sometimes they come with their joys, but not too often. As a race, we're a lot keener to share woes than triumphs. And when our comfort, help and guidance is sought, we need to pray that out of his fullness, wisdom and love the Holy Spirit will give us the right words to say, and the best help to give.

## Tree of heaven

There is a semi-tropical 'Tree of Heaven', with long leaves, each consisting of many small leaflets: a living example of the kingdom of heaven as taught by Jesus.

Where are we, on this tree? A stout branch, giving rise to smaller twigs clothed with many leaves? Or, if we're new to the faith, are we still little leaves, growing bigger each day?

Jesus taught that the kingdom of God is within us. How does it come? Perhaps, as J. C. Ryle suggests, when we pray:

> In every building the first stone must be laid, and the first blow must be struck. The ark was 120 years in building, yet there was a day when Noah laid his axe to the first tree he cut down to form it. The temple of Solomon was a glorious building. But there was a day when the first huge stone was laid at the foot of Mount Moriah. When does the building of the Spirit really begin to appear in a man's heart? It begins, as far as we can judge, when he first pours out his heart in prayer.

Our prayers, plus God's grace, and the kingdom has started to grow in us before we realize!

### Family Service Input

Encourage the young people to cut out 'leaves' for a 'Tree of Heaven' collage, and to write on each leaf how the kingdom of God can be seen to be growing in the parish. More leaves can be added, as the 'Kingdom' grows.

Father of heaven, whose love profound; Judge eternal; The kingdom of God; Thy kingdom come, O God.

## First Sunday after Trinity
*Second Service*  **How Free Is the Will?** Ps. 39; Jer. 7:1–16; Rom. 9:14–26 [Luke 7:36—8:3]

> *'For [God] says to Moses, "I will have mercy on whom I have mercy; and I will have compassion on whom I have compassion." So it depends not on human will or exertion, but on God who shows mercy.' Romans 9:15–16*

### Out of our range

We cannot buy our way into God's love: it's way out of our price-range. Neither can we ingratiate a way in: God knows the genuine article from the false one, every time. We have freedom of will, to choose to do good or to do evil. But the choice of our calling is God's: Jesus could not have spelled it out more clearly, 'You have not chosen me, but I have chosen you.' So we, as Christians, can rest in that blessed assurance; we are where we are today, because God – for reasons known only to himself – chose and called us. We could have passed up the opportunity of accepting – that's where our freedom of choice came in – but the initial decision was God's.

Does this mean that those who are presently outside the Church will always be outside? Not necessarily, for God has not fixed a date for making each decision (say, on our fourteenth birthday); he calls whom he will, when he will. Remember the workers in the vineyard: right up to the eleventh hour new harvesters were being recruited.

### In word and deed

God's call comes in many ways, often through the hearing of his word, but also by the life and witness of Christians, and sometimes actions do speak louder than words. It may be that realization of the call comes at the end of a long, gradual and growing awareness – the little inner voice that may have been whispering its message until it can no longer be ignored. Or, as in the case of St Paul, we may experience a sudden, even shattering, call, that turns around our life with *force majeure*.

Because God moves in such diverse ways, we should 'never be weary in well doing' (Gal. 6:9; 2 Thess. 3:13, AV), never let up on our witnessing and sharing; for the seeds we are sowing may take days, weeks, months, even many years, to germinate.

## Already damned?

Damnation is not our province, but God's. Paul is struggling to come to terms with it. Take Pharaoh, he says: wasn't he raised up to show the power and ability of God to deliver his chosen people out of Egypt? We may also look at Judas: hadn't there to be a betrayer, to set in motion the passion that in the end showed the tremendous resurrection-power of Jesus? Are such men as Pharaoh and Judas forever damned, because their compromise with Satan also led to such wonderful benefits for the Jews and the Christians? God alone knows: he will show mercy to whom he will show mercy.

## Our exertion

We have been given a will, and the ability to exert that will: to become enthusiastic and zealous for God, or for Satan. The impassivity of saints and angels in stained glass or oil-paint is beautiful, but it's untrue! There is no biblical foundation for – dare we say it – such boring serenity, in heaven or on earth. God is not impassive: he is the eternal Mover, who has set in motion the affairs of earth and heaven, and who encourages growth, development and ongoing action.

Yet there's an exertion that doesn't find favour with him, and St Paul has homed in on it: we are wasting our time in trying to win God's favour. We either have it, or we don't. We are either following him and obeying his laws, or we're not. We are either for him, or against him. His will is not gained by bribery, still less by corruption. Yet some people have thought otherwise, since the earliest days of the Church (e.g. Acts 8:20).

### Suggested Hymns

Father of mercies, in thy word; O Jesus, I have promised; Thy kingdom come, O God; When all thy mercies, O my God.

## Second Sunday after Trinity (Proper 7)    25 June
*Principal Service*   **Self-Preservation**
1 Sam. 17:[1a, 4–11, 19–23] and 32–49 Ps. 9:9–20; or
1 Sam. 17:57—18:5, 10–16 and Ps. 133; 2 Cor. 6:1–13;
Mark 4:35–41

> *'But [Jesus] was in the stern, asleep on the cushion, and they woke him up and said to him, "Teacher, do you not care that we are perishing?"' Mark 4:38*

### We're so useful!

Don't we often believe that we're so useful to God, he can't possibly manage without us! There comes the least whiff of danger or illness, and we feel our ministry is threatened. 'Lord, I'm doing your work! Don't throw me on the scrap-heap!' Of course, we tone it down a bit, but that's often the gist of our feeling. So it was with the disciples. They forgot that the Master of the universe had told them to go to the opposite shore (v. 35). Would he be likely to let a little storm change his plans? Would he also be likely to sleep on while his friends drowned? If the boat foundered, what of the Master, asleep on the cushion?

But commonsense had failed the men – failed them, fishermen as they were, and in their home waters. No doubt they would have argued that they knew the treachery of these freak Galilean storms. Yet surely, had the wind been really strong, Jesus would not have been resting so peacefully.

### Lord, don't you care?

A similar outburst came later in Christ's ministry, from a hard-pressed Martha, as she banged around with the kitchen-sinkery while her sister calmly sat in the parlour, listening to Jesus. 'Lord, do you not care that my sister has left me to do all the work by myself?' (Luke 10:40). Martha's problem was self-pity: the disciples', self-preservation. The culprit in each case was that inflated balloon we call 'I', 'me', 'mine', the so-important ego that so often trips us up from the inside out. If we could look at Mr/Mrs/Miss Ego, as God looks at it, Wow! – the two may not look forty-second cousin to twins.

## Hindsight

With hindsight, the disciples would look back and realize that God had them earmarked for mission: wonderful, world mission, which was to see the gospel taken out from Jerusalem to many countries; a destiny far removed from drowning in a storm on Galilee. But at the time, panic had driven all else from their minds, and, to be fair, it was near the start of Jesus' ministry, and these men still had a lot to learn.

So often when we're setting out on a work for God, we run up against opposition of one kind or another, and the thoughts do come: am I really where God wants me to be? Have I understood the Lord aright? Am I on the right track, or is he telling me not to go on?

And, yes, if the anxiety is really giant – or we tell ourselves it is – we can panic like those disciples, and say: 'Don't let me die yet, Lord!' It may sound melodramatic, but we all get to that point, sooner or later. But, 'Not yet, Lord, not just yet!'

God knows our life's work so well, can't we trust him? Of course, but preferably on a calm day!

## Physical danger

Physical danger, as also spiritual danger, is still around; and, if only because it's often more visible, can still have a great impact on us. We know, with Calvary's victory won, that we shall live eternally with Jesus; yet being human, it's natural for us to seek to prolong this life as much as possible. God has a different way of looking at things, but then, God knows what is ahead, and we do not.

Yet God is in the danger, as well as in the calm: is it all one to our indwelling Holy Spirit? Not quite; for he knows we need his help more in the spiritual danger: the temptation to listen to our ego; to compromise with Satan; to water down the uncompromised word of God; to seek for easier lives . . .

The more we concentrate on working against these temptations in the power of the Spirit, the less we'll find ourselves noticing the other dangers.

## *Family Service Input*

Encourage the young people to solve/illustrate the Word-Search (p. 161).

Be thou my vision; For ever with the Lord; Oft in danger, oft in woe; Through the night of doubt and sorrow.

# Second Sunday after Trinity
*Second Service*   **Inscrutable in All His Ways** Ps. 49; Jer. 10:1–16; Rom. 11:25–36 [Luke 8:26–39]

> *'O the depth of the riches and wisdom and knowledge of God! How unsearchable are his judgements and how inscrutable his ways!' Romans 11:34*

## The admittance of Gentiles

Paul has been tackling the thorny problem: the admittance of Gentiles to the mercy and promises of God, on a par with the Jews, his 'chosen people'. The early Church must have seen this question as its number one priority, to be solved (for Paul calls it a 'mystery', in v. 25) before the gospel could make real headway. There is a partial analogy today, as the various Christian denominations (or some of them) seek to reunite; and ongoing – as in the first century – is the question of the acknowledgement or otherwise of different faiths.

God's love, Paul teaches, is infinite, his riches and wisdom and knowledge are so far beyond ours, we cannot search them out. Who are we, therefore, to try to limit the Almighty? And Paul describes the ways of God as 'inscrutable' (a word often used to describe the Egyptian Sphinx: used for target-practice by generations of soldiers, climbed over, stared at, even vilified, the Sphinx continues to smile mysteriously, serenely, impassively on all-comers).

No, Paul, God is very different from the Sphinx; and his ways may be mysterious, but they are surely not inscrutable: full of love, rich in mercy, vibrant with enthusiasm and encouragement, God's ways are characterized by energy, and they get folk moving. With hindsight, we learn much about God and his ways, even though at the time he has often taken us by surprise.

## It had been foretold

The inclusion of the Gentiles – the whole world – in God's plan for humankind, had been foretold by the prophets, even as far back as

# Trinity Word-Search

| C | P | A | Q | B | M | O | R | D | E | C | A | I | S | J |
|---|---|---|---|---|---|---|---|---|---|---|---|---|---|---|
| C | A | A | S | I | R | S | U | R | A | Z | A | L | H | O |
| D | I | L | C | D | B | E | A | F | W | G | T | S | B | H |
| J | O | K | E | E | L | J | O | S | I | A | H | U | E | N |
| N | I | M | H | U | J | G | A | K | F | T | L | I | N | T |
| A | H | T | R | A | M | T | N | E | E | S | M | L | J | H |
| D | Q | C | P | B | O | A | W | H | L | R | A | E | A | E |
| J | E | S | U | S | S | F | S | T | E | A | D | N | M | B |
| O | P | H | Q | G | R | O | W | I | B | J | A | R | I | A |
| S | A | N | W | M | B | R | L | Q | K | C | V | O | N | P |
| F | O | T | G | I | F | S | E | P | D | N | I | C | M | J |
| P | H | B | H | S | A | O | J | I | O | J | D | K | L | I |
| H | B | P | W | C | I | S | H | M | A | E | L | M | L | S |
| C | E | A | D | S | E | R | F | H | A | N | N | A | H | T |
| M | O | S | E | S | T | G | Q | H | P | I | N | J | O | K |

| JOSIAH | MEPHIBOSHETH |
|---|---|
| MOSES | JESUS |
| DAVID | JOSEPH |
| SAMUEL | BENJAMIN |
| JOASH | ISHMAEL |
| JOHN THE BAPTIST | ISAAC |
| HANNAH | JAEL |
| MARTHA | LAZARUS |
| MORDECAI | CORNELIUS |

Abraham, who had been promised that in him all the families of the world would be blessed. Yet for centuries the Jews had either soft-pedalled on these portions of scripture, or had taken them to mean the proselytizing (i.e. converting to circumcised Judaism) of other nations. But now, with the birth of the Christian Church, circumcision was not looking the essential it had seemed; the Gentiles were not obliged to become Jews, but could keep their own nationality and status, without physical alteration. Naturally, many Jews were having a problem with this development.

## Jesus died for all

So Paul has had to go back to the cross (always a good policy), and learn from the universal sacrifice of Jesus, how the Jews and Gentiles alike have been given the hope of glory. In Jesus, our sins met, and together they were borne away, far out into the sea of God's magnificent, magnanimous forgetfulness. Elsewhere, Paul rejoices that now it's a misnomer to say 'I am a Jew', or 'I am a Greek'; in Jesus, we are all one; previous differences just don't apply any longer, not even male and female (Gal. 5:28). Two thousand years on, the world is still having difficulty in seeing life in such wonderfully simple terms: in many ways, not least in the Christian Church, we have erected more barriers, highlighting more divisions, than ever before.

Perhaps we, like Paul, could benefit from going back to the cross and 'reasoning it out with God' (Isa. 1:18), to see if we can iron out some, at least, of the differences that continue to impede the progress of the gospel.

## *Suggested Hymns*

Brother, sister, let me serve you; In Christ there is no east or west; Tell out, my soul, the greatness of the Lord; Will you come and follow me?

# Third Sunday after Trinity (Proper 8)   2 July

*Principal Service*   **Coming in Time** 2 Sam. 1:1, 17–27;
Ps. 130; 2 Cor. 8:7–15; Mark 5:21–43

> *'When they came to the house of the leader of the synagogue,
> [Jesus] saw a commotion, people weeping and wailing loudly.
> When he had entered, he said to them: "Why do you make a
> commotion and weep? The child is not dead but sleeping."'*
> Mark 5:38–39

## Only asleep

Jesus had said the same of Lazarus, even though he knew that,
physically, he was dead: 'Our friend Lazarus has fallen asleep, but
I am going there to awaken him' (John 11:11). He knew, but he
delayed, so that the miracle would be greater: just as, with Jairus's
daughter, he deliberately took time to heal the woman with haemor-
rhages, so that the little girl's miracle would be greater. To us, with
our human limitations, the moment of death seems so crucial, but
not to Jesus, the Master of Life.

It had probably been very hard for Jairus to ask a favour of Jesus:
synagogue-rulers were not prominent among the Lord's followers;
but any father worth his salt will do and dare anything if his little
child is in trouble. Then the distracted father, after gaining Jesus'
attention, would believe, when he saw the professional mourners,
that he had not come in time.

But he had: he was dealing with the Master of Time.

'Oh, I've left it too late!' is a cry very often heard today; actually
more today than ever before, because the pace of life has hotted up
to the point where practically everyone is running out of time, all
the time. Why don't we live as those who may one day die? Why
don't we live for eternity? Simply because, being human, we are
presently confined by time. But God is still pleading with us, encouraging us, to make the best use we can of the time he is giving us.

## Desperation

Desperation drove both Jairus and the sick woman, to seek out
Jesus. We are more fortunate: Jesus has already sought out us, has
called and chosen us. That's not to say we don't get desperate at
times. And, Christians though we are, don't we tend to try to work

things out ourselves first, before going to Jesus? And when we do seek his help, doesn't he sometimes seem to delay giving it? At such times, may we remember the two people in today's lesson who came to him: one had to push and shove for her healing, while the other was kept waiting in anguish until he thought it was too late. Both had their faith tested, quite severely, but both stayed with Jesus UNTIL THEY RECEIVED THE HELP THEY NEEDED.

Will our faith stand the strain? Or do we send one quick prayer to God, and then assume he doesn't want to give us what we have asked, if he doesn't send it quickly? The woman could have let the large crowd dissuade her from getting to Jesus. Jairus could have gone home, angry and despairing, when Jesus stopped to attend to the woman. Perseverance is the name of the game: God is merciful, but he is also just. Is it right to accede to someone's half-hearted request? Both recipients in our lesson were committed to their cause; one for herself, the other for his little girl. They demonstrate that if we ask the Lord in faith and trust and sheer stickability, he answers not only our prayers for others, but those for ourselves as well. We need not think, from an over-scrupulosity of modesty, that we cannot ask for our own healing, or our own troubles: God is no respecter of persons, and he loves us as well as those for whom we may intercede. If we have a problem, we can never come too late for God to be able to do something about it. When dealing with the Master of Time, we can believe we always will come 'in time'.

### Family Service Input

Encourage the young people to make a 'Prayer Tree', on which worshippers may hang their prayer requests through the week, for inclusion in the daily/weekly intercessions.

### Suggested Hymns

Inspired by love and anger; Revive thy work, O Lord; She only touched the hem of his garment; Spirit of the living God, fall afresh on me.

# Third Sunday after Trinity

*Second Service*   **Out of Debt** Ps. [52] 53; Jer. 11:1–14;
Rom. 13:1–10 [Luke 9:51–62]

> *'Owe no one anything, except to love one another; for the one who loves another has fulfilled the law.' Romans 13:8*

## Abiding by law

The laws of the land are there for the good of the nation, and we should, as good Christians, abide by them. We may not agree with either the laws or those who have made them; in this case, we have the opportunity of changing them by using our democratic right to vote in local and national elections. Every vote cast makes a difference; every one missed through apathy or disaffection is a missed opportunity. When Jesus was asked about taxes, which have been unpopular since their inception, he unequivocally taught that the physical taxes were debts due to the physical authorities, but that our debt to God needed to be paid in spiritual currency: in love, joy, peace, patience, kindness, generosity, faithfulness, gentleness and self-control (Gal. 5:22–23). Every so often, we can pay off our physical debts, until the next bill comes; but our debt of love to God is ongoing, although one great debt, that of sin, has been paid, in a one-off settlement, by Christ's victory at Calvary.

## The cheerful giver

Taxes are not usually paid cheerfully; yet the Christian should try. To part with our money willingly needs prayerful determination, and also a realization that in the faceless recipients we are dealing with men and women who, like us, are 'servants of God' (Rom. 13:4). It seems far preferable to give a donation to overseas missions or Bible translation, but God can, and will, answer our prayers if we ask him to take charge of all our finances. It's then not only ourselves paying the taxes, but God-with-us. And, yes, that knowledge does make a world of difference!

## Not in debt

There are the so-called 'blab it and grab it' or 'prosperity preachers', who teach that God wants us to be healthy and wealthy as well as wise. And they receive a fair amount of flak for such preaching. Yet, while an excess of emphasis may have sent out a distorted message from some, in the main they are holding to principles grounded in the scriptures. Jesus spent a large amount of ministry time in healing all sickness and all disease among the people. He taught that we should be 'wise as serpents, innocent as doves' (Matt. 10:16); and as far back as the time of Joshua, God was encouraging prosperity (Josh. 1:8). But it's not ours by right; God in his mercy gives us health, wealth and wisdom, according to our needs (Phil. 4:19), not because we've deserved it, but by his grace, his love, his mercy.

And when these blessings come, we are to use them for God, to his glory, not for self-aggrandizement.

> *A debtor to mercy alone,*
> *Of covenant mercy I sing,*
> *Nor fear, with thy righteousness on,*
> *My person and offering to bring.*
>
> *The terrors of law and of God*
> *With me can have nothing to do;*
> *My Saviour's obedience and blood*
> *Hide all my transgressions from view.*
>
> *The work which his goodness began,*
> *The arm of his strength will complete;*
> *His promise is Yea and Amen,*
> *And never was forfeited yet.*
> (Augustus Montague Toplady, 1740–78)

## Love is the key

Love is the key that unlocks debt's door, that sets us free from the crushing weight of debt and enables us to walk out free and tall. Remember the woman bent double with spinal paralysis for 18 years, whom Jesus freed in the synagogue one day from the crippling power of Satan (Luke 13:16). In a similar way, God takes our paralysing load of debt from us by cleansing us from sin, and setting us free to walk tall in love.

### Suggested Hymns

A charge to keep I have; Firmly I believe and truly; I danced in the morning; Soldiers of Christ, arise.

## Fourth Sunday after Trinity (Proper 9)   9 July
*Principal Service*   **So!** 2 Sam. 5:1–5, 9–10; Ps. 48;
2 Cor. 12:2–10; Mark 6:1–13

> *'[Jesus] called the twelve and began to send them out two by
> two, and gave them authority over the unclean spirits . . . SO they
> went out and proclaimed that all should repent. They cast out
> many demons, and anointed with oil many who were sick and
> cured them.' Mark 6:7, 12–13*

### Obeying the Lord

The Twelve (Judas Iscariot included) simply obeyed the Lord. Did
they wonder if the 'unclean spirits' would accept their authority?
Did they heal their first 'patients' in fear and trembling? They would
only have been human, if they did. But, however overawed they
may have been at the confidence Jesus placed in them, they did as
he had commanded. Has God given us a command that seems
beyond our capabilities? Agonize no longer: it is achievable, or he
wouldn't have given it. But he means us to go ahead in faith, like
the disciples obeyed Jesus; and then God (as then) can come through
with his power, and get the job done in us. (But let's remember,
when we're about it, to give him the glory.)

### Identifying the problem

Jesus identified the problem of sickness and disease very simply: it
was of the devil and not of God or of purely physical provenance.
Today, we don't blame God so much, as attribute it to 'natural
causes'; and as a result send sick folk into hospital, where the
'natural' illnesses are treated by 'synthetic' drugs, more often than
not. Where is Satan, in all this? Content to take a back seat, and
more than content to let others take the blame and have the hassle.
How did we get off the track? Was it when the monasteries and
their infirmaries were 'dissolved'? The monks used natural cures,
yet they, too, saw the illnesses as merely physical. So we need to
look further back into history, to the time when medicine was
gaining in credibility and doctors were no longer synonymous with
priests, or even in the Church at all. By this time we are at least in
the fourth century AD, if not earlier.

So the identifying of Satan as the cause of all sickness can be said to have lasted for a relatively short time after Jesus. Yet the teaching of Jesus to this effect has come down to us virtually unchanged through two millennia. Generations of translators have been faithful to their task, yet physical medicine has developed, and Christian healing has declined.

If we will, we can help to redress the balance. Perhaps then, we shall have a healthier world, and one better fitted to complete the task of worldwide evangelization.

## Preventive medicine

God has given us plants and herbs of many kinds to keep us healthy. There is at least a welcome trend today towards healthier eating, in a protest against the 'junk food', quick-serve boom of a decade or so ago. Eating healthily for the sake of our well-being is good; but doing it out of thankfulness to God for his rich provision, is even better.

## In faith

In faith, if we believe God is so calling us, can we not go out and minister as did the disciples? Can we not believe that the gospel brings a holistic ministry to people? that it feeds and nurtures and heals them from Satan's influence in body, as well as mind and spirit? God still reserves the right to answer our prayers in his way and in his time; we are to go in faith, not in arrogance; with prayer, not presumption; but with courage and not cowardice.

> *For my sake, and the gospel's, go,*
> *And tell redemption's story.*
> *His heralds answer, 'Be it so,*
> *And thine, O Lord, the glory.'*
> (Bishop E. H. Bickersteth)

### *Family Service Input*

Encourage the young people to abstract data from the healing ministry (a) of Jesus in the gospels, and/or (b) of the apostles in Acts, and to discuss its relevance today.

*Suggested Hymns*

Go, tell it on the mountains; Hear us, O Lord, from heaven thy dwelling-place; Jesu, lover of my soul; Thine arm, O Lord, in days of old.

## Fourth Sunday after Trinity
*Second Service*  **Loving into Life** Ps. [63] 64;
Jer. 20:1–11a; Rom. 14:1–17 [Luke 10:1–11, 16–20]

> *'Welcome those who are weak in faith, but not for the purpose of quarrelling over opinions. Let us no longer pass judgement on one another, but resolve instead never to put a stumbling-block or hindrance in the way of another.' Romans 14:1, 13*

### Reaching out in love

Reaching out to others in love is not always easy, especially to those of an argumentative frame of mind, who are critical of how we opeate, yet whose faith is kept so well under wraps that it's incognito. The Amplified Bible's rendering of 1 Cor. 13:4, 'Love is not touchy, or fretful, or resentful' is a beautiful text to take into any and every day. It may not keep us out of strife completely (for we're still human), but it does help! Can we 'love into life' those whose opinions differ from ours? With God's grace, we can but try.

### Watching ourselves

Paul is concerned not to give cause for anxiety to anyone by the way he lives out his faith. In his day, dietary rules had a higher profile than in modern times, and while Peter had been shown that nothing was unclean per se (Acts 10:15), and Paul had reached pretty much the same conclusion either by personal revelation or by hearing Peter's testimony, there were obviously a number of new Christians still struggling with their consciences about which foods they could or could not eat. Paul does not want to injure these neophytes by declaring brusquely (if truthfully) that 'anything goes', but instead sensitively teaches that if anyone could suffer embarrassment (or worse, take offence) at seeing any particular food eaten, then that food should be avoided in their company. It is all of a piece with the psalmist's teaching: 'O Lord God of hosts, do not let those who seek you be dishonoured because of me' (Ps. 69:6).

## Weak in faith

They may be weak in faith, but our insensitivity can make these people even weaker. They need, rather, as much encouragement as we can give them. We may not see a reason for their doubts and caveats, but let us remember that not everything we do or say is 'reasonable'.

Not everyone in the Church faces exactly the same challenges or has the same opportunities. Some will preach to thousands, others where 'two or three are gathered together'. Some will have 'high-profile' faith, others a faith shared in a small company. Some will have a lifetime of belief, while others will come to Christ near the end of their earthly lives. It is not for us to try to measure or evaluate any person's faith but our own, and the more frequently we run a 'time and motion' study on our own faith, the stronger it will become. But our work is to encourage, and to build up the faith of others (and in doing so we shall also be doing our own faith a favour).

## Stumbling-blocks

It should be our mission to clear the way of others from stumbling-blocks and hindrances. How? By sharing with them the uncompromised word of God; by giving them physical, spiritual and mental help wherever we see a need; by 'coming alongside' with the love and light of Christ. This last is the best position we can take, because then we are in a similar position to them, from which to see obstacles or hindrances in their way.

And if we then don't do something about these stumbling-blocks, someone one day will probably want to know the reason why.

### Suggested Hymns

Can I see another's woe; Lead us, heavenly Father, lead us; Teach me, my God and King; You will cross the barren desert (Be not afraid).

# Fifth Sunday after Trinity (Proper 10)　16 July
*Principal Service*　**Innocent for Guilty** 2 Sam. 6:1–5,
12b–19; Ps. 24; Eph. 1:3–14; Mark 6:14–29

> '*For John had been telling Herod, "It is not lawful for you to have
> your brother's wife." And Herodias had a grudge against him,
> and wanted to kill him. But she could not, for Herod feared John,
> knowing that he was a righteous and holy man, and he protected
> him.*' Mark 6:18–20

## A woman's vengeance

But Herodias' vengeance grew, and eventually she used John's vacil-
lating protector to get the Baptist killed. Had John remained silent
about Herod's illegitimate marriage, he would probably never have
got as far as the Machaerus prison-cell.

But had Henry VIII not sought a divorce, would England have
remained Catholic and answerable to the Bishop of Rome?

Had John Wesley stopped preaching before his 'second conversion' at Aldersgate, would the Methodist Church have been born?

While there are men and women brave enough to stand up and
speak out, the devil will go to work on them, but in the end, the
good that they have done will last, and have far-reaching results.
Yet, inevitably, there will be tragedy, also.

William Tyndale had a vision: to give the English-speaking people
the Bible in their mother tongue. He gave his time and talents – and
eventually his life – to the cause; and England and English-speakers
continue to thank God for Tyndale. And yet countless others lost
their lives: lawyers, ministers, merchants, academics and printers,
couriers and the gentry – all were drawn to the cause of the English
Bible. Some were burnt alive, others starved to death in prisons;
some were strangled, others thrown bound and gagged into the sea.
Did William Tyndale blame himself for the loss of these loyal
friends and helpers? Any thinking, breathing, feeling and loving
man could not help being moved, yet, with a mind that was determined and disciplined to see the great work through, he went on
with his translating.

## One ideal

Similarly, John the Baptist was uncompromising in his mission to point people to Jesus and to proclaim repentance for sins, and the approaching kingdom of God. To be true to himself and to God, he could not stay silent over Herod's sin, and so the die was cast.

Jesus, for his part, as his mission unfolded, could not stay silent over the shortcomings of the priesthood, and so another die was cast.

Paul could have faded into oblivion, to meditate on the wonder of his Damascus Road experience, but wonderful meditation would have done little for the rest of the world. So he entered the new Christian arena, and another die was cast.

If we are not to ruffle any feathers, not to stir people into finding faith, not to give anyone a reason to level the charge of 'Christian' against us, all we have to do is to stay silent, to walk away from situations: in a word, to embrace mediocrity. Mediocrity is always waiting, hands held out in sinister invitation.

And once she has us in her grasp, she is most reluctant to let us go. Many in her thrall, in fact, care little about escaping; for Satan either tones down or turns off his hassling of the 'mediocrity': they're of little threat to him.

Jesus didn't undergo the passion for his gospel to be taken up by folk who care little about whether they share it or not, or even whether or not it's true. He hung and bled for those who would not be ashamed of taking up their own cross.

And, if there's ever been a contradiction in terms, it is of the mediocrity caring enough to take up even the smallest cross.


### Family Service Input

Encourage the young folk to write and illustrate a hymn or prayer on today's gospel reading.


### Suggested Hymns

For the might of thine arm; Give me the faith that can remove; On Jordan's bank; This is the truth sent from above.

# Fifth Sunday after Trinity

*Second Service*   **A Great Lift** Ps. 66; Job 4:1; 5:6–end or
Ecclus. 4:11–31; Rom. 15:14–29 [Luke 10:25–37]

> *'I myself feel confident about you, my brothers and sisters, that
> you yourselves are full of goodness, filled with all knowledge,
> and able to instruct one another.' Romans 15:14*

## Loving encouragement

These words of Paul must have been such an encouragement to the
faithful at Rome. Paul has not yet seen them, but already he loves
them. He knows it cannot be easy for either Jews or Christians in
Rome, with the emperor and his court so close. Life is fraught
enough in Jerusalem (where Paul is going to next), with a mere
procurator in command.

The apostle's mind is racing ahead: with the business of freewill
offerings concluded, he plans to leave Jerusalem and to sail to Italy
on his way to Spain. It is unlikely that this Spanish visit ever took
place; a furore awaited Paul in Jerusalem, which would lead to his
arrest and trial. He would issue his formal 'Appeal to Caesar', and
after many vicissitudes would arrive in Rome, which was probably
the western extremity of his mission.

## Overconfident?

Was Paul being overconfident? Had he overestimated the spiritual
worth and fortitude of the believers in Rome? When he eventually
reached the city, would he be disappointed?

These are not, thankfully, merely rhetorical or hypothetical questions. Luke tells us that the believers were so excited at the prospect
of meeting Paul that they 'came as far as the Forum of Appius and
Three Taverns to meet us' (Acts 28:15) – that's a trek of around
30 miles – and that their fellowship found an appreciative response:
'on seeing them, Paul thanked God, and took courage' (Acts 28:15).
His letter and its encouragement had borne fruit! We can reverently
believe that the 'two whole years' (v. 30) he spent in Rome would
be brightened by these believers, his house arrest notwithstanding.

## The importance of fellowship

Our own Christian fellowship is important. Christ himself under-lined this, by forming an inner circle of his 12 most dearly loved disciples; and even John the Baptist, whom we may think of as a loner when he emerged from the desert, had his circle of disciples, too.

We may worship as members of a large or small congregation. And our Sunday fellowship is important, for it's principally the time of corporate worship of God. But if we have little or no Christian felowship in the week, we are depriving ourselves of valuable spiritual input and mutual encouragement. Bible, prayer, healing, intercession and study groups are a vital part of the Christ-ian's life, and worth hundreds of committee or council meetings. By these means, we are replicating the 'house-groups' of the early Church, which did so much to further the good work begun by Christ. Simply meeting together to read God's word, in a variety of the versions available today, can open up to us new truths from familiar texts, new insights from shared testimonies, new resolve from pooled resources.

## The message that counts

If ever you think that encouraging words are a waste of time, remember today's lesson, and the difference that its outcome would make to a tired old man, arriving in a country far from his home, recently shipwrecked, under armed guard, with a court appearance before the emperor on the horizon.

'On seeing [the believers], Paul thanked God, and took courage.'

We send encouraging cards and verses to each other at Christmas, Easter and birthdays. But how do we rate in the encouragement stakes for the rest of the year?

## *Suggested Hymns*

Courage, brother, do not stumble; Love is his word; Sing them over again to me; Tell me the old, old story.

# Sixth Sunday after Trinity (Proper 11)  23 July
*Principal Service*  **When Jesus Changed His Plans**
2 Sam. 7:1–14a; Ps. 89:20–37; Eph. 2:11–22; Mark 6:30–34, 53–56

> *'[Jesus] said to them, "Come away to a deserted place all by yourselves and rest awhile . . ." As he went ashore, he saw a great crowd, and he had compassion for them . . . and he began to teach them many things . . . And wherever he went, into villages or cities or farms, they laid the sick in the market-places . . . and all who touched [his cloak] were healed.' Mark 6:31, 34, 56*

## No quiet retreat

You lead a high-profile, public life, lecturing to different groups of people every day, and even on a Sunday you'll likely be in one pulpit or another, still hard at work. Then you hear that a member of your family has been brutally killed, cut off in his prime. 'Leave me alone! I must have time to think!' And, taking time off from work, you go somewhere – anywhere – to be alone with your grief.

Jesus was no different. The shock and sadness of John's execution came as a blow to his disciples; and even though, being God, he must have known (before the news arrived), he thought of his friends, and declared a retreat, a space to themselves.

But the crowd changed his plans, altered the decision of the Lord himself! He saw their need, and he put it before either his own feelings or those of the disciples. Peter and the others, in waiting on a crowd of several thousand, would have no time to brood. And from feeding the multitude, they went the next day (after a night of storms) on to a massive healing mission. Still no time to indulge in private grief!

## The luxury of solitude

Whenever it comes, grief tries to claim our full attention, and in this it can be seen as selfish. The more we pander to it, in the luxury of solitude, the greater its hold on us becomes. Jesus was no stranger to grief (e.g. Luke 19:41; John 11:35), but he was not married to it. The best antidote to grief, he taught by practice rather than precept, was work: work for others.

It's still the best way.

When Mary, wife of Dean Hewlett Johnson, died, the crowds packed into Manchester Cathedral, overflowed into the surrounding streets, and along the road to the cemtery, and in their sharing were a great comfort to the Dean. 'The glow of those days,' he wrote, afterwards,

> lit the coming weeks and months. My constant thought was that Mary had won a triumph, and nothing could rob her of her triumph. She was triumphantly secure. No shadow came until three months later, when I sat in my library on a dull afternoon. Then something broke, and overcame me, until a favourite saying of Mary's recurred: 'Don't brood, but act. Do something, the nearest kind thing you can do. Don't brood, but act.' At that very moment, an idea struck me, an act I could do, and forthwith I drove into the country, to an orphanage which Mary and her father had founded and which Mary treasured. I had seldom been to that Home. It was her work, and my spare time was very rare. However, something impelled me and I went; the matron welcomed me cordially, and the children crowded round me whilst I told them stories. After half an hour, matron burst into the room, and said: 'Do you remember your wife sought a Girl Guide to help the children?' 'Yes, indeed,' I answered, 'but she was sad that none had ever come.' 'Well,' the matron said, 'an excellent Guide has just come voluntarily and wants to begin at once, and you are here to help her by introducing her with a prayer.' Nothing will ever dissuade me that that act was not Mary's act. She said she would always be with me. Here at this critical moment she proved true. (Hewlett Johnson, *Searching for Light*, 1968)

## Family Service Input

Encourage the young folk to solve and illustrate the 'Bible Plants and Flowers' Word-Search (p. 178).

## Suggested Hymns

Blest are the pure in heart; Happy are they, they that love God; Strengthen for service, Lord, the hands; When I needed a neighbour.

# Sixth Sunday after Trinity

*Second Service*  **Because** Ps. 73; Job 13:13—14:6 or Ecclus. 18:1–14; Heb. 2:5–18 [Luke 10:38–42]

*'Therefore [Jesus] had to become like his brothers and sisters in every respect, so that he might be a merciful and faithful high priest in the service of God, to make a sacrifice of atonement for the sins of the people. Because he himself was tested by what he suffered, he is able to help those who are being tested.'*
*Hebrews 2:17–18*

## In every respect

Jesus has touched our lives in every respect, from conception through birth to the grave. But being who he is, he has gone beyond the grave, beyond the stage we call 'death' (of which we can see only the fleeting beginning) into the next life. In simple terms it means that wherever we can be, he has been; all that we can hope for, he has already experienced; all we are tested by, he has already overcome. He has completed the race, gained the winner's prize, and out of sheer love has presently given us his Spirit to see that we, in turn, make the grade.

The only way we can fail, is if we let the devil persuade us we can't win. That is all that's standing between us and victory. Jesus has done all he can. The devil seems to have ended up with a poor hand, but he tries to play those cards as best he can. And God is still allowing us the freedom to choose between Jesus and Satan, between the Master-Builder and the Destroyer.

## The important 'because'

But because Jesus has won, because he is Victor, his Spirit can show us how to win. Satan, because he has always been a loser, can only show us how to fail.

Because Jesus loved us so much, he made it possible for us to win. It's a magnificently unfair challenge, because God is on our side (Ps. 118:6). There is no way in the natural that we can win, but there is no way in the supernatural that we can lose. We can settle for a life without Jesus, or we can accept this life, and the next, with him. He is calling, he has chosen: all he is waiting for is our acceptance.

## Plants and Flowers of the Bible Word-Search

| C | P | E | O | F | N | M | H | Y | S | S | O | P | L | J |
|---|---|---|---|---|---|---|---|---|---|---|---|---|---|---|
| T | Q | S | R | U | E | A | L | R | M | H | K | I | H | P |
| R | D | O | B | W | G | D | E | P | A | R | G | E | F | O |
| C | S | L | I | L | Y | B | E | F | N | O | G | L | I | M |
| E | B | I | A | E | M | Q | B | O | C | J | E | P | J | E |
| A | W | V | Q | W | R | Q | P | Y | L | R | J | P | I | G |
| W | F | E | C | P | C | S | S | M | O | K | G | A | I | R |
| G | T | U | R | T | N | D | R | M | I | N | T | F | H | A |
| A | C | S | M | E | O | K | O | O | N | C | U | M | I | N |
| C | G | A | R | L | I | C | P | M | E | L | O | N | P | A |
| H | M | E | I | L | Y | F | J | G | K | E | L | H | C | T |
| A | L | B | F | S | C | O | R | I | A | N | D | E | R | E |
| W | A | C | D | S | I | G | E | M | B | J | F | I | G | L |
| C | P | T | D | O | R | I | N | P | O | Q | P | K | Q | M |
| W | T | B | C | W | S | A | H | W | H | E | A | T | N | R |

| | |
|---|---|
| SYCOMORE | MINT |
| FIG | RUE |
| OLIVE | HYSSOP |
| GRAPE | CUMIN |
| LILY | CORIANDER |
| WHEAT | GARLIC |
| POMEGRANATE | CUCUMBER |
| PALM | MELON |
| ROSE | APPLE |

## Giving up?

What is there in this life that we would not give up for Jesus? If he called us home today, would we feel deprived? Would we – if we had the chance – look back in sorrow? When a fuel crisis hit the country, it was noticeable that luxury items were left on the supermarket shelves, while the two items that sold out everywhere comprised basics that normally we'd take for granted: bread and toilet rolls.

Would we really long for either of these, were God to call us home?

Spiritually, we miss most the friends who are called before us. We know that nothing and no one can take their place; and sometimes we face the best part of a lifetime without them. It's natural to grieve, but because Jesus is who he is and has done what he has done, even here we can have hope and strength to carry on, because, also, he has been in our place. In the Gospels, we hear of the parting when John the Baptist, his own cousin, was killed; and we assume that, either in his teens or twenties, he lost his earthly father, Joseph.

Perhaps these lines, penned by an unknown Catholic lady on the death of her husband, may help:

> When I come to the end of the road,
> And the sun has set for me,
> I want no tears in a gloom-filled room;
> Why cry for a soul set free?
> Miss me a little – but not too long,
> And not with your head bowed low.
> Remember the love that we once shared.
> Miss me – but let me go.
> For this is a journey we all must take,
> And each must go alone.
> It's all a part of the Master's plan,
> A step on the road to home.
> When you are lonely and sick of heart,
> Go to the friends that we know,
> And bury your sorrow in doing good works.
> Miss me – but let me go.
> Perhaps if we only could but see
> The splendour of that dear land
> Where our loved ones are called from you and me,
> Far better we'd understand.
> Perhaps if we only could but hear

*The welcome they all receive,*
*From familiar voices all so dear –*
*Ah, then we would not grieve.*
*Perhaps if we only could but know*
*The reason why they went,*
*We'd smile – and we'd wipe the tears that flow,*
*And we would wait content.*

### Suggested Hymns

Conquering kings their titles take; Forth in thy name, O Lord, I go; There is a land of pure delight; Will you come and follow me.

## Seventh Sunday after Trinity (Proper 12)   30 July
*Principal Service*   **Realization** 2 Sam. 11:1–15; Ps. 14; Eph. 3:14–21; John 6:1–21

> *'When they had rowed about three or four miles, they saw Jesus walking on the lake and coming near the boat, and they were terrified. But he said to them, "It is I, do not be afraid." Then they wanted to take him into the boat, and immediately the boat reached the land towards which they were going.' John 6:19–21*

### When it dawns

We are magnificent with the dawning of realization: 'Lord, how grand it is to see you!' But we can't 'con' God. He knows that until we know for certain that it's all right, that he has stepped into the situation, we shall flounder, or resort to fear, or be so paralysed with inactivity as to be of no use at all. 'Well, Lord, I didn't know you were here. I thought . . .' Yes, we thought the Lord had left us to muddle through on our own. Oh, we of little faith!

Just look at the size of a little mustard seed. You can hardly feel it on your hand. If only you had faith 'so big', Jesus told his friends. But they were just like us, until after the joy of Easter Day, the wonder of Ascension Day and then the sheer power of Pentecost had hit them; then we never hear of them being terrified (or even mildly fearful) again.

Come on! Jesus is saying, in 2006. You also have known Easter, Ascension and Pentecost! You know what I have done, why I did it, and who I did it for! Come on!

*Oh, how beautiful their feet upon the mountains,*
*The tidings of peace who bring, who bring,*
*To the nations of the earth who sit in darkness,*
*And tell them of Zion's king.*
*Then ye heralds of the cross, be up and doing!*
*Go, work in your Master's field, away!*
*Sound the trumpet! Sound the trumpet of salvation!*
*The Lord is your strength and shield.*

(Fanny J. Crosby)

Time is ticking on, and there are still many who have never heard, who, spiritually are still in the Dark Ages. They haven't had the chance of seeing Jesus walking on the water, because not knowing him it would have no impact. All it needs, is his love shining in the eyes of a Christian, his arms giving them a loving touch, his smile lighting up their lives. We've been given all it takes, and we leave our local church each Sunday, and talk about parish shares and coffee mornings.

## Don't fear

'It is I, don't be afraid', Jesus is still saying. 'I, your Lord and Saviour, who am reminding you of these millions of souls still waiting to know who I am. It is I who am disturbing your gentle, parochial life and outlook. My people are still perishing for lack of food. My word is the imperishable bread of life, and you, my chosen ones, have it in abundance! Don't fear!' And, as soon as the disciples stopped fearing and offered Jesus a place in their boat, they were immediately where they wanted to be.

It is so today: that first realization, then the invitation, and then our Lord will have us exactly where he wants us to be. But we must make the identification; we must acknowledge God is here, come to save the situation, come to make of it something beautiful, and then: 'Oh, Lord, step right aboard! You take charge!' Oh, how gloriously sweet such an invitation must sound to Jesus! And he will come aboard, and we shall then know what he wants of us.

None of this stiff upper lip and 'I'll go it alone' stuff. Jesus wants to come on to our ship. And with him aboard, we cannot founder.

### Family Service Input

Encourage the young folk to compose/illustrate a hymn based on the gospel reading.

### Suggested Hymns

Father God, I wonder how I managed to exist; Fierce raged the tempest; Jesus calls us, o'er the tumult; Peace, perfect peace, in this dark world of sin.

## Seventh Sunday after Trinity
*Second Service*   **A Better Covenant** Ps. 74; Job 19:1–27a or Ecclus. 38:24–34; Heb. 8 [Luke 11:1–13]

> *'But Jesus has now obtained a more excellent ministry, and to that degree he is the mediator of a better covenant, which has been enacted through better promises . . . In speaking of "a new covenant", he has made the first one obsolete. And what is obsolete and growing old will soon disappear.' Hebrews 8:6, 13*

### 'Getting better all the time'

'It's getting better all the time!' is an expression referring to something that is wonderful now, and even more wonderful in prospect. There are not too many experiences like this, but the Christian life is one of them, and the best of them into the bargain.

Why? For several reasons:

(1) The victory of Christ at Calvary did away with inherited sin.
(2) It also gives us the hope of eternal life with Jesus.
(3) Satan was mortally wounded then, and is only in his death-throes now, no matter how the old devil might try to persuade us otherwise.
        and
(4) We are two millennia closer to Christ's Second Coming, and getting closer every minute.

## And the Jews?

And what of the Jews, the chosen race? To be told that the covenant they had cherished (though not fully observed) for centuries, was now obsolete, must have been difficult news to accept; that the millions of animals and birds sacrificed over the years, was now unnecessary ... It is possible to accept this, only if the sacrifice of Jesus is accepted, and the Jews in general were finding this a stumbling-block. And many still find it so today.

And who are we to point the finger, we who, in our Christian Church, have still so many divisions?

But the cross still stands at the meeting of the two covenants: as the blood of Christ dripped from his body, symbolically the old covenant with its blood-sacrifices ebbed away, became obsolete. And when the risen Jesus left the tomb three days later, the new, living covenant was up and running. One brief weekend had changed the course not only of history but of history-to-be. Men and women who could believe, were now heading for eternal life.

## Torn up for ever

Was it as though God stepping into our lives as yet unborn, at Calvary tore up the old covenant for ever, and HIMSELF IN CHRIST wrote the new covenant in his blood?

Not quite.

The old covenant, it's true, had been a blood covenant, made in blood and regularly commemorated in blood. The new covenant, no less truly, was also made in blood (Christ's own blood), but its commemoration did not need blood; all the blood necessary for it had already been shed; new covenant commemorations would be, as Christ had shown only the night before in the cenacle, in bread and wine. All the blood had been shed. All the sacrifice had been offered. All the suffering had been done.

## For our sins

But there was also another difference. Where the blood of animals had sufficed in the old covenant, for the sins of the people, and though Jesus' sacrifice had washed away inherited sin – we were (are) now responsible for any further sins we commit; and no amount of animal blood releases us from the responsibility of coming to God in repentance and receiving his forgiveness.

It's all a matter of getting better, all the time, not only on Yom Kippur.

### Suggested Hymns

A new commandment I give unto you; Forgive them, O my Father; Once, only once, and once for all; There is a fountain filled with blood.

## Eighth Sunday after Trinity or, The Transfiguration of our Lord (q.v.) (Proper 13)  6 August
*Principal Service*  **Heavenly Food** 2 Sam. 11:26—12:13a; Ps. 51:1–13; Eph. 4:1–16; John 6:24–35

> *'[Jesus said], "For the bread of God is that which comes down from heaven and gives life to the world." They said to him, "Sir, give us this bread always." Jesus said to them, "I am the bread of life. Whoever comes to me will never be hungry, and whoever believes in me will never be thirsty."' John 6:33–35*

### More than manna

The manna, in the time of the wilderness wanderings, had kept the Israelites alive; but the food on offer from Jesus is sufficient to give life to everyone on earth until God's kingdom comes.

What is this life-giving heavenly food? Jesus himself. More precisely, his words, for he is the Word; and, as he says, later on in this chapter: 'The words that I have spoken to you are spirit and life' (v. 63). They are words that call life into being, and sustain it to the end. They can defeat Satan; they can encourage us to do and dare the impossible; they can heal the body and raise the spirit; and they are imperishable. Even when heaven and earth have gone, the words of Jesus will remain (Mark 13:31; Luke 21:33). They and they alone are indestructible.

And we, as Christians, have them in abundance. Do we value them? Do we share them? Do we even acknowledge that we've been given them?

When we hold our Bibles, between the pages from Genesis to Revelation we have words that can change the world – even more than it has been changed already. We cannot know the full extent of the power that Christ has vested in us, but we should at least attempt to use it as much as possible.

184

How often do we thank God for this heavenly food? But for his grace, we would still be among the millions in ignorance of Jesus and the gospel.

But, by his grace, we have been saved, called and chosen. We've been given the means to bring life to others, light in their darkness, knowledge to replace their unknowing, healing for body, mind and spirit, hope for eternity. This is our commission, and we are serving officers: light and salt for the world.

When the disciples were told all this, they didn't sit around too long overwhelmed at the prospect. They believed that the power had been given them; the building had been shaken (Acts 2:2), the fire had come down (Acts 2:3), and languages hitherto unknown were theirs (Acts 2:4). They received everything God was giving them. And we, in faith, can receive the same, usually without fire and earthquake, but by the acceptance of the Holy Spirit. Look back and see what you have already done for Jesus.

'Was that really me?'

No, it was the heavenly power energizing you into doing what you yourself could never have done. It's a 'surprising' force, in more ways than one: every time it persuades and enables us to act for God, the results are surprising; and, surprisingly, we usually either take the credit ourselves, or give it to someone else. God must surely find this not only surprising, but also hurtful.

'Wasn't it good that I stopped in time?'

'Didn't the operation go well!'

'Isn't it a miracle, that the war was averted?'

Yes, it was, it is, and it always will be miraculous, while God takes a hand in the affairs of humanity.

> *Give him the glory, give him the praise,*
> *Great is his holy name!*
> *Sing of his love, when veiled as a child,*
> *Jesus to Bethlehem came ...*
> *Child in the manger, come to our hearts,*
> *Come and unite us in love;*
> *Flame of the Spirit, keep us alight,*
> *With power from heaven above.*
> *Give us wisdom to know you, love to embrace,*
> *Strength to keep straight on the road;*
> *Joy to endeavour great things for your name,*
> *Feed us with heavenly food.*

## Family Service Input

Encourage the young people to transcribe and illustrate the above lines, for a parish prayer-focus. (They can be sung to the tune: Skye Boat Song.)

## Suggested Hymns

Bread of heaven, on thee we feed; Bread of the world in mercy broken; O Bread of heaven, beneath this veil; We hail thy Presence glorious.

# Eighth Sunday after Trinity
*Second Service*   **Fact of Faith** Ps. 88; Job 28 or Ecclus. 42:15–25; Heb. 11:17–31 [Luke 12:13–21]

> *'By faith Abraham . . . considered the fact that God is able even to raise someone from the dead – and figuratively speaking he did receive him back.' Hebrews 11:17a, 19*

## Ahead of his time

Abraham's faith was centuries ahead of his time: he was so convinced that 'God is able', he believed that if his 'point of no return' with Isaac was passed, it was not God's limit; the Lord could raise the dead.

We know he can, but then, we've had proof, in the life and ministry of Jesus, and the miracles done in his name since. But Abraham's was sheer naked faith, albeit faith that had already been strengthened by the birth of Isaac outside the natural child-bearing age of his parents, after a long, faith-filled wait of 25 years. Abraham had been brought to the realization that if God is able to bring life to birth from nothing, he is surely able to restore it to a body that has already lived.

We don't know how long Abraham had agonized over the whys and hows and wherefores, or whether he had just set them aside and gone straight ahead in believing. Nor do we know what were his thoughts as he trekked up the mountain with Isaac, built the altar, stacked the timber and then bound the lad and prepared his knife. Who would want to be in such a position? Who would want to know? God, in his mercy, shielded Sarah from the agony.

## Nearer home

Abraham's challenge makes our own testing on the home front seem mild by comparison. Yet we may ask: if we are not being challenged in our faith, how strong is it? How intently are we listening out for God? At various times in Christian history, there have been those who have actually sought martyrdom, often as an expiation for their sins. If we believe that God is a God of love, we surely cannot accept that self-sought martyrdom is within his will. Neither Abraham nor Isaac, given the choice, would have planned or executed the sacrifical challenge themselves.

Yet God is forever presenting us with lesser Calvaries, simpler challenges; and Satan is forever pleading with the Almighty to increase the testing, just as he did in the case of Job. It's the Christian's constant blessing, that 'God is faithful, and he will not let you be tested beyond your strength, but with the testing he will also provide the way out so that you may be able to endure it' (1 Cor. 10:13). It does mean that to cry to God that we are being hassled beyond our strength, is a non-starter!

So, if we're going through a terrible time just now, do we dance for joy and praise God for counting us strong enough to win through? Yes, by faith, in the power of the Holy Spirit, that's exactly what God is saying. We were not enlisted by Christ in the Royal Army to be side-liners, but crack troops in whatever fighting position the Lord would direct.

## The hard way

Paul had learned this lesson the hard way. At the height of his ministry, he was hassled by something he called a 'thorn in the flesh'. What it was exactly we don't know, but three times (at least) Paul prayed for God to take it away. But God didn't, yet he didn't ignore the request, either. 'My grace is sufficient for you,' he told his apostle, 'for [my] power is made perfect in [your] weakness' (2 Cor. 12:9).

Yes, we are weak. We are human. But God-in-us supplies all we need but haven't got in the natural. If only we'd get this truth into our hearts more thoroughly, it would save us an awful lot of anxiety.

## Suggested Hymns

Faith of our fathers; God of mercy, God of grace; Grace! 'Tis a charming sound; O, for a faith that will not shrink.

# Ninth Sunday after Trinity (Proper 14)   13 August
*Principal Service*   **Don't Complain!** 2 Sam. 18:5–9, 15, 31–33; Ps. 130; Eph. 4:25—5:2; John 6:35, 41–51

> *'Jesus answered them, "Do not complain among yourselves. No one can come to me unless drawn by the Father who sent me, and I will raise that person up on the last day."' John 6:43–44*

## God's decision

The fact of our Christian calling has been God's decision, not ours. Others may have been used by God to bring us to a knowledge of him, to guide us to Calvary, but it is God who reserves to himself the right to call whom he will. Some reject his call. Others, including ourselves, have said, 'Yes.' We don't know all that this acceptance will lead to: think what Mary's 'Fiat' produced (Luke 1:38)!

Who are we, to question God's decisions? We sow the gospel seed, and it seems to fall on unresponsive land; yet germination may only have been delayed, and, if so, we should believe that the delay is necessary for God's particular purpose to have the best result.

Nor should we who have faced many years of challenge complain when others come late in life to the faith. Both we and they have come 'in time', in God's time. And the heavenly bread is there to nourish, literally from the cradle to the grave; what use we shall put it to after that, is in God's hands.

## On the last day

As Christ won the victory of Calvary, so he has the privilege of raising us to glory. We need not agonize about it; if we have been faithful to him here, he will not disown us on the last day. We need the faith of the old bishop of Smyrna, Polycarp, who declared, when being given the opportunity to recant or be burned to death: 'Eighty-six years have I served my king, and he has proved faithful. Will he desert me now?'

## Suggested Hymns

O love that will not let me go; There's a wideness in God's mercy; Make me a channel of your peace; Bread of heaven, on thee we feed.

# Ninth Sunday after Trinity
*Second Service*   **Family Members** Ps. 91; Job 39:1—40:4 or Ecclus. 43:13–33; Heb. 12:1–17 [Luke 12:32–40]

*'Endure trials for the sake of discipline. God is treating you as children; for what child is there whom a parent does not discipline? If you do not have that discipline in which all children share, then you are illegitimate and not his children.' Hebrews 12:7–8*

## Always children?

Children, in a sense, never grow up in their parents' eyes. By the same token, the child who is loving and dutiful respects his parents for as long as they live. It is a natural bond that strengthens with time, and families whose parents and children grow apart are the poorer for the lack of this bond.

Similarly, God has bound us to himself, and with a love that far exceeds the strongest of human ties.

> *I've found a Friend, oh, such a Friend!*
> *He loved me ere I knew him.*
> *He drew me with the cords of love,*
> *And thus he bound me to him.*
> *And round my heart still closely twine*
> *Those ties which nought can sever;*
> *For I am his, and he is mine,*
> *For ever and for ever.*
>
> (Revd J. G. Small)

The Father heart of God, the saving heart of Jesus, the loving heart of the Holy Spirit, all reach out to those chosen and called by God. One would think these cords could not be broken, and in a way, that's true: God will not break them, though at times we may test his patience. But it is possible to wriggle free; Judas Iscariot, and others since, managed to escape, to their own detriment.

## Love and respect

As an earthly father looks for the love as well as the respect of his children, so does God from his larger family. We may call him 'Dad' (Abba), and love him as a constant companion and 'best Friend', but he's God, and as such we owe him respect, awe and wonder. We may (in fact he has invited us to) come boldly to the throne of grace, and find grace to help in time of need, but we are not to come arrogantly.

It has been said that 'God tests those most whom he most loves.' And we can all look round and see others – often non-believers – seemingly leading less fraught lives than we are experiencing. 'It's not fair, Lord! After all I've done, or tried to do!' We don't always sing it out to the heavens, but doesn't the thought cross our minds? And don't we feel even a bit aggrieved? Or perhaps we 'progress' to the virtuous stage, and, yes, that probably helps us through! But all these feelings, though natural, are less than God's best. He wants us to see nothing unusual in our disciplining, but instead to see it as the normal challenge of 'growing up'.

## Our guide

Our guide through 'growing up' is our 'Big Brother', the Lord whose sacrifice admitted us into the King's family, the 'Pioneer and perfecter of our faith' (Heb. 12:2).

In heaven, Jesus has told us, there will be no marriage as we understand it. We shall be children no longer, but perfected citizens of heaven. Yet God will surely still be our Father, and still he will be in charge of our eternal life. Every present trial, every minute of testing, is a preparation in some way for what is to come. It only serves to heighten the anticipation, if we try to learn more of the Hereafter by analysing our present challenges. God is speaking to us, directing us, through these testings. Are we reading his signs, or just careening from one trial to the next in an attitude of resignation, or, even worse, rebellion?

### *Suggested Hymns*

Father God, I wonder how I managed to exist; Love of the Father; Oft in danger, oft in woe; Through all the changing scenes of life.

## Tenth Sunday after Trinity (Proper 15)   20 August
*Principal Service*   **Life in Us** 1 Kings 2:10–12; 3:3–14;
Ps. 111; Eph. 5:15–20; John 6:51–58

> *'So Jesus said to them, "Very truly, I tell you, unless you eat the flesh of the Son of Man and drink his blood, you have no life in you."' John 6:53*

### How shocking!

He knew his questioners were shocked, yet Jesus went on to shock them further. And, like Nicodemus and the 'born again' question, these Jews were not on the Lord's wavelength. They reduced his teaching to their own level, that of physical flesh and blood. He, on the other hand, was dealing with participation by belief. Those who would believe in him, would by faith be sharing his sufferings, his very real Calvary flesh-and-blood sufferings.

### The Eucharist

The Eucharist has always been hard to explain, for believers and others alike. We may understand what we are remembering, and why; but in general we make a pretty poor fist of explaining it. A major part of the problem is that it means different things to different people, which is not really surprising, given its uniqueness and originality. And these differences can be – and throughout history have been – magnified out of all proportion. Dare we say, it matters less whether we understand the rite as a memorial or a sacrifice, or the elements as physical or as transubstantiated, than if we approach it with reverence and love, as a means of meeting our Saviour and feasting on his strength and resurrection vitality.

'I come with joy to meet my Lord', says the hymn, and surely joy should be the keynote of our Eucharist. Surely it is a commemoration of an event that took place when Jesus' arrest was imminent. Yet in the cenacle that night, he and his closest friends gathered for a Passover celebration, the last they would share as a group.

And not even the betrayer was excluded

It was an occasion that Jesus decreed should be replicated, while ever his Church was on earth. One day it will be superseded by the great Marriage Supper of the Lamb; but for the present we are to continue the commemoration. Its message is one of joy, rather than sorrow.

*The cross he bore is life and health,*
*Though shame and death to him;*
*His people's hope, his people's wealth,*
*Their everlasting theme.*

(T. Kelly)

## Where there are two or three

From great gatherings in lofty cathedrals, to where two or three are gathered in a cottage or in the open air, the Eucharist is in essence the same. It may be accompanied by high ceremonial and liturgy, or be a simple thanksgiving in a nursing-home or hospital ward. But it has endured through 2,000 years of satanic onslaught, and it will endure, for it is divinely ordained. And each time the faithful meet to remember, and to celebrate the Lord's victory, the devil loses ground. May we never forget this. Satan recoils, for this eating of our Lord's flesh and drinking of his blood – this participation by belief – is too poignant a reminder for Satan, of the Calvary battle he fought and lost.

That, if nothing else, would be a sufficient reason to perpetuate our Eucharists.

Our attendance at the Eucharist is one way in which we show to the world where we stand. And, at the same time, it shows to our fellow-believers that we love them enough in Jesus to want to share his special meal with them.

For the Eucharist – whether or not we include the 'Peace' and its embrace – is a fellowship meal. It may be possible to maintain even an 'armed neutrality' with someone in the workplace; but as we go to and from the altar, and kneel together at the rail, it's very difficult to cherish thoughts of strife against fellow-participants at the feast . . .

. . . which adds to the Eucharist's importance.

### Family Service Input

Encourage the young folk to illustrate the veil, burse, paten, ciborium and other items associated with the Eucharist, and to discuss their use.

And now, O Father, mindful of the love; Author of life divine; My God, and is thy table spread; Soul of my Saviour.

# Tenth Sunday after Trinity
*Second Service*   **Word Without Price?** Ps. [92] 100; Ex. 2:23—3:10; Heb. 13:1–15 [Luke 12:49–56]

> *'Keep your lives free from the love of money, and be content with what you have; for he has said, "I will never leave you or forsake you." So we can say with confidence, "The Lord is my helper; I will not be afraid. What can anyone do to me?"'*
> *Hebrews 13:5–6*

## A shining example

As one reads this text, surely examples of self-sacrificing lives will come to mind: lives dedicated to God, and unmindful of money and its lure. A shining example is surely William Tyndale (*c.*1494–1536), who forfeited health, wealth, country and even his life, to give the English-speaking world the Bible in their mother tongue. The priests of the time in England were desperately ignorant; an examination conducted by William Warham, Archbishop of Canterbury, in 1550, uncovered alarming figures, some priests having no idea of where the Decalogue was to be found, or what it comprised; many not being able to recite the creed; and a number not only ignorant of where to find the Lord's Prayer, or who had written it (!), but also unable to recite it!

## The boy who drives the plough

The venom of the local Gloucestershire clergy, who felt threatened by Tyndale's attack on the errors of the Vulgate – their precious Latin Bible treasured since Jerome had translated it, the best part of a thousand years before – had Tyndale up before the Chancellor; and only the standing of his employer, Sir John Walsh, together with his own stout defence, helped Tyndale to win that round.

'We had best be without God's law, than the pope's!' one cleric irately told Tyndale, who famously replied: 'If God spare me, ere many years from now I shall see that the boy who drives the plough knows more of the Bible than do you!'

Having fled to the Continent, Tyndale laboured in poverty, cold and hunger, flitting between Worms, Cologne and Antwerp, to get his New Testament translated into English from the best Greek texts of the day. Back in England, Cuthbert Tunstall, Bishop of London, and the sinister John Stokesley, his successor, apprehended as many of Tyndale's Testaments as they could, on their arrival in England. Tunstall publicly burned the books in a bonfire at St Paul's. Stokeley went further, and burned men and women (alive) who either had the English Testaments in their possession (or any of Tyndale's other books), or who had assisted their passage to England in any way.

## The traitor

It was an egregious graduate in civil law, Henry Phillips, who in 1535 was dispatched – by, it is thought, John Stokesley – to Antwerp: his mission, to find and arrest Tyndale. By infiltration and the basest treachery, Phillips accomplished the task, Tyndale then being incarcerated in the fortress of Vilvorde for 16 months. In August, 1536, he was formally stripped of his priesthood, and early in the morning of 6 October the same year was strangled and then burned.

## The victory

Had Tyndale known that, barely a year earlier, Miles Coverdale's complete English Bible (of which the Pentateuch and New Testament were Tyndale's) had been dedicated to King Henry VIII, and was even then circulating in England, he would have rejoiced. As it was, he could rejoice that the work begun by him would continue unstoppable. 'The Lord is my helper', had been the strength that sustained him, and whatever man did to him, William Tyndale would not deny his God.

## *Suggested Hymns*

A safe stronghold our God is still; Father of mercies, in your word; Lord, thy word abideth; Who would true valour see.

# Eleventh Sunday after Trinity (Proper 16)
27 August
*Principal Service*  **Useless Flesh** 1 Kings 8:[1, 6, 10–11]
22–30, 41–43; Ps. 84; Eph. 6:10–20; John 6:56–69

> *'[Jesus said], "It is the spirit that gives life; the flesh is useless. The
> words that I have spoken to you are spirit and life."' John 6:63*

## What price this life?

These are strong words from Jesus. No wonder the verdict among
his listeners had been: 'This teaching is difficult; who can accept
it?' (v. 60). Only those to whom God gave the grace, would in fact
accept it. The others would shrug, and turn the other way: perhaps
a few would 'regretfully ponder' it for a while. But only a very few
would remain faithful.

And, according to today's gospel, Jesus knew exactly who these
would be (v. 64). But it was not his way to condemn anyone before
they had been given every opportunity to believe. He knew that
Judas would betray him; not that Judas himself had been 'pro-
grammed' from ages past, but his betrayal had been prophesied,
and so someone would commit the crime. With his ability to see
ahead, Jesus knew now who it would be.

So, what is this life, if our Lord calls the flesh 'useless'? If he
knows in advance what we are going to make of it?

In the second part of this two-in-one question, lies the key. He
knows that we are going to use the grace we have been given. He
knows – dare we believe – that we are going to do 'greater works'
than the ones Jesus did (John 14:12). But only if we disregard the
permanence of the flesh.

'But that's obvious! Of course I don't believe the flesh is everlasting!' Don't we? The way we try to preserve the flesh, with implants,
transplants and the like, one would think we were trying to prolong
this fleshly existence for ever. We value the lives and examples of
the saints: men and women who died a martyr's death, often when
quite young, or who suffered unspeakable tortures for the sake of
the gospel, or who simply lived for others, unmindful of themselves
– content to suffer cold, hunger and thirst, so long as they were
serving others. Without exception, they were living examples of
Jesus' teaching, that the flesh is useless, and a new life without the
flesh was the reason for Jesus' incarnation.

They were not perfect, these self-forgetful saints, but they simply gave God their best. Did they do more than they needed? God, in his mercy, doesn't give a datum-line between what is and what is not 'necessary' to qualify for heaven, because such a line would be a contradiction of Calvary's sacrifice. By grace we are saved. If we go further, witness more, give up more luxuries, suffer more for the gospel than anyone for miles around, we are only doing our duty. God gives to each person a unique mission, with grace sufficient to carry it through; and we are to resist the temptation to evaluate our mission against anyone else's, or to try to tell anyone else what we think they should be doing (cf. John 21:20–22).

## When 'the flesh' gets in the way

The red light should flash when we start putting convenience, comfort and luxury before our work for God. 'Go on, you've EARNED a break!' whispers the devil. Have we? Well, perhaps we have been overworking a bit . . . And then the temptation increases to taking a longer break, or more frequent breaks . . . And the danger spreads.

'I'm sure the Lord doesn't want me to wear myself out!' Doesn't he? Well, just get serious with him in prayer (Isa. 1:18), and get his divine thoughts on it.

Rest assured, that if the flesh is useless, God won't let us hang around in it for too long.

### *Family Service Input*

Encourage the young people to solve the 'Books of the Bible' Word-Search (p. 198), and if time permits to illustrate/discuss their favourite verses.

### *Suggested Hymns*

Dear Lord and Father of mankind; Forth in thy name, O Lord, I go; Will you come and follow me; You will cross the barren desert (Be not afraid).

# Eleventh Sunday after Trinity
*Second Service*  **A Beautiful Prayer** Ps. 116;
Ex. 4:27—5:1; Heb. 13:16–21 [Luke 13:10–17]

*'Now may the God of peace, who brought back from the dead our Lord Jesus, the great shepherd of the sheep, by the blood of the eternal covenant, make you complete in everything good so that you may do his will, working among us that which is pleasing in his sight, through Jesus Christ, to whom be the glory for ever and ever. Amen.' Hebrews 13:20–21*

## Carrying complete assurance

In complete assurance, Paul (or whoever wrote these lines to the Hebrews) prays for his readers to be made 'complete'. Why can he be so sure? Simply because he channels this prayer to God 'through Jesus Christ'. It is the powerful name of Jesus that makes everything possible. Hadn't the Lord said, time and again, that whatever was asked of the Father, in his name, he would do it (see, e.g., John 14:13, 14; 15:16; 16:23, 24, 26)?

At the start of the disciples' mission, they'd been given authority to cast out demonic spirits in the name of Jesus, and the results had been so wonderful they were ecstatic as they shared the debriefing on their return. And Jesus joyed with them: 'I watched Satan fall from heaven like a flash of lightning!' he told them (Luke 10:18). What a wonderful affirmation of the power of his name!

## Whatever we ask

But, later in the ministry, when he was about to return to glory, he gave the disciples authority not only to baptize in his name (and in the name of the Father and the Spirit (see also Acts 2:38), but also to ask for anything, providing, of course, that it was in accordance with God's will. And so we have the 'gi-normous' prayer of today's reading, made in complete confidence in this great name of our Lord. We have his authority to use it: power of attorney, for he has given it to the Body of Christ.

# Books of the Bible Word-Search

| S | N | A | I | S | E | H | P | E | I | Y | C | J | A | P |
|---|---|---|---|---|---|---|---|---|---|---|---|---|---|---|
| G | A | L | A | T | I | A | N | S | M | D | K | B | L | H |
| H | E | B | R | E | W | S | Q | O | P | N | O | S | M | I |
| L | B | I | H | A | T | G | N | R | E | S | N | F | W | L |
| C | S | D | R | E | V | O | R | P | F | O | E | G | D | I |
| L | N | M | K | J | R | H | L | E | I | K | E | Z | E | P |
| E | O | D | P | E | Q | I | R | T | I | T | U | S | B | P |
| I | E | D | T | C | H | S | A | T | A | W | B | A | C | I |
| N | E | U | F | C | G | T | H | N | H | R | J | O | B | A |
| A | E | G | A | J | N | I | T | I | S | Q | J | P | P | N |
| D | F | L | Z | E | P | H | A | N | I | A | H | T | S | S |
| H | A | I | M | K | S | L | M | K | N | C | E | O | A | R |
| M | H | A | N | O | J | L | G | M | F | T | N | W | L | Q |
| J | L | L | K | G | E | N | E | S | I | S | D | O | M | A |
| C | O | R | I | N | T | H | I | A | N | S | P | B | S | C |

| | |
|---|---|
| GENESIS | PHILIPPIANS |
| PROVERBS | ACTS |
| EPHESIANS | ZEPHANIAH |
| CORINTHIANS | EZEKIEL |
| PSALMS | DANIEL |
| JOB | JONAH |
| HEBREWS | DEUTERONOMY |
| MALACHI | TITUS |
| GALATIANS | LAMENTATIONS |

198

## We are to be bold in using Christ's name

A striking instance of the boldness with which God empowers us to use the name of Jesus, is given in the earliest days of the Church. Peter and John, having healed a lame man at 'the Beautiful Gate' of the temple, in the name of Jesus, had been arraigned before the Council and had been warned not to continue using this name. On being released, the apostles returned to their congregation and prayed: 'Now, Lord, look at their threats, and grant to your servants to speak your word with all boldness . . .' (Acts 4:29)

The answer came very immediately, very convincingly, in an earthquake that shook the building: 'they were all filled with the Holy Spirit and spoke the word of God with boldness' (v. 31).

## Holy boldness

And today's prayer continues in this boldness. It's a combined petition, for the readers of the letter and also for the ministry team, that the work of God may go forward as a combined operation. Those are, indeed, the best prayers that ask for others as well as ourselves, and in the asking draw both sides closer together in God.

An industrial disagreement, in which a key safety force was threatening withdrawal of its labour in strike action, was teetering on the brink of a protracted dispute. Throughout one long night meetings had been held in which the shop stewards and employers had brokered a deal. Then inexplicably in the morning the deal was scuppered by an unseen, unknown third party, and the strike went ahead. One of the shop stewards interviewed that day said: 'It was as though an unseen hand took the pens away from the signatories, before the deal could be ratified.'

Satan had stepped in so fast, he hadn't had time to masquerade as anyone else. Had the signatories, in faith, committed the deal to Jesus, the outcome may have been very different.

## *Suggested Hymns*

At the name of Jesus: How sweet the name of Jesus sounds; Jesus, the name high over all; Name of all majesty.

# Twelfth Sunday after Trinity (Proper 17)

3 September

*Principal Service*   **The Core of the Problem** S. of Sol.
2:8–13; Ps. 45:1–2, 6–9; James 1:17–27;
Mark 7:1–8, 14–15, 21–23

> '[Jesus said], "for it is from within, from the human heart, that
> evil intentions come: fornication, theft, murder, adultery, avarice,
> wickedness, deceit, licentiousness, envy, slander, pride, folly. All
> these evil things come from within, and they defile a person."'
> *Mark 7:21–23*

## Cutting through ritual

Jesus cut right through the ritual of hand-washing and the like, so
cherished and elevated by the Pharisees, but which could be used
as a smokescreen for inner filthiness. It's one thing to feel ill, pray
for healing and believe we receive when we pray, then to go out
declaring belief in that healing. That is faith. But to harbour evil
thoughts, or to act dishonestly or commit any sin in secret, and then
pretend in public that we are keeping God's law, is sheer hypocrisy.
Yes, we all do it at times, for we are all human. But let's come clean
about it to God, and repent and seek his forgiveness, for we can't
have any secrets from him, anyway. We may be able to con some
of our friends some of the time – or even to con some of them all
of the time – but God is not for conning. Long before Röntgen, the
Lord was not only reading out bodies but also our minds.

## 'Clean dirt'

'It's clean dirt. It'll wash off. But beware of the dirt that won't wash
off.' This sage advice was given to a child by her godly father, and it's
so true today. A bit of grime under the fingernails may look awful,
but it's not a permanent disfigurement. But grime in the soul is serious, and needs repentance and the blood of Jesus to eradicate it.

## Can we be too scrupulous?

The religious of former days were at times accused of being over-
scrupulous in their self-examination; and some religious houses, for
charity's sake, had sessions where one's fellow-monks or nuns

would scrupulously point out the faults that one had (in)conveniently overlooked. Can we really go over the top with such navel-gazing? Only if we get an inverted sense of guilt and begin imagining faults we really haven't got.

And, let's face it, most of us are streets away from that particular danger.

We need the discipline of regular self-examination; but we also need to do it prayerfully, asking God in his mercy as well as his judgement to show us where we are veering off-track. He will show us, because it's not in his interest any more than ours, to let us carry on carrying a load of sin's grime.

> *Wash me, and make me all thine own;*
> *Wash me, and mine thou art;*
> *Wash me, but not my feet alone,*
> *My head, my hands, my heart.*
> (Charles Wesley, 1707–88)

## A temple of the Holy Spirit

It's a nasty thought that in admitting evil into our hearts, we have admitted Satan into what has been so beautifully called 'a temple of the Holy Spirit' (1 Cor. 6:19). It should be sacrosanct, but nothing is sacred with Satan; not being in any sense of the word a gentleman, he'll push his way in wherever and however he can. And again, it's only the cleansing blood of Jesus' forgiveness that can dislodge him.

> *The temple has been yielded,*
> *And purified of sin;*
> *Let thy shekinah-glory*
> *Now flash forth from within,*
> *And all the earth be silent.*
> *The body henceforth be*
> *Thy silent, docile servant,*
> *Moved only as by thee.*
> (Frances Ridley Havergal)

## *Family Service Input*

Encourage – and help, if necessary – the young people to solve the crossword (p. 202), and the youngest to illustrate (some of) the clues as they are found.

## Trinity Crossword

---

### Suggested Hymns

A charge to keep I have; Not for our sins alone; O, for a closer walk with God; To the name of our salvation.

## The Twelfth Sunday after Trinity
*Second Service* **Beacons in the Night** Ps. 119:1–16;
Ex. 12:21–27; Matt. 4:23—5:20

> *'[Jesus said], "You are the light of the world. A city built on a hill cannot be hidden. No one after lighting a lamp puts it under the*

## Clues Across

1. Rarer. (7)
5. Caper. (5)
11. Tied up. (7)
12. Owl-calling. (7)
13. Timer. (5)
14. Applied to practical use. (9)
15. Burial place. (10)
16. Type of brake. (4)
19. Ireland. (4)
20. Engineering. (10)
23. Basic. (9)
24. Components. (5)
26. Support. (7)
27. Sweet-smelling flower. (7)
28. Near. (5)
29. Demonstrate. (7)

## Clues Down

2. World of believers. (6, 8)
3. Ride on soft turf? (4, 4)
4. Finish Martha's sister? (3, 4)
6. Ruth's mother-in-law. (5)
7. Thomas a Kempis's masterpiece. (8, 7)
8. Deaden pain. (4, 4)
9. Designer. (6)
10. Church moulding. (4)
17. Destination of a Pauline letter. (8)
18. Case before court? (2, 6)
21. Here today. (6)
22. Town in Yorkshire. (7)
23. When the tide flows back to the sea. (4)
24. Leaves. (5)

*See page 205 for solution*

---

*bushel basket, but on the lampstand, and it gives light to all in the house. In the same way, let your light shine before others, so that they may see your good works and give glory to your Father in heaven."' Matthew 5:14–16*

## False modesty

'Oh, I don't want to push myself forward!' Isn't it a common expression, and very often the recipients of this protest want it as little as the protester; probably they want it far less. But, in letting our light 'shine before others', Jesus isn't looking for our personal halo to be burnished, but for HIS light to shine through us. Let's agree on one basic truth: we don't have any personal light worth speaking of. Any brightness we give out, is his, not ours. And, as Christians, we have an obligation not to hide his light. It's not ours to hide. Christians worth their salt (and we are salt, as well as light, v. 13) have a duty to shine Christ's light to the world.

*Do not be ashamed to own him,*
*Or obey your Lord's command;*
*In your every word and action*
*Show the world just where you stand.*

*When temptations throng around you,*
*Closer hold his nail-pierced hand;*
*You have joined his blessed service,*
*Show the world just where you stand.*

*Do not be ashamed to own him,*
*Tell it out through all the land.*
*Loyal ever to the Master,*
*Show the world just where you stand.*
(Lizzie de Armond)

## Lights in the darkness

If it takes only a very little light to make an impact on darkness, a stronger light – or a number of lights – can make even greater impact. We may not think our beacon-light is very strong; but if we only let Christ shine in our eyes and on our lips, there's a fair chance he'll beam out from our lives as well. We may not see the light, but others will. Not one of Christ's followers is recorded in the New Testament as going around proclaiming, 'I've got the light of Christ!' but others noticed it (e.g. Acts 4:13). As a beacon's light guides the ships away from dangerous rocks and into safe harbour, so the light of Christ shining out from us has a twofold mission: (a) it sends a warning rocket across Satan's bows, that if the devil is spoiling for a fight he'll have to tangle not merely with us but also with Christ. And (b) it tells others whose side we are on: God's side of light and love and mercy. What a privilege, to send out such powerful messages!

## Glory to God

It's fine to shine for Jesus, and to do 'good works' in his name. But it's also very tempting to take the credit for all this goodness, or even to accept the occasional compliment: the world is often so chary in its praise, that 'occasional' is probably the right word. But Jesus warns us against taking even the occasional whiff of glory for ourselves. All the credit, all the glory, belongs to God.

We don't need to agonize over how we can shine for Jesus, but just to ask God in his name to show us. God is not short on ideas. He'll give us plenty of opportunities.

### Suggested Hymns

Glorious things of thee are spoken; Jesus bids us shine; O, the love of my Lord is the essence; Shine, Jesus, shine.

## Thirteenth Sunday after Trinity (Proper 18)
### 10 September
*Principal Service* **Those in Need** Prov. 22:1–2, 8–9, 22–23; Ps. 125; James 2:1–10 [11–13] 14–17; Mark 7:24–37

> 'From there [Jesus] set out and went away to the region of Tyre. He entered a house and did not want anyone to know he was there. Yet he could not escape notice.' Mark 7:24

### Meeting Jesus

Jesus spent his ministry time in meeting people's needs, and those who needed him were always led to him, even on one occasion breaking up a roof to get a need met (Mark 2:4). So it is today.

---

Solution
Across: 1. Scarcer. 5. Antic. 11. Trussed. 12. Hooting. 13. Pacer.
14. Applicate. 15. Churchyard. 16. Disc. 19. Erin. 20. Mechanical.
23. Elemental. 24. Parts. 26. Bastion. 27. Freesia. 28. Close. 29. Explain.

Down: 2. Church Universal. 3. Risk race. 4. End Mary. 6. Naomi.
7. Imitatio Christi. 8. Stop ache. 9. Shaper. 10. Ogee. 17. Colossae.
18. On appeal. 21. Extant. 22. Halifax. 23. Ebbs. 24. Exits.

Some things have changed; there are many more people around today, with many more needs. But what has not changed is the fact that Jesus is still here in every one of his followers, still eager to meet every need – and the basic needs have not changed: they are still forgiveness for sins, healing of mind and body, and hunger for the gospel. Every person ever born has these needs, though relatively few are honest enough to admit the fact.

## No undercover work

Jesus does not put his itinerary up in neon lights, but neither does he go around incognito, pretending to be someone else. Why should he? Our Lord has nothing of which to be ashamed. If we find ourselves in a place where we feel unable to share the gospel of Christ, we're in the wrong place, and we'd better do something about it. Either we take the plunge, and make Christ known, or, we are in the wrong place. Yet since Christ has full authority in all of earth as well as all of heaven, is there really any place where he may escape notice? If God has brought us to a place, rest assured we can make Jesus known there.

## Evil lives on?

> *The evil that men do lives after them.*
> *The good is oft interred with their bones.*
> (Shakespeare, Julius Caesar)

Is this so? Don't we nowadays tend to speak well of the dead? But we shouldn't leave this good until the funeral oration; the more of Christ we can share and make known to the living, the better it will be. True good is very difficult to hide, and this is a big 'plus' as we move forward in ministry. The first steps are the most difficult, and from there it becomes easier all the way! When she came out of Ravensbrück Concentration Camp, Corrie ten Boom at first found it difficult to witness for Jesus, especially when God told her to go back into Germany after the War. But she carried on, for the best part of 30 years, until she would witness to anyone and everyone, from hotel porters to aircraft personnel, and passers-by to university professors. Practice may not make our witnessing perfect, this side of eternity, but it certainly helps along the way to perfection.

## Making Jesus known

Making Jesus known is our first priority as Christians. We have God on our side (Ps. 118:6), and his Holy Spirit ever ready to do the spadework: together, this gives us a back-up that surely encourages us to press on. We have not an abundance of time: the 'cut-off' comes, says Jesus, when the gospel has been published to all nations; and it's making progress.

If we will, we can help it on its way. Every word we speak for Jesus, every thing we do for him, makes a difference in the evangelization of the world.

> *I am only one,*
> *But I am one.*
> *I cannot do everything,*
> *But I can do something.*
> *What I can do,*
> *That I ought to do.*
> *And what I ought to do,*
> *By the grace of God I will do.*
> (Dean Farrar)

And we don't get too much done by starting tomorrow.

### *Family Service Input*

Encourage the young people to write out and illustrate/ illuminate Dean Farrar's lines.

### *Suggested Hymns*

And can it be; I heard the voice of Jesus say; Teach me, my God and King; Thou art coming, O my Saviour.

## Thirteenth Sunday after Trinity
*Second Service* **Seeing Is Believing** Ps. 119:41–56; Ex. 14:5–31; Matt. 6:1–18

> *'Thus the Lord saved Israel that day from the Egyptians, and Israel saw the Egyptians dead on the seashore. Israel saw the great*

*work that the Lord did against the Egyptians. So the people feared the Lord and believed in the Lord and in his servant Moses.'*
*Exodus 14:30–31*

## Short-lived faith

It was a belief that was to be pretty short-lived for many of these Israelites. Moses was to be given a hard time in the wilderness wanderings, and God was not only going to lose patience with the people, but with Moses as well. Yet all that was in the future. For the present, God had acted with *force majeure*, and had cowed the people into fearful respect and belief.

Faith, when thus mixed with fear, is not usually long-lived. When Jesus came, he preached a gospel of love, and it was love that would draw Christians to his side and keep them there. His message was that faith casts out fear (and vice versa). Take, for example, the storm on Galilee. When the disciples panicked, and roused the Lord from sleep, his question to them implied that their fear was continuing to prevent them having any faith (Mark 4:40). When Thomas refused to believe without seeing, he was in a sense descending to the 'seeing is believing' mind-set of his ancestors, in our Old Testament reading. That such a mind-set was volatile and easily upset, was shown by future events, when the crowd could get paranoid even when recalling non-essentials like the vegetables they had enjoyed in Egypt.

It's easy to decide that those ancient Israelites were 'young in the faith'. They were, to an extent. But they also had a visible, flesh-and-blood prophet of the Lord; and they had had ample faith-building experiences in the 'plagues' that God had sent on Egypt. Then, to crown everything, they had been miraculously brought across the Red (or Reed) Sea, while the Egyptians, hard on their heels, had perished.

Isn't it more difficult in many ways for Christians in 2006 to believe? No doubt much mileage could be spent in arguing this one out. But the principle of God is the same as it has always been: some believe by sight, but the ones who are really blessed are they who believe by faith (like Abraham, Peter, Francis of Assisi, Mother Teresa, and you and I).

## Because of faith

And what does our faith lead to? What do we do with it, once we have it? How, in fact, do we know we have it? Over 200 years ago, John Wesley struggled with these very questions. He would leave a meeting-house after preaching and sharing God's word; and he would be in despair. Very honestly, he wrote of his anguish in his Journal. 'I find myself thinking that the members of my congregation have more faith than I. What am I to do?' In desperation, he sought out a Moravian whom he had met on his voyage to America, and for whose quiet, firm faith he had great respect. Peter Bohler listened to Wesley's trouble, and then said, quietly: 'On no account neglect the gift that appears to have been given you. Preach faith, until you have it. And then preach it because you have it.' Soon after this, Wesley experienced a 'strange warming' at Aldersgate, which has been termed his 'second conversion', from where he went on to become one of the greatest preachers of all time.

Can we not pray that God may use us, to be a 'Peter Bohler' of encouragement, to someone in need?

### Suggested Hymns

Give me the faith that can remove; I watch the sunrise lighting the sky; O, for a faith that will not shrink; Soldiers of Christ, arise.

## Fourteenth Sunday after Trinity (Proper 19)
### 17 September
*Principal Service* **A Hearing of Convenience**
Prov. 1:20–33; Ps. 19 or Canticle: Wisd. 7:26—8:1;
James 3:1–12; Mark 8:27–38

> 'Then [Jesus] began to teach them that the Son of Man must undergo great suffering, and be rejected by the elders, the chief priests, and the scribes, and be killed, and after three days rise again. He said all this quite openly. And Peter took him aside, and began to rebuke him.' Mark 8:31–32

### The hidden future

By God's mercy, the future is hidden from us. We couldn't cope with knowing it. God knows we couldn't. And Jesus proved that Peter couldn't take it, either. What a frazzle our lives would be in, if we could see ahead!

So, why did Jesus predict the future so openly? Perhaps it was to test his disciples' faith. Perhaps it was a type of divine insurance, so that when the passion and resurrection came to pass, the disciples with hindsight would remember. Well, they did remember, eventually, but not before the events had first caught them unawares. Not even the shock of being rebuked by Jesus fixed the inevitability of the events to come in Peter's memory. We must not criticize. Don't we hear news of a catastrophe that could occur, declare, 'Oh, it may not happen!', and promptly implicitly decide that it won't happen? And if it does come to pass, aren't we as surprised as anyone? No, the veiling of the future is a very loving, understanding and caring gift of our heavenly Father.

But Jesus had no such veiling. For him, the agony of the passion was real before it happened, yet so also was the joy of the resurrection, and all that his victory brought to millions of believers. And the joy was greater than the agony (Heb. 12:2).

## No short-cuts

Some people are so keen to see and know what God has ordained should be hidden from us, that they take illegal short-cuts; illegal, in that they are outside God's laws for us. They seek out a medium of one sort or another, in much the same way that King Saul, at the end of his tether and believing God had deserted him, sought out the Witch of Endor (1 Sam. 28:7). If the occultists of our day would learn from what happened to Saul as a result of this, they may reconsider their position. God shows us in this experience that it is not impossible to call up spirits from 'the other side', but it is wrong. We are not to take this short-cut to future knowledge: the future will come without it.

## The Jesus experience

There are (at least) two ways of looking at the experience that Jesus had, namely, of full past, present and future knowledge. On the one hand, it may have made the coming passion more terrible, knowing in advance not only the pain of torture but also the pain of desertion by his friends. On the other hand, it gave him not only knowledge of the victory to come, but also the opportunity to prepare the disciples. That they appear to have ignored his fore-casting, was probably also known in advance by him, yet he still forewarned them.

## Into the air

Is Jesus speaking 'into the air' to us on any matter? Is he warning, preparing, encouraging us for something to which we are closing our spiritual ears? Does what he is saying seem so outlandish, so improbable, if only because we'd never have thought of it ourselves? We'd do well to reflect today on the obtuseness of Peter and the other disciples . . . We need also to reflect that it's highly unlikely that in glory Jesus has taken a vow of silence. He is, through his Holy Spirit, still at the helm of this great ship called his Church, still directing, still encouraging . . . let us listen to what he is saying.

### Family Service Input

Encourage the young people to solve the 'New Testament Men and Women' Word-Search (p. 212), and then to illustrate/discuss how Jesus spoke to some of these.

### Suggested Hymns

Come, ye faithful, raise the anthem; I heard the voice of Jesus say; Jesus calls us, o'er the tumult; Lord, speak to me that I may speak.

## Fourteenth Sunday after Trinity
### Second Service    A Word to the Wise Ps. 119:73–88;
Ex. 18:13–26; Matt. 7:1–14

> 'Moses's father-in-law said to him, "What you are doing is not good. You will surely wear yourself out, both you and these people with you. For the task is too heavy for you; you cannot do it alone."' Exodus 18:17–18

## Good advice

It was good advice, and Moses was wise enough to act on it – and everyone was happy, at least for a while. The Israelites of those

# New Testament Men and Women Word-Search

| C | G | P | F | A | S | I | L | A | S | S | R | F | S | P |
|---|---|---|---|---|---|---|---|---|---|---|---|---|---|---|
| L | H | B | Y | L | N | E | O | E | A | Q | G | T | W | U |
| I | K | R | J | L | T | D | B | N | H | A | D | E | W | E |
| M | A | N | G | A | O | E | N | I | C | J | M | A | R | K |
| M | K | O | L | H | P | A | J | R | F | O | D | S | G | U |
| R | Q | I | T | O | J | U | D | E | L | H | T | H | B | L |
| W | P | R | P | L | N | M | E | O | I | N | C | J | A | K |
| S | A | C | A | I | A | P | H | A | S | W | P | L | J | M |
| B | I | T | A | M | A | T | T | H | E | W | H | C | O | B |
| P | J | H | N | G | R | J | F | I | E | R | I | D | S | E |
| J | A | O | N | A | T | H | A | N | A | E | L | L | E | Q |
| Q | M | K | B | M | C | K | L | H | N | D | I | S | P | P |
| S | E | W | R | H | E | R | O | D | D | O | P | G | H | E |
| A | S | T | A | B | B | M | P | H | I | L | E | M | O | N |
| C | S | U | M | E | D | O | C | I | N | F | G | T | F | W |

| | |
|---|---|
| MATTHEW | CAIAPHAS |
| MARK | ANNAS |
| LUKE | HEROD |
| JOHN | JOSEPH |
| BARTHOLOMEW | MARY |
| NATHANAEL | JAMES |
| PHILIP | JUDE |
| NICODEMUS | PHILEMON |
| PILATE | SILAS |

wilderness wanderings were an unsettled crowd, and seemed to look for problems. Their counterparts are not hard to find today, but still today God knows how to handle the situation. Moses would never have delegated the responsibility of judging his people's disputes, but the Lord knew the right person to bring along at the right time.

It's very tempting to go it alone, taking on more and more work until we have overreached our capacities. And it's not God's way. He knows exactly how much we can do, and how much we should do. Many workers in the vineyard are in no danger of over-stretching themselves, but for those who are, God at the crucial time brings along the twenty-first-century counterpart of Moses' deliverer. We may ignore his or her advice; but if we are wise, we shall take it. Perhaps God is asking us to rest for a while, or to take up some different work. If we are open to his promptings, we shall receive a blessing, and probably many other people will receive one, too.

## Spoiling ourselves

It's fine, so long as we're not trying to spoil ourselves, and operate a policy of self-persuasion. 'I really do need a holiday; it's at least a couple of weeks since I got back from Spain!' God's not likely to fall for that one! We are taking up precious oxygen to WORK for him, not to be a part-time ambassador for Christ.

## The Christian work ethic

What, then, is the Christian work ethic today? After all, we're not 'Moses look-alikes', stuck in the desert with thousands of volatile migrants. Most of us have our daily secular jobs. Many of us have homes and families to manage. How can we be full-timers for Jesus?

Only if we see every situation, every experience that God brings us into, as an opportunity to show and grow our faith. In fact, 'Show it and Grow it!' is not a bad slogan to have in our minds each day. If more Christians put this into practice, the Church would impact more on the world at large. God is constantly giving us experiences, leading us into new places, leading us to meet new people, giving us new challenges, joys and encouragements. Do we attribute these to 'someone else'? The person I ran across the other day . . . Now, what did he say? Something about . . . ? Well, if we can't remember, how important was our response? Did we miss the point? Was it, could it have been really vital?

## Christ-awareness

If Moses had been too preoccupied with his workload, he might not have taken on board what his father-in-law was saying, or he might have been so uptight as to reject the advice out of hand. We need to have a 'Christ-awareness': the ability and openness to see where God is working in our lives; it can save so much hassle, if we see the point before we sit on it.

### Suggested Hymns

Dear Lord and Father of mankind; Give me oil in my lamp; Glad that I live am I; Jesus, the very thought is sweet.


# Fifteenth Sunday after Trinity (Proper 20)
## 24 September
*Principal Service*   **Open House!** Prov. 31:10–31; Ps. 1; James 3:13—4:3, 7–8a; Mark 9:36–37

> *'Then [Jesus] took a little child and put it among them, and taking it in his arms, he said to them, "Whoever welcomes one such child in my name welcomes me, and whoever welcomes me welcomes not me but the one who sent me."'* Mark 9:36–37

## The divine hospitality

It's 'open house' in heaven, when we give Jesus first place in our lives: our loyalty to him is evident in our acceptance of his 'little ones' here on earth, and God in turn sets all eternity waiting to welcome us. What a beautiful 'chain-reaction' of hospitality, openness and welcome! And yet so often we let preoccupation with work and worry get in the way of simply living, simply loving.

There are still countries where it is illegal to give children religious instruction. The media carry daily news of paedophilia and pornography as it affects the young. Children go missing, and the outcome is all too often tragic. How God must weep, at such un-Christlike treatment of his little ones! Are we engaged on a prayer-and-practical offensive against these injustices and crimes?

## A child's view

What is a child's view of the world today? A seven-year-old quickly responded with his view of heaven: 'I think heaven is like a railway station where the train comes in on time, and God's waiting there to meet it.' Bless him, but how many miles has his train to travel on earth, before that heavenly station is reached? How many branch-lines will it need to trundle along? How many signals will be set at 'red'?

## View of Jesus

A child's view of Jesus is different from an adult's, and to a large extent inexplicable: one has only to ask a class of primary school-children about how they see Jesus, to discover that God has already been at work giving them precious revelations that excite our awe and wonder. And then, what happens? As the child grows older, we get to work with our so-called 'wisdom', and too often a far less exciting (even, dare we say it, an almost boring) picture emerges. Let us not be too quick to smother the ideas of childhood revelations. Let us listen, as these young people tell us of wonder, colour, scents and sounds that we have either forgotten or have never known. There is a whole new world of God's love in the mind of a child, and we neglect it at our peril. What did Professor Karl Barth choose, as the most profound truth of Christianity, when asked by an equally august scholar?

> *Jesus loves me, this I know,*
> *For the Bible tells me so.*

When we're too old to see things as a child, we're too old.

## Healing for all

A class of youngsters was asked if any of them wanted to be a doctor when they grew up. No hands were raised. When asked who then would heal all the sick people, a six-year-old said, promptly: 'Jesus!' Do we, with our too-often neglect of healing in the Church, believe otherwise?

## Trinity Crossword

## God is light

'God is light, and in him there is no darkness at all,' says John (1 John 1:5). What does this mean to us? Have we ever stopped to think? A five-year-old gave her opinion: 'It means, in heaven there's no sun, because God's always shining!'

On this Sunday, when Mark shares with us the beautiful scene of Jesus with the child in his arms, can we take time to reflect on just how much time we give simply to listening to our children?

## Clues Across

1. Thanksgiving service. (7, 8)
9. Fire. (7)
10. Template. (7)
11. Tug. (4)
12. On one's own. (4)
13. Precedes Epistle. (7)
16. Result. (5)
17. Land of the Pharaohs. (5)
18. Bible-stand. (7)
19. Up to. (5)
21. Girl's name (colloq.) (5)
23. Bright red. (7)
26. Harbour. (4)
27. Biting insect. (4)
30. Man of Italy. (7)
31. Conjuring wonder. (7)
32. The New Jerusalem. (11, 4)

## Clues Down

1. Eldest son. (4, 11)
2. Games of chance. (7)
3. Deserve. (4)
4. Gardening tool. (6)
5. Make certain. (6)
6. Oak. (4)
7. Success. (7)
8. Sweet-scented white flower. (4, 2, 3, 6)
13. Prison rooms. (5)
14. In a while. (5)
15. Principle. (5)
20. Sauce. (7)
22. Old Testament prophet. (7)
24. Stages. (6)
25. Hosea's second son. (6)
28. Corn is ground here. (4)
29. Alert. (4)

*See page 219 for solution*

---

### Family Service Input

Can the whole congregation be involved in solving the crossword, with the young people giving their ideas on the clues.

### Suggested Hymns

All things bright and beautiful; Jesus, good above all other; Loving shepherd of thy sheep; Will you come and follow me.

# Fifteenth Sunday after Trinity

*Second Service* **You Will See, and Live** Ps. 119:137–152;
Ex. 19:10–25; Matt. 8:23–34

> *'Then the Lord said to Moses, "Go down and warn the people*
> *not to break through to the Lord to look; otherwise many of*
> *them will perish. Even the priests who approach the Lord must*
> *consecrate themselves or the Lord will break out against them."'*
> *Exodus 19:21–22*

## The old dispensation

These were the terms of the old dispensation: God was almighty
and unreachable. Only Moses could meet him, and even Moses'
view was limited (Ex. 33:23). The people were to worship him as
God and Lord (Ex. 20:2), and to accord him due respect and worship. He was a God of the unusual and unique; a God of mighty
miracles and mountain-shaking: a God to be feared more than
loved.

## The new dispensation

And then Jesus came, and showed us what God is really like: a
'Dad' in whom we can take delight: a loving Father who has given
us a kingly inheritance out of his unmerited favour (= grace); a
Lord to whom we may come, not as grovelling slaves but boldly,
as inheritors of a kingdom; a God who is not unknowable, impassive or aloof, but who wants us to share everything with him: all
our time, all our talents, and all of ourselves.

Would Moses have recognized this God? Of course he would,
for he is the same yesterday, today and forever. The difference is
not in God, but in his revealing and in human perception.

## The Transfiguration

The Transfiguration of Jesus bore this out. It was a meeting of the
old and the new, as Moses and Elijah met and conversed from the
past, in the present, about the future.

The disciples found it impossible to grasp, at the time. We have
the advantage of knowing what happened as a result: the passion
of Jesus that had been discussed at that meeting, did take place.

And the victory of the passion opened the door to glory for all believers.

## Thousands of years

It has taken thousands of years for God to be known as he is today; and the world as a whole still doesn't know him. But the promises are still operative, that one day we shall know him fully (1 Cor. 13:12), face to face. As a modern hymn has it: 'You will see the face of God, and live' (Robert J. Dufford, SJ).

## And what will he be like?

Just like Jesus. 'Whoever has seen me, has seen the Father,' said Jesus (John 14:9). The sight will not be blinding, not destroying, but wonderful, full of life and living, beauty, joy and fulfilment. We shall really, really live.

## In a glass darkly?

But for the present, it's veiled in glory, and we're not yet in glory. Yet in the eyes of a child, the smile of a friend, the wonder of a tiny flower, we get a glimpse of sheer unadulterated glory and joy. Treasure these glimpses, keep watch for as many as God gives; and God is no niggardly giver. In a lifetime we can, if we will, receive – and share – a lot of glory.

## *Suggested Hymns*

From glory to glory advancing; Glorious things of thee are spoken; God of grace, and God of glory; To God be the glory.

---

**Solution**

**Across:** 1. Harvest festival. 9. Inferno. 10. Stencil. 11. Pull. 12. Solo. 13. Collect. 16. Ensue. 17. Egypt. 18. Lectern. 19. Until. 21. Emmie. 23. Scarlet. 26. Port. 27. Flea. 30. Italian. 31. Magical. 32. Everlasting city.

**Down:** 1. Heir presumptive. 2. Raffles. 3. Earn. 4. Trowel. 5. Ensure. 6. Tree. 7. Victory. 8. Lily of the valley. 13. Cells. 14. Later. 15. Tenet. 20. Tartare. 22. Malachi. 24. Arenas. 25. Lo-ammi. 28. Mill. 29. Agog.

# Sixteenth Sunday after Trinity (Proper 21)
1 October
*Principal Service* **Salted with Fire** Esther 7:1–6, 9–10;
9:20–22; Ps. 124; James 5:13–20; Mark 9:38–50

> '*[Jesus said], "For everyone will be salted with fire. Salt is good;
> but if salt has lost its saltiness, how can you season it? Have salt
> in yourselves, and be at peace with one another."* ' Mark 9:49–50

## The Spirit's testing?

Is this the Holy Spirit's testing for saltiness by fire? Some have seen
it this way. At Pentecost, the Spirit descended in tongues of fire on
the assembly, who went on to become the early Church: local and
missionary. With the Spirit, people became the salt of the earth:
Jesus-in-them giving fire and zest for living, cleansing (purifying) of
sin, halting both the putrefaction and insipid evils of Satan; and
preserving what was good that it might become better – all things
that physical salt does in the physical realm.

Salt, too, is social, in that most people don't take their meals in
solitary state. Family and celebration eating would be unthinkable
without salt. Just so, says Jesus: have the spiritual salt among yourselves, and love each other.

Also, salt in ancient times formed an integral part of many covenants: they were sealed by the sharing of salt, whether taken with a
meal or as part of the bargain (centuries before the Romans termed
a man's wage as his *salarium*, or salt was given in lieu of wages).

## The indispensability of the Spirit

Jesus knew that he would send his Spirit as the indispensable
enabler of the body of believers, when he returned to Glory. Similarly, salt is essential: we could not live without it; and if something
is amiss with our body and we are prescribed a no-salt diet, the con-
stituents of salt need to be found for us in other ways. Fortunately,
we no more need to wonder how a world without salt would manage,
than how the Church without the Holy Spirit would get on.

Salt – true salt – cannot be hidden: it broadcasts its presence by
its unique flavour. There are some kinds of 'adulterated' or false
salt that look like the real thing but have no flavour: they are like
Christians who may show all the outward signs of a believer –

attending Church Bible Class, wearing a cross, displaying a Christian symbol on the car – but who in the privacy of their home watch smutty films, use bad language, eat or drink bad substances. Their saltiness would not stand the litmus-test of the Holy Spirit.

## Testing by fire

Any reviewing of our spiritual saltiness is surely time well spent, for Jesus has promised that we shall all be 'salted with fire'. Does our saltiness in private reflect how we are in public? Is there a part of our lives we feel we'd not like to share? Well, rest assured, God knows of it already, so let's get it straight with him first, and be willing to attend to it as he directs.

## Unsalty salt

Implicit in Jesus' teaching, is the warning that unsalty salt has gone beyond the point of no return. This is serious. No one has yet been able to re-salt unsalty salt. Judas Iscariot lost his saltiness for ever. While our salt is still worthy of the name, may we put it to the best use the Spirit directs.

And then he'll carry on replenishing our reserves.

## *Family Service Input*

Explore the physical uses of salt with the young people, and discuss/illustrate its spiritual applications.

## *Suggested Hymns*

Crown him with many crowns; Firmly I believe and truly; Take my life, and let it be; The King of love my shepherd is.

## Sixteenth Sunday after Trinity
*Second Service*   **Paralysis of Sin** Ps. 120, 121; Ex. 24; Matt. 9:1–8

> *'And just then some people were carrying a paralysed man lying on a bed. When Jesus saw their faith, he said to the paralytic, "Take heart, son; your sins are forgiven."' Matthew 9:2*

## Speaking faith

The faith of these carriers spoke louder than words, and Jesus rewarded them by healing their friend; healing him not in the conventional way, but by first absolving him from sin. We may reverently believe that in some way the man's paralysis was linked with sin; but we do not know. Jesus was demonstrating his power over spiritual as well as physical illness, and there are many instances today where there is a visible link between the two (e.g. in the case of drugs, or other abuse); and many more, where the connection is not obvious. Worry (which is also a sin) can paralyse the mind, and do all sorts of harm to the rest of the body.

But the buck for illness of body, mind or spirit stops with Satan (e.g. Luke 13:16), and therefore Jesus in his ministry operated holistic healing across this spectrum. That it took some by surprise (and probably not least the patients themselves), is seen in today's reading.

## Fear or suspicion of the unknown

It was easier for the onlookers to understand healing by command: 'Get up and walk', was amazing in itself when directed to a paralytic, especially when the man acted on it; but, 'Your sins are forgiven', was another matter. What sins? Why? How could these words act on physical inability? And who had the authority to issue such a command? With all these imponderables, fear and suspicion erupted in protest.

Who are we to criticize? If it happened today, we'd probably be equally mystified.

## Holistic healing

Like the paralytic, people today may find their healing is blocked or delayed by unconfessed sin; and it's a wise practitioner – medical, Christian, holistic or however (s)he is termed – to explore this possibility first. If we are at one with God, healing can flow; but sin, even manifested as worry, which all too often is thought relatively harmless, is the most effective deterrent to healing and wholeness. This much has not altered: it is a constant, until the end of time. We need 'a healthy mind' for 'a healthy body': let's never consign this to the dustbin of obsolete cliches.

## As ever was

As he was in the time of Jesus (and long before that), Satan is still at work using a variety of spiritual weapons ranging from fear and anxiety to delusion and doubt, to deprive us of our physical, mental and spiritual health. He knows, even better than we do, that our defences buckle as our health deteriorates; situations and problems are magnified out of all proportion; and unless we seek help from the only Source who knows exactly what Satan is doing, our problems will increase.

The amount of time that Jesus devoted to healing, in his relatively short ministry, is an indication of the importance of good health to his followers. God would be untrue to himself, if it was his intention to cripple us in his service. Can we reflect on this, as we see again with the eye of faith, the paralytic getting up and carrying his bed?

### Suggested Hymns

Forth in thy name, O Lord, I go; I, the Lord of sea and sky; Strengthen for service, Lord; Thine arm, O Lord, in days of old.

# Seventeenth Sunday after Trinity (Proper 22)
## 8 October
*Principal Service*   **What Is Legal?** Job 1:1; 2:1–10; Ps. 26; Heb. 1:1–4; 2:5–12; Mark 10:2–16

> *'Some Pharisees came, and to test him they asked, "Is it lawful for a man to divorce his wife?" Jesus answered them, "What did Moses command you?"' Mark 10:2–3*

## Talking it through

Yes, it was a very Jewish trait to follow a question with a question, and this is by no means the only occasion that Jesus employed this tactic. But it's good 'faith-sense'; God himself advocates it (Isa. 1:18, 'Come now, let us argue it out'). Let us never be shy of asking God questions in return for the ones he sets us; he would far rather we enter into dialogue with him, and show him our interest in the enterprise, than stoically accept everything without comment. Jesus

NEVER MINDED dialoguing with earnest enquirers: look, for instance, at the questions raised by Nicodemus (John 3:1ff.)

## The questioning Pharisees

These Pharisees had seemingly overlooked the fact that it takes three to make a marriage: a man, a woman and God. In their tasselled robes, and with haughty bearing, the Pharisees were the 'legal eagles' of the time. Out to trap Jesus, they had pitched on the question of divorce, always a thorny problem. They knew full well that the interpretation of Moses' day had been an accommodation, but they wanted Jesus to endorse it. And Jesus told them directly, that divorce is possible; legal, as man interprets the term, but it's still not God's best.

It's not God's way of operating, to remove all the options but the right one. What would be the point of making it impossible for us to sin? Into whatever situation he calls us, he expects us to ask: 'Is what I am going to do/say lawful in the sight of God?' – and then to choose the right. It has been his modus operandi from the start. He gave then – and continues to give – the challenge: Keep my rules, and live life to the full. Break my rules, and you will struggle.

## Even in Eden

God could have left the forbidden tree out of Eden. Adam and Eve would never have known what they were missing, and anyway, there was plenty more vegetation to keep them going. Instead, the Lord presented them with the challenge: Here's the fruit, but I've said don't touch it. You have the choice, but don't do it!

He gave Adam a companion, a woman, because in his Father heart of love he believed it wasn't right for Adam to be the only form of humankind. God, being God, could have populated the earth without women, but he chose otherwise. He didn't remove the capacity of Adam to separate from Eve, but he said: 'I've given you to each other, as man and wife. You have the choice to alter that union, but don't do it!'

## Any justification?

There would be some listening to Jesus – probably in all innocence, and what they would call 'legal' justification – who had taken advantage of the Mosaic accommodation. But Jesus didn't subscribe to accommodations. God had intended equality in the sharing of life and love between men and women.

'The blood of Jesus . . . cleanses us from all sin' (1 John 1:7). 'All sin' surely includes divorce. But this doesn't mean that we can condone divorce. It is less than God's best. The Church has a great opportunity here to promote the sanctity of marriage, because, if we don't rise to the challenge, it will fall by default.

In heaven, marriage as we know it does not exist (Matt. 22:30; Mark 12:25; Luke 20:35). We shall know our loved ones there, but the wedding-feast will be the Marriage-Supper of the Lamb. Angels for millennia have managed without marriage; we can be sure that God won't deprive us of anything that is essential. Quite how he will work out the matter can safely be left with him. He's in charge of eternity.

### Family Service Input

Let the young folk solve the Word-Search (p. 226), and then either (a) illustrate it, or (b) compile one of their own, possibly for the Parish Magazine.

### Suggested Hymns

Awake, my soul, and with the sun; Help us to help each other, Lord; I danced in the morning; O perfect love, all human thought transcending.

# Seventeenth Sunday after Trinity

*Second Service*  **Crossing Over** Ps. 125, 126; Josh. 3:7–17; Matt. 10:1–22

> *'The Lord said to Joshua, "This day I will begin to exalt you in the sight of all Israel, so that they may know that I will be with you as I was with Moses."' Joshua 3:7*

## The right exalting

'I will exalt you . . .'
  So that you can receive acclamation? No.
  So that life will be easier for you? No.

# Trinity Word-Search

| M | H | J | I | L | A | O | D | I | C | E | A | D | B | A |
|---|---|---|---|---|---|---|---|---|---|---|---|---|---|---|
| I | Y | N | O | D | E | C | L | A | H | C | E | S | C | R |
| C | N | K | S | L | S | Q | M | R | F | L | U | P | E | G |
| H | T | O | P | O | M | E | G | A | Y | S | N | P | M | J |
| A | G | W | M | E | A | D | B | R | E | Q | S | O | I | L |
| E | E | T | F | D | C | O | E | H | S | A | P | H | R | P |
| L | A | H | F | B | G | B | P | T | J | W | K | A | S | E |
| P | H | I | L | A | D | E | L | P | H | I | A | M | A | R |
| K | S | I | L | H | R | F | I | E | J | A | Y | K | R | G |
| T | J | P | E | M | E | R | A | L | D | R | L | B | D | A |
| L | H | M | Q | W | P | G | O | D | N | N | C | M | I | M |
| A | T | H | Y | A | T | I | R | A | C | N | D | O | S | U |
| N | T | O | S | A | R | D | O | N | Y | X | E | P | F | M |
| W | M | S | J | S | A | P | P | H | I | R | E | G | Q | H |
| L | A | K | B | M | E | L | A | S | U | R | E | J | I | R |

PATMOS
EPHESUS
SMYRNA
THYATIRA
LAODICEA
PHILADELPHIA
SARDIS
PERGAMUM
JERUSALEM

MICHAEL
ALPHA
OMEGA
JASPER
SAPPHIRE
CHALCEDONY
EMERALD
SARDONYX
BERYL

So that the Israelites 'may know' that Joshua has a similar relationship with God that Moses had; not quite the 'favoured' relationship that Mary was to have (Luke 1:28), but a no-nonsense, 'macho', commander-in-chief to company commander relationship. God was not losing sight of his aim, which was to get the Israelites into the land which he had promised them. Moses had led them to a point from which they could see this land; Joshua was God's chosen instrument to lead them across to fight for it and to take possession. Any power, any miracles, that God gave to Joshua, would be designed to show both him and the troops he led, exactly who was still in charge of the operation.

## Army of occupation?

Our own relationship with God today may not seem quite so war-like. And yet, in a way, it is. We may not be marching into the promised land of Canaan: instead, we are part of the vast Christian 'army of occupation', yet on our home-ground, a land to which Satan has no claim, land that is under the authority of Jesus. Yet, in his frenzy at losing the war in the heavenlies (Rev. 12:7ff.), Satan tries to deceive us into believing otherwise. So we ARE battling on our patch, warring against the prince of evil. At the same time, we are marching constantly towards our promised land of eternity.

Yet Jesus, having shown us the beautiful face of God's tender loving care, we are privileged to see our Commander-in-Chief in a gentler way than perceived by Joshua. God is no longer waiting for his people to come to a knowledge of him on their own; he has sent Jesus, and Jesus has completed his mission. Joshua could not worship God the Son as Saviour and loving Redeemer.

But we can, and let's thank God for this all-important difference.

## Only the beginning!

Notice, too, how God encouraged Joshua, and how much that would mean, as Joshua prepared to enter the promised land: 'I will BEGIN to exalt you . . .' The crossing of the Jordan may be a great miracle, but it was not to be the only one. God was going to be with Joshua the full distance. He had already given an earnest of this, in seeing Moses through the wilderness; there had been no divine desertion when the Red Sea had been negotiated!

So God's power would continue to go with Joshua for as long as it took. Can we not take this truth into our own hearts? You've been trusting God for help in a particular situation. Has it blinded you to what may be ahead? Once the danger or testing is over, do you career along the intervening straight, only remembering to resume your dialogue with God when the next problem shows up? Our heavenly 'Dad' wants to share all our life, not just the sticky bits; for his part, he's promised to be with us, not only until we reach our promised land, but also for all the time we shall be there.

That's the Dad of rain, and shine.

### Suggested Hymns

From glory to glory advancing; Let saints on earth in concert sing; Oft in danger, oft in woe; Swing low, sweet chariot.

## Eighteenth Sunday after Trinity (Proper 23)
### 15 October
*Principal Service*   **War Against Greed** Job 23:1–9, 16–17; Ps. 22:1–15; Heb. 4:12–16; Mark 10:17–31

> *'Then Jesus looked around and said to his disciples, "How hard it will be for those who have wealth to enter the kingdom of God! . . . You lack one thing; go, sell what you own, and give the money to the poor . . . then come and follow me."'*
> *Mark 10:23, 21*

### The right way round!

Are these two verses the wrong way round? No; they've merely been juxtapositioned so that not only Jesus' comment, but also his command, speak to us today. It's still hard for wealthy folk to be good Christians (even harder than for poor folk); but the resolving command is still the same; the wealthy have the chance, as ever, to store up treasure in heaven, by presently relieving the poor. And still today, excuses abound as to why this 'simple' solution cannot or should not be taken.

### All things common

St Luke tells us that the early Church began by its members pooling their resources (Acts 2:44, 45); the way such communal sharing is resisted today, one would think we were destined to live this earthly life for ever! Even from the BCP funeral service, the following texts are now almost invariably excluded (because they had begun to ring so hollow?):

> *We brought nothing into the world, and it is certain*
> *we can carry nothing out. The Lord gave, and the Lord*
> *hath taken away; blessed be the name of the Lord.*
>
> (1 Tim. 6:7; Job 1:21, AV)

## To the poor

This is the clearest teaching on poverty that Jesus gives in the Gospels. At no point does he 'heal' poverty, by producing (miraculously or otherwise) funds to lift any poor person above the breadline. He would heal all sickness and all disease; he would turn death into life for a corpse (even a four-day-old corpse, John 11:17, 43, 44). But he told John's disciples that the poor had the gospel preached to them (Matt. 11:5), and an assembled dinner-party that they always had the poor with them (Matt. 26:11; Mark 14:7; John 12:8).

No doubt the preaching of the gospel would bring hope and new resolve to the poor; but today's text actually tells us how Jesus envisaged the poor getting immediate, practical help from the generosity of the rich.

And note that it was not merely a 'hand-out' that was in our Lord's mind, but the rich actually depriving themselves to enrich (or at least alleviate the plight of) the poor. That is tough talking, the sort of toughness that separates muscle from bone (cf. Heb. 4:12)!

Is Jesus saying that it's up to us to deal with poverty? No – for it's virtually humanly impossible to employ such self-sacrifice. It's the sort that needs prayer (and probably fasting as well), so that God can move in on the act and make possible the impossible.

If the wealthy do not take this seriously, shall we have the poor always with us?

Yes.

It's as serious as that.

## The Church's awakening

Worldwide, the Church needs to awake to this problem. What sort of a Christian message does it send out, for a worship service with great pomp and circumstance to be offered to God, a street or a street-and-a-half away from 'Cardboard City'?

In parts of the world, a lot is being done, let's be fair. But the other parts give both poverty and the Church a bad name.

### Family Service Input

Discuss a specific area of poverty with the young folk, and how a difference is being/could be made.

### Suggested Hymns

Brother, sister, let me serve you; For my sake and the gospel's, go; Take my life and let it be consecrated, Lord, to thee; When I needed a neighbour, were you there?

## Eighteenth Sunday after Trinity
*Second Service*   **Implicit Trust** Ps. 127 [128]; Josh. 5:13—6:20; Matt. 11:20–30

> *'So the people shouted, and the trumpets were blown. As soon as the people heard the sound of the trumpets, they raised a great shout, and the wall fell down flat, so the people charged straight ahead into the city and captured it.' Joshua 6:20*

### 'You cannot mean it!'

No, Joshua never said: 'You cannot be serious!' With exemplary humility, he had given his 'Fiat', and simply asked the Commander-in-Chief what he wanted done. None of, 'I'm in charge here!' God had known his man, when he had chosen Joshua to lead the army of invasion. Yet what an amazing set of orders! The days of silent marches, then using voices and instruments to make a great din, and then the taking of a city that had looked impregnable! And all without a word of questioning from Joshua.

But the people had seen how the Lord had taken them over the Jordan, and they appear to have accepted without question the strange orders for the Jericho operation.

### Logic, reason and commonsense

Just as Jericho did not fall by logic, reason or commonsense, or force of arms, so God doesn't limit his dealings with us today by such restrictive practices. He is a master of the ingenious, the unexpected, even the outlandish and the humorous. He will shock us into belief, if he has to. He will laugh us into it, too, on occasion. He has a million and more ways of getting anything done, so we need to be prepared to be surprised (if that's not a contradction in terms!).

## Not by might . . .

Jericho was certainly taken by *force majeure*, but it was divine might, not human might or cold steel. When we have stopped looking for the most ordinary answer to our problems, we shall be on the road of faith. Yes, it's hard to step over the human bounds, of logic, reason and commonsense. But we can do it, because our bodies are temples of the Holy Spirit, and with such a divine resident we are more than human. We can stand with Paul in affirming: 'I can do all things through him who strengthens me' (Phil. 4:13). Just pause a while to let the implication of these words penetrate to the part that the doctor's scalpel doesn't reach.

'All things' means exactly that.

## The message sent out

Joshua and the invading Israelites would not be unmindful of the clarion-call of a message that the fall of Jericho would send to neighbouring towns and communities. How often do we stop to consider what messages God-in-us is transmitting, through his dealings with us and us with him? Do other Christians want to be involved in our lives? Do non-believers come to us with questions that are exercising them, of faith, life and living, death and dying? They will, if God's light is shining out through us, as it shone out through Joshua. If the Lord is having his way with us, we shall find we are increasingly being used to help others, we are being stretched in ways we should never have dreamt of before.

Stopping to take stock of how God is loving us into more living, is a good thing; it deepens our dependence on him, for it's only by his grace we are being so used, not because of any worth or merit of our own.

Our 'Jericho' may not be forty-second cousin to Joshua's, but we can be certain that if we haven't experienced it yet, it's on the horizon!

Crown him with many crowns; Fight the good fight; I wonder as I wander; Spirit of God, as strong as the wind.


# Nineteenth Sunday after Trinity (Proper 24)
## 22 October
*Principal Service*   **Men of Feeling** Job 38:1–7 [34–41]; Ps. 104:1–10, [26, 35c]; Heb. 5:1–10; Mark 10:35–45

> *'And [James and John] said to him, "Grant us to sit, one at your right hand and one at your left, in your glory." . . . When the ten heard this, they began to be angry with James and John.' Mark 10:37, 41*


## Far from perfect

The 'inner circle' of Jesus' disciples were very human and far from perfect; yet in this honest gospel reportage of Mark, we can take hope ourselves. We are not plaster saints, nor even oil-painted ones, yet, and probably never will be. There are folk outside the Church who live better lives than we do, but who may not see eternity.

Yet we have our Commander as our Guide, and one day he will perfect us, his powerful sacrifice enabling him to work a miracle on us. As Mediator, he will stand between us and our Father; as Advocate, he will plead for us before our Judge, and heaven's courtroom is unlikely to be littered with cases that the divine Advocate has lost.


## The best we can

Yet this is no reason for any slacking on our part now. We are still after that 'impossible ideal', and our aim should be to come as close to it as possible. It's no use raising our eyebrows at the temerity or self-seeking of James and John; have we never jockeyed for position? And, as for the other disciples: have we never said, or even thought, an angry or digruntled word? Perhaps not within the last half-hour . . .

Yet Jesus loved these men: loved them enough to entrust his mission into their hands; loved even Judas enough to include him in the Last Supper; loved them, warts and all. Just as he loves us, for if he were to wait until we were perfect before showing us his love, he'd be in for a long wait.

## Keeping up our spirits

At times, it's tempting to get downhearted at our lack of progress. ('Lord, I've messed it up, yet again!') James and John may have wished the earth could have opened and swallowed them up. Matthew, in his account of the faux pas, puts the question in the mouth of their mother (Matt. 20:20). But they had to put it behind them, just as the others would need to let their protests drop into history's forgetfulness. Have we made a gaff? Confess it, repent of it, accept God's forgiveness, and carry on. We can't rewrite history, but we can resolve to do better next time. It's thoroughly counter-productive to brood. God is constantly planning us a full and fruitful future, that doesn't need cluttering up with hang-ups from the past.

## 'We are able'

Oh, the confidence of James and John (v. 39)! They had but the merest idea about what they were committing themselves to, but Jesus would at least appreciate their enthusiasm. He could work on men like that: men, like Peter also, who may get into trouble in their eagerness; but who, as history was to show, still had enough spirit and zeal to make good.

> 'Are ye able?' said the Master,
> 'To be crucified with me?'
> 'Yes,' the sturdy dreamers answered,
> 'To the death we follow thee.'
>
> 'Are ye able?' still the Master
> Whispers down eternity.
> And heroic spirits answer,
> Now, as then in Galilee.
> (Earl Marlatt, b.1892)

The Master still asks, and there are still the Jameses and Johns of today who undertake more than in the natural they can deliver. Perhaps we are among them. If so, we are in better company than the mediocre set of believers at Laodicea, who were too laid back to show enthusiasm over anything (Rev. 3:16).

Encourage the young folk to design invitation cards for the 'All Souls' Remembrance' service(s) in a fortnight's time.

### Suggested Hymns

A sovereign Protector I have; Filled with the Spirit's fire; O Jesus, I have promised; O love, how deep, how broad, how high.

# Nineteenth Sunday after Trinity
*Second Service*   **The Strength of the Lord** Ps. 141; Josh. 14:6–14; Matt. 12:1–21

> '*[And Caleb said], "I am still as strong today [at eighty-five] as I was on the day that Moses sent me; my strength now is as my strength was then, for war, and for going and coming." ' Joshua 14:11*

## Joy in life

Caleb's joy in life and zest for living had been evident when, 45 years earlier, he had given an up-beat report on the land of Canaan and the fasibility of possessing it. He had been outvoted by the pessimistic souls who had suddenly seen the wilderness as the lesser of two evils; but he had bided his time, determined, no matter how old he became, to be in the invading force when eventually it did move into the promised land.

And Joshua honoured Caleb's loyalty and commitment, by giving him land and property.

Nehemiah, years later, was to prove that 'the joy of the Lord is [our] strength' (Neh. 8:10), as he and his men struggled to rebuild the walls of Jerusalem against severe opposition. It's joy that comes from knowing our heavenly back-up is always on duty; joy that lifts us to get up and get on, when in the natural it's impossible; joy that can meet anxiety with a serenity that knows God is in control of the situation, not from light-years distant, but God-in-us.

In 1910, as tension was growing in Europe, a little girl was born, the last of nine children in a country-labourer's cottage where money was tight but faith was high. The child was so frail, that the vicar was called to the house to baptize her, in case she didn't live until Easter. She went to her rest 92½ years later at the end of a life packed full to overflowing of service to God, having brought joy to everyone who had known her.

Similarly, Caleb, at 85, had a joyful zest for living that belied his years.

## Fruit of the Spirit

It's surely significant that 'joy' comes hard on the heels of 'love', when Paul enumerates the fruit of the Spirit (Gal. 5:22). Joy kept Paul going, as joy had seen Jesus through Calvary and out of the tomb on Easter morning. Joy will see us to the finishing-post of this life, not at our last, tottering step, but content that we have done what we could with the time at our disposal, and ready and eager to begin the next phase, bring with it what it will.

Those who have lost their zest for living, are like the woodsman trying to hand-cut a tree with a power-saw; operating in their own inadequate strength, without the power (in the case of believers, the Holy Spirit dynamo) switched on.

There is no joy of the Lord outside the operation of the Holy Spirit, only an ephemeral, frothy happiness that takes flight at the first whiff of trouble. That sort of joy isn't going to get us within business-distance of the pearly gates.

## God's volunteers

God is after volunteers like Caleb, who will put all their energies into seeking out his will, putting his joy (= strength) to work, and getting the mountains moved. Perhaps we feel like Caleb, when his enthusiasm was voted down. If we do seem to be the only live wires in a cat's cradle of inactivity and apathy, let us remember the patience of Caleb: we may not have to wait 45 years for things to change.

We may see our way clear to changing the situation ourselves.

> *God grant me the courage*
> *to change the things I can;*
> *Serenity to accept the*
> *things I cannot change;*
> *And the wisdom to know the difference.*

## *Suggested Hymns*

Give me oil in my lamp; Love divine, all loves excelling; Jesu, the very thought of thee; Thou art coming, O my Saviour.

# Last Sunday after Trinity (Bible Sunday)   29 October
*Principal Service*   **Unseen Pedigree** Isa. 55:1–11;
Ps. 19:7–14; 2 Tim. 3:14—4:5; John 5:36b–47

> *'[Jesus said], "I have come in my Father's name, and you do not accept me; if another comes in his own name, you will accept him. How can you believe when you accept glory from one another and do not seek the glory that comes from the one who alone is God?"' John 5:43–44*

## Where are you from?

Human beings are inquisitive animals, often spending energy in seeking after useless or wrong information. We think we are obsessed with data-collecting today, but these Jews of the first century were keen to know the pedigree of a stranger. They believed that they had successfully 'grounded' Jesus, in establishing the identity of his parents and family (Matt. 13:56; Mark 6:3). But when he claimed another Father, they were out of their depth.

If someone turned up this afternoon in our parish, claiming that he had come from God, wouldn't eyebrows be raised, shoulders be shrugged, and probably backs be turned? Yet every day we go out in the name of Jesus, expecting folk to accept that we have come from him, armed with his commission, walking in his authority, using his name. It's good policy, every so often, to try to see ourselves as others are seeing us. Perhaps it might make a difference!

## We are different

'Oh, I didn't ask you to come to that film, it wasn't your sort!' We often hear this, or variations on the theme. And our reactions are pretty predictable: 'Well, why did you go, then?' or, 'Thanks for being so considerate!' or, 'What was the film?'

But how often do we go further? How often do we care enough about the other person, actively to persuade him or her not to see another smutty film? It's all right to bask in the compliment they've paid us, but that doesn't do much for the good of their soul.

When we have recognized the sheer value and impact of our Christian way of life on others, we are on the way to doing something about closing the differential gap; not, of course, subsuming our values under theirs, but of raising theirs to get in line with those of Jesus.

But that's patronizing, isn't it?

No, it's ministry.

Did Jesus come to live among us, and talk about the state of the economy, or global warming? He came to issue a challenge: 'Take up the cross, and follow me' (e.g. Matt. 16:24; Mark 8:34; 10:21; Luke 9:23); and to warn that those who were not (actively) with him, were (actively) against him (Matt. 12:30).

When we get discouraged at people's seeming inability to believe what to us is all of life, let us remember that even after Jesus had risen and appeared to hundreds of people, some still doubted him (Matt. 28:17). It's a measure of Satan's power that he can make people disbelieve what they can see; how much easier the devil must find it, to attack faith in what is presently invisible!

## Not in his own name

Jesus was not concerned over his own name. He was secure in the knowledge of who he was and from where he came, and it was this Source, his Father, whom he wanted people to understand and to focus on. But it was a terrible indictment of his listeners that they would elevate a person proclaiming his own 'gospel', above Jesus who was preaching God's.

Would it – could it – happen today?

Surely not.

Yet it is happening; people are running in all directions after other 'gospels', other messages.

What are we, as Christians, doing about it?

### Family Service Input

Encourage some of the young people to solve the 'Old – and New' Word-Search (p. 239), while the rest discuss/illustrate the answers.

### Suggested Hymns

O Breath of Life, come sweeping; The Church of God a kingdom is; Thine be the glory, risen, conquering Son; Thy kingdom come, O God.

## Last Sunday after Trinity (Bible Sunday)
*Second Service* **Giving Thanks** Ps. 119:1–16; 2 Kings 22;
Col. 3:12–17 [Luke 4:14–30]

*'Let the word of Christ dwell in you richly; teach and admonish one another in all wisdom; and with gratitude in your hearts sing psalms, hymns and spiritual songs to God. And whatever you do, in word or deed, do everything in the name of the Lord Jesus, giving thanks to God the Father through him.'*
*Colossians 3:16–17*

### With a grateful heart

'Give thanks with a grateful heart', we sing, probably more often than we put the words into practice. Whatever we do, whatever we say, Paul tells us that this is a way of saying 'Thank you' to God for making it possible. When we receive a coffin into church for either the lying-in or the funeral itself, we pray that the thoughts and prayers of those who are remembering the departed, 'be guided toward that place where all love meets' – in [God's] Father heart of compassion and mercy. And God is there powerfully in the meeting of hearts and wills.

But when our mortality is not concentrating our minds to this degree, they are often so full of daily business, worries and plans that our 'grateful heart' may at best be in suspended animation, at worst a misnomer.

### For the word

Yet on Bible Sunday, we have one of God's greatest gifts claiming our attention. As we thank him for the scriptures, in the plethora of versions, translations and editions that no earlier age has enjoyed, can we reflect on just how much this word means to us? How much time every day do we spend in it, not only using it as sermon or lesson material, but simply enjoying it with God, and being open to what he may be telling us in it?

How often do we share the word with children, our own, or others? How often do we take it into hospitals and nursing-homes, to read with the elderly who are no longer able to read it for themselves? Does our church operate a 'Talking Bible'? Do we have

## Old and New Word-Search

| D | E | A | C | D | Y | R | O | T | S | E | R | E | L | C |
|---|---|---|---|---|---|---|---|---|---|---|---|---|---|---|
| I | E | S | T | H | E | R | S | F | P | R | N | O | A | E |
| O | S | N | A | B | T | I | W | O | X | G | P | T | Q | C |
| C | O | B | O | D | H | F | H | G | L | I | H | M | M | C |
| E | L | C | J | M | E | S | H | K | J | E | L | K | N | L |
| S | O | I | S | A | I | A | H | R | D | Q | A | O | W | E |
| E | M | B | T | B | S | N | P | R | I | E | S | T | P | S |
| C | O | D | H | C | O | F | A | W | A | S | H | R | J | I |
| E | N | C | D | C | B | L | T | T | G | N | Q | I | O | A |
| F | R | G | A | E | M | A | I | R | I | M | S | K | P | S |
| A | F | E | H | D | K | C | J | M | B | O | Y | L | R | T |
| G | D | L | E | H | A | I | M | E | H | E | N | W | A | E |
| M | H | N | P | H | A | R | A | O | H | A | O | A | T | S |
| M | E | T | H | W | S | E | L | A | H | T | D | I | L | Q |
| S | E | L | C | I | N | O | R | C | H | P | O | R | A | S |

METHUSELAH
SOLOMON
NEHEMIAH
ISAIAH
ESTHER
MIRIAM
PHARAOH
ECCLESIASTES
CHRONICLES

ARCHBISHOP
PRIEST
DEACON
DIOCESE
CATHEDRAL
CLERESTORY
ALTAR
DENOMINATIONAL
SYNOD

Bible read-a-thons? Are there regular events and competitions in our local schools for Bible reading and learning?

So many, many questions!

But, just one more, and can we take it seriously: What would you give up for your Bible? No need to confess to your next-door neighbour, but tell God, before Bible Sunday is over.

## Richly indwelling

Paul didn't have the New Testament to hand; he was more than playing his part in writing it at the time. Yet he was obviously a 'man of the Book' (or the old scrolls); he knew the blessing of the memorized word deep in his heart, rich in joy and strength and all the fruit of the Spirit.

It's drawing closer to another Christmas. Many cards have a topical verse printed in already. Perhaps we could add another (or two), and thus double the value of every card we send. Most cards, after all, concentrate on Christmas verses – but the Bible has thousands more from which to choose, and which can often be linked to the main Christmas message of love.

Whatever else we send, the word of God is surely the best Christmas gift of all.

> *He smiles within his cradle,*
> *A Babe with face so bright*
> *It beams most like a mirror*
> *Against a blaze of light;*
> *This Babe so burning bright . . .*
>
> *O Jesus, dearest Babe of all*
> *And dearest Babe of mine,*
> *Thy love is great, thy limbs are small,*
> *O, flood this heart of mine*
> *With overflow from thine!'*
> (Austrian, 1649, Tr. R. Groves)

## *Suggested Hymns*

Holy Spirit, truth divine; Now thank we all our God; Praise and thanksgiving, Father, we offer; Tell out, my soul, the greatness of the Lord.

## Fourth Sunday before Advent (or All Saints' Sunday (if trans. from 1 Nov.), q.v.)  5 November
*Principal Service*  **Much More Important** Deut. 6:1–9; Ps. 119:1–8; Heb. 9:11–14; Mark 12:28–34

> *'Then the scribe said to [Jesus], "You are right, Teacher . . . this is much more important than all whole burnt-offerings and sacrifices." When Jesus saw that he answered wisely, he said to him, "You are not far from the kingdom of God." After that no one dared to ask him any questions.' Mark 12:32–34*

### Q and A

It had been a 'Question and Answer' session, and for once Jesus' questioner had emerged with praise: high praise, and well deserved, for in getting his priorities right he was breaking with tradition. There would be some within earshot who would disapprove, some who placed an inordinately high value on burnt-offerings and sacrifices; but this man had been quick to see that Jesus was right. One would like to believe that he went on to become one of the earliest disciples of the Christian Church.

### Letting go

Letting go of long-held and greatly esteemed traditions is still difficult. Usually ours don't go back anywhere near as long as the Jewish burnt-offerings and sacrifices; but if, say, we've grown up with a certain liturgical form, or a particular version of the Bible, or a set of really favourite hymns . . . it can be hard to accept even minor changes, much less the sea-change that Jesus put over on his questioner. There is a danger, of course, of changing for changing's sake; but if we resist a change that would take our faith forward, we may miss out on a blessing.

### A new sacrifice

The number of innocent animals that had been sacrificed in Jewish history must have run into millions. What had all the bloodshed achieved? It had given the Jews a feeling of exclusivity, yet other, pagan beliefs included animal (and even human) sacrifices. The Jews held up their hands in horror at such practices by what they saw as heathen Gentiles. Yet Jesus came and offered himself as a human sacrifice on the most infamous slaughter-weapon of the time, a cross! For every Jew, like the questioner in today's text, who was bold enough to believe in the new order, hundreds – thousands – could not.

And we spend interminable arguments on a single word-change in the Lord's Prayer, or the altering of a long-established service time, or the position of the celebrant at the Eucharist . . .

## Our priorities

If we had our minds focused on (1) loving God with all we have; and (2) loving our neighbour with as much zeal as we can muster, there wouldn't be too much energy left over to waste on non-essentials.

When William Tyndale was in constant danger of his life, shuttling between Worms, Cologne and Antwerp, cold, hungry and with enemy agents seeking him, he went on calmly translating more and more of the Bible into English. It was his life's work, his sole occupation, and his disciplined mind could shut out non-essentials while he got on with the job in hand.

Can we be so disciplined? Not often. We usually try to do at least three things at once. And only two are permitted: loving God and our neighbour. It's perfectly possible to combine these; they were always together in the life of our Lord. He could see God in other people; and through his love they were brought to a knowledge of God.

Feel you can't do it? Then pray God to show you how. He's ready and waiting.

> Let us walk hand in hand with the Master,
> Who is mindful and loving and kind,
> With the light of his sunshine to cheer us,
> And the shadows will all fall behind.
> For his love pardons every transgression,
> His sweet friendship will comfort and cheer;
> And his peace passeth all understanding,
> For with him there is nothing to fear.
>
> (Clara Simpson)

Encourage (with mature help, if available) the young folk to solve/illustrate/discuss the crossword (p. 244).

## Suggested Hymns

Holy, Holy, Holy, Lord God Almighty; O love, how deep, how broad, how high; Ten thousand times ten thousand; When I needed a neighbour.

# Fourth Sunday before Advent

*Second Service*   **Who Are These?** Ps. 145; Dan. 2:1–48 (or 1–11, 25–48); Rev. 7:9–17 [Matt. 5:1–12]

> *'Then one of the elders addressed me, saying, "Who are these, robed in white, and where have they come from?" I said to him: "Sir, you are the one that knows." Then he said to me: "These are they who have come out of the great ordeal; they have washed their robes and made them white in the blood of the Lamb."' Revelation 7:13–14*

## Where are they?

We look at the polished wood and gleaming brass handles of the coffins, and we ask, 'Where are they? What are they doing?' Yes, we know the departed are in good hands, in the best of all keeping; but it's still a mystery. Yet John's visions give us an inkling of the glory that is theirs. Their 'robes', the clothing of their souls, have been made white in the blood, and that's another mystery.

It's as though God is saying: 'You haven't seen anything yet!' He is challenging us to be prepared for so many new experiences, we shall literally be in the seventh heaven of wonderment. Can't we trust him to give us the best? We cannot pinpoint the longitude and latitude of heaven: it's enough, surely, to believe we shall be there.

And Christ will be there: the reason for our inheritance. And that will be wonderful.

> *When, by his grace, I shall look on his face,*
> *I shall be satisfied then.*
>
> (James C. Moore)

## Advent Crossword

---

## And who are they?

The blessed assembly consists of those who have followed Jesus all the way; who have fought the good fight and have kept faith with him. They are there through no merit or value of their own, but by their willingness to be kept loyal to Jesus. All the credit for their lives is his; all the strength that they have needed, has been his; and all the pains and persecutions they have suffered, have been on his behalf. They have been faithful servants, so faithful, he has called them 'friends'. Many folk with whom they have shared the gospel are there too, but many more are not.

Yet they have done what they could.

And now they are enjoying the reward.

## Clues Across

1. Moses' sister. (6)
4. The resurrection-day. (6)
7. Girl's name. (3)
8. Implement. (4)
9. Snug. (4)
10. Popular drink. (3)
12. Shed tears. (3)
13. Tumult. (5)
15. St Thomas is said to have died here. (5)
17. View. (3)
19. What he owns. (3)
20. At the end of a foot. (3)
22. Solid. (6)
23. He has a diocese. (6)
26. Limb. (3)
28. Bind. (3)
29. Question. (3)
30. Enthusiastic. (5)
31. Fortunate. (5)
32. Tribe of Israel. (3)
34. Before. (3)
36. Vessel. (4)
37. Metal. (4)
39. Tin. (3)
40. Limb of a tree. (6)
41. Eden, for instance. (6)

## Clues Down

1. Where coal is found. (4)
2. Rodent. (3)
3. Old Testament prophet. (7)
4. Church officer. (7)
5. Morning and afternoon. (3)
6. January to December. (4)
11. Monkey. (3)
12. Moggie. (3)
14. Requiring. (7)
16. The Jerusalem monarchy. (7)
18. Come in. (5)
21. Wind instruments. (5)
24. Pull out. (7)
25. Parting with, for a price. (7)
27. Adam and Noah. (3)
29. Yes. (3)
33. Hebrew month. (4)
35. Showers. (4)
36. Snake. (3)
38. Inclination. (3)

*See page 247 for solution*

## Each new opportunity

Every day brings a new opportunity (or even a host of new opportunities). What for? For us to get a day nearer glory? No, we shall be a day nearer glory however we use each day. If we set our sights on earning glory, we shall one day get near enough to miss it. Each new day is God-given for one purpose: to make Jesus known to others. It is to this end that God gives us opportunities: to this one end. When we have disciplined and focused our minds on this, then truly we are on the road to heaven.

## Jesus is Lord!

Yes, the times we affirm that he IS Lord, you'd think we were already focused on this truth. But just reflect on the digressions and preoccupations that an average day can bring; before we know where we are, we're worrying over something that has precious little to do with Jesus being Lord.

'But it's never been so hard to get a bit of peace and quiet to think!' You're right, it's never been so vital that we should fight against the set and current of the times. Satan is evilly content if he can get our minds off God.

He's been successful so many times, it's gone to his head.

Today, as we focus on those white-robed success-stories of eternity, Satan will have to take a back seat.

Won't he?

### Suggested Hymns

Angel-voices, ever singing; Around the throne of God a band; Jerusalem the golden; There is a land of pure delight.

## Third Sunday before Advent (or, the Sermon for Remembrance Sunday, q.v.) 12 November

*Principal Service* **Believe It!** Jonah 3:1–5, 10; Ps. 62:5–12; Heb. 9:24–28; Mark 1:14–20

> 'Now after John was arrested, Jesus came to Galilee, proclaiming the good news of God, and saying: "The time is fulfilled, and the kingdom of God has come near; repent, and believe in the good news."' Mark 1:14–15

### Is this all?

'Repent, and believe.' Is this all we have to do? No, but it's a start. Unless we acknowledge our sins and shortcomings, we can't repent; so realizing what they are is a prerequisite. If we've developed a good 'forgettery', we need to get serious with God, and pray that the Holy Spirit will bring any darkness in our lives to the light. And then we can confess, and receive God's forgiveness.

Then comes the hard part: leaving the confessed sins deep in the sea of God's merciful forgetfulness, and starting over, resuming our lives as though we had never sinned. If we insist on raking up old sins, worrying over them as though we've neither confessed nor been forgiven, we are not only acting a lie, but hurting our Lord into the bargain. We need to come to the point where we can say, with Paul: 'There is therefore now no condemnation for those who are in Christ Jesus . . .' (Rom. 8:1). No condemnation! The slate has been wiped clean, and is now as though we had never sinned! How could Paul say that? He'd hounded the early believers, persecuted them to prison and to death! If he'd forgotten, there were plenty of folk with good memories around to remind him. But no, Paul had been 'apprehended' by God, convinced and convicted of his sins, and forgiven. Yes, he'd done more than any of the other apostles; he'd preached more, travelled more, suffered more . . . To make up for his awful past? No! Nothing he could do would 'make up'. Jesus had done it all, through grace. Paul's mission was simply to believe in the gospel, and to share it.

## Stage two

After stage one (repentance), then comes belief. 'Believe in the good news (= the gospel)', Jesus says.

> Redemption! Oh, wonderful story!
> Glad message for you and for me,
> That Jesus has purchased our pardon,
> And paid all the debt on the tree.
> Believe it, O sinner, believe it!
> Receive the glad message, 'tis true!
> Trust now in the crucified Saviour,
> Salvation he offers to you.
>
> (S. M. Sayford)

---

**Solution**

**Across:** 1. Miriam. 4. Sunday. 7. Ada. 8. Tool. 9. Cosy. 10. Tea. 12. Cry. 13. Panic. 15. India. 17. See. 19. His. 20. Toe. 22. Steady. 23. Bishop. 26. Arm. 28. Tie. 29. Ask. 30. Eager. 31. Lucky. 32. Dan. 34. Ere. 36. Boat. 37. Iron. 39. Can. 40. Branch. 41. Garden.

**Down:** 1. Mine. 2. Rat. 3. Malachi. 4. Sacrist. 5. Day. 6. Year. 11. Ape. 12. Cat. 14. Needing. 16. Davidic. 18. Enter. 21. Oboes. 24. Stretch. 25. Selling. 27. Men. 29. Aye. 33. Abib. 35. Rain. 36. Boa. 38. Nod.

Believe in his nativity, his mission, his miracles, his passion, resurrection and ascension. Believe it, because it was done for you. Don't blue-pencil, red-pencil or mess it about in any way. Those who fell to arguing that 'black was white, and blue was no colour at all', making problems where there were none, obstructions where the way was clear, were so caught up in their devious machinations, that the Saviour was born among them, and they didn't notice; the Messiah preached and healed in their midst, and they found fault. The Son of God was sent to the cross by folk who thought they were doing God's service; and the Christ rose from the dead; and they said it was a lie. Whatever we may feel like being, let's not join the ranks of such unbelievers.

## Stage three

And after belief, what then? Then comes the practical stage three, that Jesus spent his whole ministry on: sharing the gospel, taking our belief into the lives of others. Heaven is not so short of space that God has reached the end of his accommodation lists. While we have breath to share, and love to reach out, and compassion for others, God will give us the grace to go on. Repent; believe; share.

And after that, the glory.

We can believe it.

### Family Service Input

Encourage the young folk to solve the Word-Search, 'What Life Is About' (p. 250), and then to compile a further list of their own.

### Suggested Hymns

Dear Lord and Father of mankind; I heard the voice of Jesus say; Sweet sacrament divine; Tell out, my soul, the greatness of the Lord.

# Third Sunday before Advent

*Second Service*   **No Present Justice?** Ps. 46 [82];
Isa. 10:33—11:9; John 14:1–22 [23–29]

> *'His delight shall be in the fear of the Lord. He shall not judge by what his eyes see, or decide by what his ears hear . . . They will not hurt or destroy on all my holy mountain; for the earth will be full of the knowledge of the Lord as the waters cover the sea.'*
> *Isaiah 11:3, 9*

## Now – and then

There are two 'settings' in these verses, the present and the future; earth and heaven. And yet, with a sort of divine alchemy, they can also be read as descriptive of both then and now. When the light of Christ has come into a person, by faith we see things differently; we understand people differently; and our very lives send out a different message than that which was sent before we believed. To this extent, we can experience something of the glory of eternity now; we can 'broadcast' the message of peace before we are translated into peace in all its fullness. We can show Christ to others, and give them a foretaste of glory. Yes, we can, because we have our Lord's own promise, that we are 'the light of the world (Matt. 5:14). Unless we are making a difference, we are not fulfilling our mission as Christians. And the more of our Lord's light that we show, the more this present time will take on the aura of glory.

## The world as God sees it

As God looks on our world today, how much of it can he see as being already cognizant of him? To how much of the globe has the Bible spread? Well, it has still some way to go: to many hundreds of places where minority languages and dialects still do not have the scriptures; to many places where the Christian gospel is being denied freedom of publication; to many other places where the gospel is being adulterated by heresies, suffocated by persecution, or left to die by neglect. Looking on our world, God will see areas where Christ's light is shining out brightly (such as from this parish!), but also other places where it is flickering, sputtering or going out.

## What Life Is About Word-Search

| | | | | | | | | | | | | | | |
|---|---|---|---|---|---|---|---|---|---|---|---|---|---|---|
| L | A | R | P | S | S | E | N | E | V | I | G | R | O | F |
| B | O | Q | P | R | O | P | H | E | C | Y | N | K | L | E |
| G | E | N | T | L | E | N | E | S | S | H | M | O | J | V |
| C | S | D | G | E | T | F | W | G | T | E | H | I | L | A |
| B | D | M | O | S | I | J | H | I | F | A | C | I | A | N |
| C | E | A | O | K | U | L | A | G | E | V | F | D | B | G |
| G | B | F | D | C | N | F | Q | C | D | E | O | E | N | E |
| E | P | A | N | S | E | L | F | C | O | N | T | R | O | L |
| T | H | B | E | R | O | S | P | E | A | C | E | K | P | I |
| E | A | O | S | I | H | P | L | T | R | W | Q | F | L | S |
| R | I | G | S | W | J | D | I | E | K | I | J | M | G | T |
| N | N | T | F | J | U | D | G | E | M | E | N | T | Q | E |
| I | B | M | T | S | C | S | H | R | O | R | H | G | V | I |
| T | A | T | W | S | L | R | T | Q | L | J | J | O | Y | N |
| Y | W | S | Y | N | A | G | O | G | U | E | L | K | M | P |

LOVE
JOY
PEACE
LONGSUFFERING
GOODNESS
GENTLENESS
MEEKNESS
FAITH
SELF-CONTROL

HEAVEN
JUDGEMENT
LIFE
LIGHT
ETERNITY
FORGIVENESS
SYNAGOGUE
PROPHECY
EVANGELIST

## Making a difference

If we take stock of how our parish-light of Christ is burning brightly, can we use these data to help someone else? Perhaps it's the broad spectrum of services we have . . . or the Bible groups . . . or the mission outreach, the ministry to the sick, prisons or the handicapped . . . Is there another parish in the deanery/diocese/further afield with whom we could do spiritual business? (Or have they got a 'lightning-conductor' that would help us shine better?)

## God is the Judge

'There ain't no justice in this world!' is still a protest heard far too often – and it's all the worse for being true by human standards – because humans judge by what they see, unlike God (v. 3). Invite God into a situation, and the world is shown up for its shallowness. Hypocrisy is seen for what it is, as the Lord's scrutiny goes to the heart of the matter. We cannot hide anything from God, but we know that when he judges, he is always right. And under his glorious rule, all nature as well as ourselves will be brought into a right order (vv. 6–9).

We surely get a glimpse in these verses, of how it must presently grieve God, to see both the human and animal world out of kilter with his original designs. We may look forward to glory with longing, but how much greater must be the longing of our Father! Can we not help forward the good work, by extending the gospel's reach in every way we can (Matt. 24:14; Mark 13:10)?

## *Suggested Hymns*

God is working his purpose out; Mine eyes have seen the glory of the coming of the Lord; Spirit of God, as strong as the wind; Teach me, my God and King.

# Second Sunday before Advent   19 November

*Principal Service*   **Just the Beginning** Dan. 12:1–3; Ps. 16; Heb. 10:11–14 [15–18] 19–25; Mark 13:1–8

> *'[Jesus said] "For nation will rise against nation, and kingdom against kingdom; there will be earthquakes in various places; there will be famines. This is but the beginning of the birth-pangs."'* Mark 13:8

## Before birth

Even Mary had not been spared the birth-pangs, though hers continued after the nativity. When she presented Jesus at the temple, 40 days later, Simeon foretold her anguish: 'A sword will pierce your own soul, too' (Luke 2:35). Before every birth, there is anguish. Therefore, it is only to be expected that pain will precede the birth of Eternity. Humankind, ever hopeful that thier generation has got its sums right, have for centuries seen the present age mirrored in today's verses. 'Surely we are in the Last Days!' This has been said for so long, the 'Last Day' must be the longest on record.

## God's time-span

'Do not ignore this one fact, beloved,' says St Peter, 'that with the Lord one day is like a thousand years, and a thousand years are like one day' (2 Peter 3:8). Millennia which seem long to us, are put into a different perspective by the Lord of Eternity. Jesus has said that the Last Day will come when the gospel has been published to all nations (e.g. Matt. 24:14; Mark 13:10). We may, therefore, be in the 'Last Days', but only if these are reckoned by God's time-span rather than ours. It's not our business to wonder when the Last Day will dawn: even Jesus disclaimed such knowledge (Mark 13:32). There have been many false estimates, and false christs leading people astray; in recent years, hundreds, thousands of expectant people have been led to watch on mountain-tops for the dawn of the Last Day only to be cruelly disillusioned when it did not come as the false prophets had tricked them into believing.

It will come. God does not lie. But meanwhile, we are to continue working for the gospel, working with new zeal, looking for no respite or holiday, until we have done all we can.

## What will be?

If the beginning of the birth-pangs is characterized by earthquakes, famines and wars, what may we expect to follow? The pessimists have read into Jesus' words a threat of even worse disasters, but are they justified in this? The birth-pangs are painful, no one would deny the hurt and damage caused by the present trials; but birth-pangs by their nature are not permanent. Look at the teaching of Jesus on this: 'When a woman is in labour, she has pain, because her hour has come. But when her child is born, she no longer remembers the anguish, because of the joy of having brought a human being into the world' (John 16:21). The pangs in some cases, it's true, precede a difficult birth, but in many other cases the birth is far less traumatic than this preliminary anguish. Who is to say that it will not be so at the Last Day?

## The 'hour'

'My hour has not yet come', Jesus told his mother, when she wanted his help at the Cana wedding-breakfast (John 2:4) – but he helped her, nevertheless. By contrast, our own 'hour' is now here. As a wise person has written: We 'pass through this world once'. Whatever we are going to do for God here, we need to do it now. He'll find us plenty of other work to do in eternity: new work, perhaps different from what we have learned to do here (but perhaps not very different).

We sometimes make a mess of deciding how best to use this 'hour'. If we're up-front with God about the matter, he'll redirect us as and where necessary; and, rather than getting overawed by the thought that our life and work is making a difference, he'll get us up and out and doing.

Wherever we are – here or 'there' – we shall not miss the Last Day, that's for sure.

### Family Service Input

Encourage the young people to design an Advent Card for the parish, including details of services, etc.

### Suggested Hymns

Father God, I wonder how I managed to exist; Give me the faith that can remove; Thy way, not mine, O Lord; Will you come and follow me.

253

# Second Sunday before Advent
*Second Service*   **The Hand of the Lord** Ps. 95;
Dan. 3:[1–12] 13–30; Matt. 13:24–30, 36–43

> *'If our God whom we serve is able to deliver us from the furnace of blazing fire and out of your hand, O king, let him deliver us.'* Daniel 3:17
> *'In [the Lord's] hand are the depths of the earth . . . the sea . . . and the dry land, which his hands have formed . . . He is our God, and we are the people of his pasture, and the sheep of his hand.'* Psalm 95:4–5, 7

## The weak hand

Nebuchadnezzar measured the strength of his hand by the power of a man-made furnace. The language in Daniel 3:19 shows the king's chagrin, as his human-generated heat left the men of God unmoved. The king's 'strength', such as it was, proved puny and ineffectual when it came against the mighty hand of God, though it sufficed for the stokers of the boiler (v. 22).

## The strong hand

The strong hand of God is seen in today's psalm, familiar from the service of Morning Prayer. In the Lord's hand is the entire earth: land and sea, and everyone he has ever (and will ever) make. Our times are his.

> *My times are in thy hand,*
> *My God, I wish them there;*
> *My life, my friends, my soul I leave*
> *Entirely to thy care . . .*
>
> *My times are in thy hand:*
> *Why should I doubt or fear?*
> *My Father's hand will never cause*
> *His child a needless fear.*
> (W. F. Lloyd)

If only we could focus more on this truth, it would save us an awful lot of anxiety. When the sun shines and life is good, we're in

God's hands. When the storm howls around us, and sickness, grief and worry all vie for our attention, we are still in God's hands.

Do we know what this means? No, because most of us most of the time don't know how to give our heavenly Father 100 per cent of our trust. We're usually very bad at even defining what 'trust' is. If we rely on something we can see and feel, that is not trust.

Whoever said it was? Haven't we forgotten, because relying on the visible and tangible has become such a habit, we've lost count of when it began.

## Real trust

Real trust is to rest assured in what is not visible, not tangible, but very truth. Listen to how the author of Hebrews describes the trust of Moses: 'By faith he left Egypt, unafraid of the king's anger: for he persevered as though he saw him who is invisible' (Heb. 11:27).

We can see plenty with 'the mind's eye', when it comes to making business or holiday plans; when we telephone, e-mail or fax a friend, can we not visualize that person as though he or she were sitting across the table from us? Yet ask us about God – Father, Son and Holy Spirit – and our mind's eye (= the eye of faith) seems to shut down. We can see what God has made: does his handiwork tell us nothing about him? We, who in this technological age, are obsessed with data-collection and evaluation, can we not go to work in the same way, and learn how to trust from what God is constantly working in our lives?

Of course we can. If we are willing.

## Working at trust

We need to work at our trust, just as we work at much that is far less important, and certainly less durable.

> *Trust God when your wants are many;*
> *Trust him when your wants are few;*
> *Trust him, when to trust him only*
> *Seems the hardest thing to do.*

### Suggested Hymns

Give me the faith that can remove; Put thou thy trust in God; Take my life, and let it be; When we walk with the Lord (Trust and obey).

# Christ the King (Sunday next before Advent)

26 November

*Principal Service* **King of the Universe** Dan. 7:9–10, 13–14; Ps. 93; Rev. 1:4b–8; John 18:33–37

> *'Jesus answered, "My kingdom is not from this world. If my kingdom was from this world, my followers would be fighting to keep me from being handed over to the Jews. But as it is, my kingdom is not from here."' John 18:36*

## A little distance

Pilate has just told Jesus, 'Your own nation and the chief priests have handed you over to me' (v. 35). Yet here, Jesus appears to put some distance between himself and 'the Jews'. He had come to 'what was his own', but 'his own people' had shown they did not accept him (John 1:11), so now he was undergoing a passion not only for his own people, but for all people of the world. By neglect, animosity, distrust and downright vengeance, his own people had forfeited any right they may once have had to be treated as a special case. The man now standing before Pilate was as much the Roman's King as he was of Caiaphas. And today, both disowned him, and it would be left to a penitent thief to acknowledge his sovereignty.

## King of our lives

> *King of my life, I crown thee now,*
> *Thine shall the glory be.*
> *Lest I forget thy thorn-crowned brow,*
> *Lead me to Calvary.*
> *Lest I forget Gethsemane,*
> *Lest I forget thine agony,*
> *Lest I forget thy love for me,*
> *Lead me to Calvary.*
>
> (Jenny Evelyn Hussey)

Yes, for it's only at Calvary that we see the thorn-crowned brow, only at the cross that we hear the anguished cry, full of loving trust: 'Jesus, remember me, WHEN YOU COME INTO YOUR KINGDOM' (Luke 23:42). Is there Paradise in our hearts? Has Christ the King come 'not to sojourn, but to abide with us' (H. F.

Lyte)? He cannot come, until there is a kingdom-sized space ready and waiting for him in our hearts.

## Heart-preparation for the King

When he comes, in a month or so's time, as a child, we shall have the manger ready, lined with soft hay and waiting to receive him. But it is as King he comes knocking today. And a king needs a right royal welcome, a heart free of confessed sin that's been left with God; free of preoccupation with matters that just don't matter; a heart where the Spirit has already a 'reception-force' of his fruit: love, joy, peace, patience, kindness, generosity, faithfulness, gentleness and self-control (Gal. 5:22–23).

## Service for the King

And in this Spirit-enriched heart, is there not also a zeal for service in the army of our King? Are we ready for what he may call us to do? Are we willing to be used for any service? An eminent surgeon enrolled on a 'mercy team' to an Asian country where the anti-Christian government had a policy of neglecting its many orphanages; and for three months, until his humility and genuine love for the children had won the confidence of the authorities, the surgeon was employed exclusively in cleaning out the toilets. But he dedicated the work to Jesus: 'All for Jesus!' – and saw to it that those toilets were as clean and hygienic as the best of his operating theatres back home.

Are we as willing, to serve Jesus in any capacity?

> *Teach us, O Lord, to serve thee as thou deservedst;*
> *To give, and not to count the cost;*
> *To fight, and not to heed the wounds;*
> *To toil, and not to seek for rest;*
> *To labour, and not to ask for any reward,*
> *Save that of knowing that we do thy will.*

## *Family Service Input*

Encourage the children (using the gospels as an aide-memoire) to formulate Christ the King's laws for his followers, and if time permits, to illustrate them.

Suggested Hymns

Christ is the King! O friends, rejoice; King of glory, King of peace; The King of love my shepherd is; Thou didst leave thy throne.

# Christ the King (Sunday next before Advent)
*Second Service*   **Chains of Office** Ps. 72; Dan. 5; John 6:1–15

> *'The king cried aloud to bring in the enchanters, the Chaldeans, and the diviners; and the king said to the wise men of Babylon, "Whoever can read the writing and tell me its interpretation shall be clothed in purple, have a chain of gold around his neck, and rank third in the kingdom..." Then Daniel answered ... "let your gifts be for yourself, or give your rewards to someone else! Nevertheless, I will read the writing..."' Daniel 5:7, 17*

## What money cannot buy

God made people, but man made money. Belshazzar, like many before and since, had made money his god. Whatever he wanted, money would achieve it for him; until he met Daniel, that is. Daniel was not as abrupt as was Peter, centuries later, when he told Simon the magician: 'May your silver perish with you, because you thought you could obtain God's gift with money!' (Acts 8:20), but he showed great dignity, brushing aside the royal bribe, and making sure that everyone knew where the real power lay: power that mere money couldn't buy.

## Worldly impedimenta

On this Sunday next before Advent, as we share this story of Daniel, can we reflect on any worldly impedimenta that have been allowed to get in the way of our service for God? Can we examine our lives to identify any 'chains of office' that may be blocking other people's view of God-in-us? We may genuinely believe these 'chains' are actually helping our ministry. Would Jesus – Christ the King – agree? He was a king without a crown, without royal regalia or robes; a king who came with no fanfare of trumpets; a monarch who came to serve. How would we describe our own ministry? Do we invite folk to a meal without a thought of a return invitation? Do we lend time, money or talents without thought of recompense? Do we give of ourselves freely, unconditionally, with absolutely no strings attached?

Suppose we were parachuted down in a far-off country, with no ID cards and unable for any reason to divulge our identity. Would the 'natives' realize by our words and actions that we belonged to Christ? Probably not. But suppose we walked into a church, say, 30 or 40 miles away from our own ... Oh, yes! Identification would be simple! We'd not only be speaking the same language, but also talking about the same things – services, quotas, missions, PCCs, and the like ...

## Christ-the-King-speak

But are those the subjects that Christ the King would discuss, were he to join our worship today? Well, he might talk of mission, but he'd probably be just as keen to discuss matters nearer home: the folk in 'Cardboard City', the drug-users, prisoners, sick and house-bound; the children and young people ... and what about the 'Drop-In' centres, the soup-kitchens ... ? ('Lord, don't you want to hear about the new road system, the computer centre, the leisure complex ... ?')

... And what about the hospice, the rest-homes? the families living in that row of houses destined for demolition ... ?

('But, Lord, we must tell you about the hyper-market that's opening next week ... !')

## Priorities

Before another Advent starts another new Christian year, let's sit down with God, and 'argue out' our priorities (Isa. 1:18), getting them as much as possible in line with his.

There is then every chance that the coming year will be the best one yet.

## *Suggested Hymns*

Another year is dawning; Jesus, stand among us; Meekness and majesty; The royal banners forward go.

# SERMONS FOR SAINTS' DAYS AND SPECIAL OCCASIONS

## St Andrew, Apostle   30 November
**Proclaiming Jesus** Isa. 52:7–10; Ps. 19:1–6; Rom. 10:12–18; Matt. 4:18–22

> *'But how are they to call on one in whom they have not believed? And how are they to believe in one of whom they have never heard? And how are they to hear without someone to proclaim him? And how are they to proclaim him unless they are sent?'*
> *Romans 10:14–15a*

### Answering the call

St John's Gospel has Andrew as the first of the Twelve to hear Jesus and follow him. And, since Andrew went immediately to find his brother Simon Peter, and bring him to Jesus, we can see also in Andrew the first Christian missionary. He became one of the 'inner circle', with Peter, James and John. At the feeding of the 5,000, it was Andrew who had faith enough to present the boy with his little bag of fish and bread to Jesus, even though he wondered how such a small amount of food could satisfy such a large crowd of hungry people.

### From Pentecost onwards

Andrew is among those present when the Holy Spirit descended at Pentecost, and from then onwards the biblical record is silent about him; but according to tradition he went to Scythia with the gospel, and from there to Greece and Byzantium. In or around AD 60, he is said to have been crucified on an X-shaped cross at Patras, in Achaia. His relics are believed to have been brought to Scotland in the eighth century, soon after which the country adopted him as its patron saint.

## Missionary zeal

From the little Galilean fishing community, to Scythia and eventually to Patras, is a good distance to travel with the good news of Jesus. Could folk hear without a preacher? No. Therefore Paul, Andrew and the others needed to leave home and country and go as far and as fast as they could. Their knowledge of the world beyond Judaea, or even the Roman Empire, was such that some of them at least would believe that the world would have the gospel preached to it in their lifetime, so speed as well as distance was important.

It is still important, for we are now so much closer to world-evangelization than were those early disciples, so much closer to the end of war and bloodshed, that this in itself is surely a great incentive to keep the gospel message rolling.

## A quiet learner

Through the years of Jesus' ministry, Andrew had been quietly learning from the Master, so that when the time came for him to launch out on his own, he not only had plenty of teaching stashed away in his memory – but he also knew (and this would bolster his confidence even more) that the Holy Spirit given at Pentecost was forever in him to remind him of any of that teaching that he forgot (John 14:26). If we will also only remember this, and pray the Spirit into action, instead of thrashing about trying to do everything by ourselves, we should not only be honouring the gift, but also the Giver.

So far as we know, Andrew did not return to his Galilean home, once the missionary zeal got full hold of him. Others, like William Tyndale who fled to the Continent and was persecuted even there, also left home and country for the gospel. On this Festival of St Andrew, can we – dare we – ask God to make our own path clear? For it's possible that he wants us, too, to get the gospel message rolling further.

> *'For my sake, and the gospel's, go,*
> *And tell redemption's story.'*
> *His heralds answer, 'Be it so,*
> *And thine, O Lord, the glory.'*
> *They preach his birth, his life, his cross,*
> *The love of his atonement,*
> *for whom they count the world but loss,*
> *his Easter, his enthronment.*

## Suggested Hymns

A Man there lived in Galilee; I heard the voice of Jesus say; Jesus calls us, o'er the tumult; Will you come and follow me.


# St Nicholas, Bishop of Myra c.326    6 December
## The Gentle Bishop Isa. 61:1–3; Ps. 68; 1 Tim. 6:6–11; Mark 10:13–16

> *'For the love of money is the root of all kinds of evil, and in their eagerness to be rich some have wandered away from the faith and pierced themselves with many pains. But as for you, man of God, shun all this; pursue righteousness, godliness, faith, love, endurance, gentleness.' 1 Timothy 6:10–11*


### Lover of children

Born into a wealthy family at Patara in Asia Minor, Nicholas in the fourth century became Bishop of Myra. Most of what we know about him comes from a ninth-century hagiographer, according to whom Nicholas was a lover of children, giving help and food especially to the youngsters of poor families. He is often portrayed holding a bag of gold, in illustration of the tradition that, hearing of a poor man in the city, whose daughter could not marry for lack of a dowry, visiting the house one night Nicholas threw a bag of gold in through the open window. He did the same when the second daughter became engaged. But when the third daughter's marriage was due, the father sat up all night, and thus discovered the identity of their benefactor. Nicholas is thought to have suffered martyrdom in the Diocletian persecutions. His festival came to be associated with the exchanging of gifts, in his honour; and later became subsumed into the Christmas celebrations. The Dutch name for him, 'Sinter Claes', has been anglicized into 'Santa Claus'.


### Patron saint

Nicholas has been adopted as the patron saint of Greece and Russia, and cities such as Freiburg and Moscow. According to one tradition, he rescued some sailors from a ship foundering on the rocks, and is also revered as the patron saint of sailors.

In many parts of Europe during the Middle Ages, his feast day saw the election of a 'Boy Bishop', whose 'reign' lasted until the feast of the Holy Innocents.

## Using money for God

Nicholas knew what it was to have a lot of money, but wealth did not blind him to the plight of the poor; and he used his wealth and position to help the underprivileged wherever he could. He could use money, without being a slave to it: use it as God directed for the benefit of others. And, what's more, he could share it unostentatiously: the value lay in the deed itself, and not in the giver. Today, many Christians shy away from wealth, believing it to be an inhibitor to glory. Yet wealth per se is not evil; any evil comes in the misusing of wealth: the hoarding of it, or the squandering of it, or the accumulation with it of evil things. If God has given us power to get wealth, we can be sure that he knows exactly how much good we can do with it.

We only have to ask him to show us.

## Painful progress

Paul cautions Timothy against emulating those who are determined to get wealth at all costs, trampling on others or even stealing to get it. That is not 'getting on in the world', nor is it 'an insurance for the future'. It is plain sinful and, worse, it's slavery, for we have then made money our master.

Let us remember Nicholas, not only on 6 December, but whenever we are tempted to use money for anyone but the God who has provided it.

### Suggested Hymns

A charge to keep I have; All for Jesus, all for Jesus; All I have, I give to Jesus; Take my life, and let it be.

# St Ambrose, Bishop of Milan, Teacher of the Faith
397    7 December
**The 'Poor' Bishop** Isa. 41:9b–13; Ps. 20; 2 Cor. 5:16–21;
Luke 22:24–30

> *'So we are ambassadors for Christ, since God is making his appeal*
> *through us; we entreat you on behalf of Christ, be reconciled to*
> *God. For our sake he made him to be sin who knew no sin,*
> *so that in him we might become the righteousness of God.'*
> *2 Corinthians 5:20–21*

## Of the aristocracy

Born to a wealthy aristocratic family in Trier, in 340, Ambrose lost
his father at an early age, and went to Rome with his widowed
mother. Having trained for a legal career, he was made governor
of Liguria and Aemilia, based in the capital, Milan. This was a time
of tension in the Church. When the Bishop of Milan died, rival
candidates were put up, from the orthodox and Arian wings of the
Church. So heated became the episcopal debate, that a 'wild cat'
election was proposed, to settle the issue: Ambrose was voted into
office by public acclaim, even though he had not yet been baptized.
Quickly the Church elevated him through the ranks, from deacon
to bishop in eight days.

## A worthy choice

It had been a good decision. Ambrose brought quiet peace and
sobriety to the office. Although, for the rest of his life he was to
mediate between the factions, he did it with a gentleness and charity
that melted hearts and cooled tempers. His diplomacy was such
that he even had the Emperor Theodosius I doing public penance,
after a mob at Thessalonica had killed the Roman governor in
AD 390, which had been followed up by a savage massacre of
civilians on the emperor's unwise orders.

## Church and state

Ambrose was insistent that the state did not meddle in Church
matters (though the Church could, when occasion demanded,
inveigh against the state!). When the Emperor Valentinian II was

asked to sanction a new statue of the goddess of Victory for erection in Rome, Ambrose leaned on the emperor to forbid it. Nor would he take notice of the regent Justina when she wanted one of Ambrose's churches for the Arian heretics.

It is a sad irony that the two greatest Christian preachers of the time – John Chrysostom and Ambrose – should have had such different fortunes: John, at Constantinople, was far too close to the Court and the Empress Eudoxia for his own safety; and was exiled several times, dying eventually from the cruelty of his guards. Ambrose, on the other hand, had a relatively peaceful life, and was able to rule prelates and poor alike – with kindly but firm justice.

## The 'poor' bishop

Ambrose gave his wealth to the poor and to good causes, and consciously sought poverty and humility. He was determined to make a success of his office – and he succeeded. He had leisure and opportunity to write many hymns; when admitting new members into the Church, he humbly washed their feet, as Christ had done for his disciples. A close friend of Monica's, he did much to encourage Augustine (later Bishop of Hippo) in the faith.

We have much in Ambrose for which to thank God.

### *Suggested Hymns* (all Ambrosian)

Come, Holy Ghost, for ever one; Come, thou Redeemer of the earth; O strength and stay; O Trinity, most blessed Light.

# Conception of the Blessed Virgin Mary
## 8 December
**Into Trust** Gen. 3:9–15a; Ps. 97; Eph. 1:3–6, 11–12; Luke 1:26–38

> *'And [the angel] came to her, and said, "Greetings, favoured one! The Lord is with you." But she was much perplexed by his words and pondered what sort of greeting this might be.'*
> *Luke 1:28–29*

## Natural wonderment

And well might Mary wonder, for no one had ever been asked to do what God was asking of her. Whether or not we believe that she herself was 'immaculately' conceived, without original sin, her early life must have been such to persuade God that she would be the fitting mother for his Son. If Mary was not recognized as 'special' before Gabriel's visit, that was to change, imperceptibly at first, but then as the early Church was formed and expanded, so the knowledge of the *Theotokos* (Mother of God) enlarged.

## Honouring Mary

> *To live, and not to love thee,*
> *Would fill my soul with shame,*

wrote John Wyse. And today we as a Church are gradually recovering from the damage that over-wrought feelings and attitudes of the Reformation period did to the honouring of Mary. We give thanks today for her conception. They are not mentioned in the New Testament, but according to the Proto-Gospel of James, her parents were Anne (Anna) and Joachim. In the account, there are similarities with the story of Hannah, the mother of Samuel.

## Highly favoured

But the Gospels tell us quite a lot about Mary herself, though who has not longed to know more? It would appear that Luke, the author of the third Gospel and Acts, had access either to Mary or to someone very close to her; and to Luke we are indebted for most of the Christmas stories, the Candlemas presentation, and the fact that Mary played a not inconsiderable role in the early Church. From Matthew, comes the angel's visit to Joseph, and the story of the Magi; and from John the amazing courage of Mary in practically ordering her son to perform a miracle at the Cana wedding-breakfast. John, too, gives the touching account of Jesus, in his hour of agony at Calvary, giving Mary over into the care of his beloved disciple.

## The carpenter's wife

Since Joseph appears to have died before the start of Jesus' ministry (and to have been anything but talkative prior to that! There is no word from him recorded in the gospels), Mary must have often found life hard, especially when Jesus was claiming to be Son of God, and the critics homed in on Mary and her husband's lowly trade. Did Jesus shield her from as much of the criticism and questioning as possible? At any rate, Mary loyally stayed in his mission team, and courageously was right there at the cross on Good Friday afternoon.

> *Maiden, yet a mother,*
> *Daughter of thy Son;*
> *High beyond all other,*
> *Lowlier is none.*
> *Thou the consummation,*
> *Planned by God's decree,*
> *When our lost creation*
> *Nobler rose in thee.*
> (Dante Alighieri, 1285–1321,
> Tr. R. A. Knox)

### Suggested Hymns

I'll sing a hymn to Mary; Mary Immaculate, Star of the morning; O purest of creatures, sweet Mother, sweet Maid; Virgin wholly marvellous.

## St John of the Cross, Poet, Teacher of the Faith
### 1591   14 December
**Not I, But Christ** S. of Sol. 2:8–17; Ps. 121; 1 Cor. 2:1–10; John 14:18–23

> *'For I decided to know nothing among you, except Jesus Christ and him crucified . . . My speech and my proclamation were . . . with a demonstration of the spirit and of power.'* 1 Corinthians 2:2, 4

## The priority of the message

Paul is thought to have been a smallish man; one tradition says he had bandy legs. Since he was once let down from a wall at Damascus 'in a basket' (Acts 9:25; 2 Cor. 11:33), he probably was compact in size. If so, he had something in common with John of the Cross, who was also of small build. But both men were big on proclaiming the gospel. John was born into a poor but noble family near Avila, in 1542. As Juan de Yepes, he left his charity school to become a nurse, studying meanwhile with the Jesuits in order to enter the monastic life. Before he was 21, he had joined the Carmelites, but studied further at Salamanca University, afterwards being ordained and meeting the woman who was to have a major influence on his life – Teresa d'Avila. John assisted Teresa in her reforms of the Carmelite order, incurring the wrath of the religious authorities, who imprisoned him for a time; and it was during his incarceration that John wrote much of the work for which he is now famous. In the *Dark Night of the Soul*, John describes how a soul can separate itself from the world and its attractions, undergoing a deep experience of the sufferings of Christ, through which it emerges into the transport of God's glory.

## Leaving the world

Through his writings, John became more and more detached from the world and the bitterness which was at that time so much a part of the local scene, as Spanish Catholicism worked through its differences from the Roman practices. Yet he was persuaded for a time to become Vicar Provincial of Andalusia and a prior at Segovia. Mysticism, however, continued to tug at his heart, and when internal disputes erupted among the Spanish Carmelites, John retired into solitude. He died after a painful illness, in Andalusia, in 1591.

## Benefits of the *Dark Night*

In the first place, the soul learns to commune with God with more respect and more courtesy, such as a soul must ever observe in converse with the Most High ... And here we must taste another excellent benefit ... in this dark night of the desire ... God will enlighten the soul, giving it knowledge, not only of its lowliness and wretchedness, but likewise of the greatness and excellence of God. For, as well as quenching the desires and pleasures and attachments of sense, he cleanses and frees the understanding that it may understand the truth . . . (*Dark Night of the Soul*, I.xii)

## Suggested Hymns

Breathe on me, breath of God; My soul, there is a country; Through all the changing scenes of life; Through the night of doubt and sorrow.

## St Stephen, Deacon, First Martyr   26 December
## Anticipation of Glory   Acts 7:51–60; Ps. 119:161–168; Gal. 2:16b–20; Matt. 10:17–22

*'But filled with the Holy Spirit, [Stephen] gazed into heaven and saw the glory of God and Jesus standing at the right hand of God. "Look," he said, "I see the heavens opened and the Son of Man standing at the right hand of God!"' Acts 9:55–56*

## What a welcome!

What a welcome, for the table-waiter-cum-fearless-preacher! What joy for the first Christian martyr, to see Jesus on his feet waiting at God's right hand to greet his faithful servant! And what a blessing, that Stephen was given the vision before he had even died, otherwise we might never have shared it.

Many people keeping vigil at the bedside of a dying person have reported seeing the fading eyes brighten just before they close for the last time. The patient cannot speak, but the light in the eyes has told a story, and don't we wonder what they saw! On occasion, the lips have smiled, and some in extremis have actually managed to say, 'Jesus!' And then they have gone, leaving us to ponder what they saw, who they were greeting, and where they are now.

As Christians, we don't need such glimpses, to convince us that death is not the end, but yet we treasure them, every one. It's as though between this life and the next is a giant jig-saw of unknowing, but, every so often, God gives us another little piece to add to a picture that will not be complete until we are actually the soul crossing that divide.

Will Jesus be on his feet, to welcome us? We don't know. But one thing is certain: we shall know him when we see him.

*When my life-work is ended, and I cross the swelling tide,*
*On that bright and glorious morning I shall see,*
*I shall know my Redeemer, when I reach the other side,*
*And his smile will be the first to welcome me.*
*I shall know him, I shall know him,*
*And redeemed by his side I shall stand;*
*I shall know him, I shall know him,*
*By the print of the nails in his hand.*

(Fanny J. Crosby)

## Without fear

There was no recrimination from Stephen: no, 'Lord, I've only just begun my ministry; don't call me home yet, there's so much to do!' And there was no fear: he could look the stone-slingers in the eye, and their missiles left him unmoved. He'd not been long in the vineyard, but his life's-work on earth had been completed. God had plans for this young man, plans that Satan had tried to thwart; but the devil had instead only succeeded in advancing Stephen into the waiting arms of Jesus.

Throughout Christian history, there have been those who, in a mistaken urge of zeal, have 'engineered' their martyrdom. That is not God's will for anyone. He will make martyrs of those whom he has chosen to be martyrs; we are not to deny Christ if faced with that 'life or death' decision. But we are not to seek death before God's time, even for the loftiest of reasons.

Stephen certainly did not seek death, but when martyrdom was inevitable, he not only bowed to God's will, but embraced it joyfully.

## *Suggested Hymns*

Around the throne of God a band; For all the saints; Let saints on earth in concert sing; Ye holy angels bright.

## St John, Apostle and Evangelist  27 December
## The Johannine Festival  Ex. 33:7–11a; Ps. 117; 1 John 1; John 21:19b–25

*'This is the message we have heard from him and proclaim to you, that God is light and in him there is no darkness at all.'*
*1 John 1:5*

### Who was John?

We do not know whether there were three Johns – the evangelist and apostle, the writer of the Letters, and the writer of Revelation – or two, or just the one. But traditionally the Church has honoured the writer(s) of all the Johannine books on this day.

John was the most 'theological' of the evangelists. His Gospel not only quotes the Old Testament more than Matthew, Mark or Luke, but it gives us the spiritually challenging doctrine of Jesus as the Logos, or Word, of God. John seems to have no knowledge of the birth stories (perhaps unusual, since at the request of Jesus, he took Mary into his home after the crucifixion).

One of the 'inner circle' of the apostles, John was with Jesus throughout his ministry. The brother of James, he was called from mending the family's fishing-nets on Galilee. He witnessed the transfiguration, was present at the Last Supper, the agony and the crucifixion, and witnessed the resurrected Christ.

If he and John of Patmos were indeed the same, he was exiled to the island in or around AD 95, presumably for refusing to worship the emperor. On 'The Lord's Day' (Rev. 1:10), he received the visions recorded in the Book of Revelation.

### John's light

Common to the Gospel, letters and revelation, is the importance of light: God's light, the light of Jesus (the Word) and the light of the Holy Spirit. John has thought deeply about the light that God has brought into the world, from creation until his day, and also the light afforded by the visions, of the world to come. He sees God as being total light, with not a hint of darkness. For John, the whole message of the incarnation was the gift of divine light: physically in the ministry of Jesus, and spiritually in its shining in the darkness that evil had brought. It 'shone in the darkness, and the darkness did not overcome it.' This is the core of John's teaching, and he returns to it throughout the writings.

## Light for today

And his verses give the same message for us today. There may be more Christians in the world than ever before, but there are still many places in desperate need of the light of Christ, and their need is all the greater in the degree it is not yet recognized. Wherever God's light has shone, the seeds of the gospel have been sown. They may take years, even centuries, to germinate, but, gospel seed being indestructible, their time will come.

> *The good, the fruitful ground*
> *Expect not here nor there;*
> *O'er hill and dale by plots 'tis found;*
> *Go forth, then, everywhere.*
> *Thou canst not toil in vain;*
> *Cold, heat, or moist or dry,*
> *Shall foster and mature the grain*
> *For garners in the sky.*
> (James Montgomery, 1771–1854)

The best way in which we can honour the memory of John is to pray for grace to sow more seed, in as many places as the Lord gives us opportunity.

### Suggested Hymns

Christ is the world's true light; Jesu, our hope, our heart's desire; Living Lord; Thou whose almighty Word.

## Holy Innocents   28 December
**Prophecy Fulfilled** Jer. 31:15–17; Ps. 124; 1 Cor. 1:26–29; Matt. 2:13–18

> *'Then Joseph got up, took the child and his mother by night, and went to Egypt, and remained there until the death of Herod.'*
> *Matthew 2:14–15a*

## Happy ever after?

Especially at Christmas, we want things to go well, and every situation to have a happy ending. It's an effort to focus on an episode as tragic as the seemingly senseless massacre of the innocent boys of Bethlehem. Of course, we're glad that Joseph and Mary got Jesus safely away and into Egypt out of Herod's clutches, but why did innocent children have to die in such a brutal way? Prophecy had foretold it, but it was a crying shame, nevertheless. Yet God would have his reasons. Throughout history, people of all ages have been crossing the line between this world and the next; when we get there, we shall see why; but for now we simply don't know the reason.

Would some of the parents or sisters of these innocent children meet a man some 30 or so years later in Jerusalem, Nazareth or Capernaum? Would they remember that it was for him their families had been bereaved? We don't know.

## Random evil?

There appears a randomness – even a chaos – about evil, which is difficult to grasp. Yet from God's dialogue with Satan at the start of Job's problems, we may infer that God has fixed parameters beyond which Satan cannot go. There were limits fixed in the case of the innocent children. We may consider them too wide, but Satan would be able to go only as far as God allowed. God prevented him from acting, until the Holy Family had put a safe distance between themselves and Bethlehem; and the carnage, though dreadful for the families involved, was limited by gender, age and location.

## God's pattern

If evil seems chaotic, God's working by contrast has a pattern: that of prophecy and fulfilment. Everything prophesied and promised by God comes to pass. But, because the Master of time will not be limited to our human timescale, the fulfilment of these promises often catches us unawares.

'Oh, Lord, if only I'd known . . . !'

But the Lord doesn't intend for us to know. He'd far rather surprise us. He'll be seeking to surprise us this Christmas. We may be so preoccupied with the secular busyness of the season, that we fail to see or hear his counsel. No matter. He will try, again and again.

## Personal prophecies

Has it occurred to you that you are a part of the fulfilment of prophecy? 'In your descendants, all the families of the earth will be blessed,' God told Abraham. Unless we are of another planet, this includes us. The little boys of Bethlehem had not progressed far enough along life's way, to have a well-formulated understanding of prophecy; they were so young. But we shall meet them one day, and perhaps then we shall understand. For by then, God willing, we shall have more in common with them

### Suggested Hymns

A great and mighty wonder; In vain the cruel Herod's fear; Jesus, grant me this, I pray; Unto us a Boy is born.

# Naming and Circumcision of Jesus  1 January
## The Name It Had To Be Num. 6:22–27; Ps. 8; Gal. 4:4–7; Luke 2:15–21

> 'After eight days had passed, it was time to circumcise the child; and he was called Jesus, the name given by the angel before he was conceived in the womb.' Luke 2:21

## The precious name

It was not chosen by God because it was unique: Jesus (Jeshua) was quite a common name at the time. No, Jesus had come to be a man, one of us. He would have plenty of 'special' names: Messiah, Saviour, Redeemer, Advocate, Mediator ... but Jesus ('saviour') was chosen as his familiar name, because it highlighted his chief purpose: that of saving the world. At the name of Jesus, everyone and everything would bow, in heaven, and on earth and under the earth.

'Whatever you ask the Father, in my name, he will do it', Jesus was to promise his disciples. When he sent them out on their first mission, they returned in great excitement, saying that even the devils obeyed them when they used the name of Jesus. Hadn't our

Lord a smile on his lips, as he replied: 'I saw Satan as lightning fall from heaven!'

It's this name of Jesus that makes Satan quail, for it brings home to the devil his defeat at Calvary.

## At the Beautiful Gate

When Peter and John healed the lame man at the Beautiful Gate of the temple (Acts 3:6), Peter told him, boldly: 'I have no silver or gold, but what I have I give you; in the name of Jesus Christ of Nazareth, stand up and walk.' The apostles were brought before the authorities, who angrily forbade them to minister in that name.

'But it was through faith in the name of Jesus, that this man was healed! We're going to continue using it!' the apostles declared, and the baffled authorities merely let them go.

## Saul's conversion

When Saul had had his dramatic blinding on the Damascus Road, and the Lord told Ananias to go and restore his sight, Ananias (naturally enough) protested. But the Lord said to him: 'Go, for he is an instrument whom I have chosen to bring MY NAME before Gentiles and kings and before the people of Israel; I myself will show him how much he must suffer for the sake of MY NAME' (Acts 9:15, 16).

And, as the Book of Acts unfolds, Saul (= Paul) went from being the Church's arch-persecutor, to its most travelled, most persecuted, most ardent preacher of the gospel. The last thing we hear of him doing, when he had been under house-arrest in Rome for two years, was his 'preaching about the Lord Jesus Christ with all boldness and without hindrance' (Acts 28:31).

## The power of the name

It's of little us a Christian going around merely declaring: 'There's power in the name of Jesus!' Even the devil knows that. The precious name needs to be applied. One doesn't get a car going by sitting in the driving-seat and saying, 'There's petrol in the tank!' The ignition needs activating to prove that there's petrol available. So the name of Jesus needs to be applied: Whatever we ask, in the name . . . We have to be dynamic about it, and then the power of Jesus thrusts in and gets things moving.

At the name of Jesus; How sweet the name of Jesus sounds; Jesus, the name high over all; There is a name I love to hear.

# Epiphany   6 January
## Wise to Discern Isa. 60:1–6; Ps. 72; Eph. 3:1–12;
Matt. 2:1–12

> *'Then, opening their treasure-chests, they offered him gifts of gold, frankincense and myrrh. And having been warned in a dream not to return to Herod, they left for their own country by another road.' Matthew 2:11b–12*

## Open to signs and wonders

These men of learning were open to signs and wonders; they had interpreted the meaning and importance of the star when many other people would have disregarded it, or would not have gone to the trouble of researching its relevance for the anticipated 'King of the Jews'. And they took seriously the dream that they had, heeding its warning to make quick tracks for home, and giving Herod a wide berth.

And they had come bearing gifts, as one does when a king has been born: the best gifts to hand. Perhaps Mary and Joseph used these gifts to finance their journey to Egypt, and the time they spent there, for it is not certain that Joseph would have taken any tools with him; and certainly on a journey of over 200 miles they would need food and lodging.

## God's provision

As God provided for the Holy Family, so he continues to provide for his children. He has given us the power to get wealth, but what is the sort of wealth he has designed for us?

> *I own not the riches of silver or gold,*
> *Nor the glittering jewels of time;*
> *But I am content with the Treasures of Old,*
> *For the wealth of all heaven is mine.*
>                                   (Alfred H. Ackley)

God would sell every one of those cattle 'on his thousand hills' (Ps. 50:10), before he would see one of his children starve. The choice is ours. If we allow money to rule us, if we trust in the wealth we can see, then God will let us carry on until we discover our mistake. But if we roll our trust for everything over to him, asking him to take charge of our time, our talents, our finances, then he will.

'Well, just in case ... I'll take out this insurance ... I'll put something by, for a rainy day ...' That is not trusting the Holy and Undivided Trinity. The Magi set out on a journey that had no maps, no carefully planned itinerary. We're not even told they had a pocketful of travellers' cheques, still less travel insurance. They were not even Jews. We don't know if they had any religion, or none. But they had the star; they were in God's will (whether they realized it, or not); and they were open and alert to the signs and the dreams that he gave them.

No, a travel insurance firm may well have looked askance at their lack of detail. Yet they ended up making one of the most important journeys of all time.

As we reflect on their visit to the young Jesus, we may reverently wonder what God may have in store for us.

Can we – dare we – be as open and alert to his directions, as were the Magi?

### Suggested Hymns

As with gladness men of old; Brightest and best; O, worship the Lord in the beauty of holiness; Unto us a Boy is born.

## St Antony of Egypt, Hermit, Abbot 356   17 January
## 'With Long Life Will I Satisfy Him' 1 Kings 17:2–6; Ps. 91; Phil. 3:7–14; Matt. 19:16–26

*'Yet whatever gains I had, these I have come to regard as loss because of Christ. More than that, I regard everything as loss because of the surpassing value of knowing Christ Jesus my Lord. For his sake I have suffered the loss of all things ...' Philippians 3:7–8*

## The rich young man

Born into a wealthy family in Egypt, in 251, Antony inherited a fortune when his parents died in or around the year 276. But when he read Jesus' command in the gospels to sell everything and follow him, Antony obeyed to the letter, retreating into the desert for a life of solitude. His fame, however, was such that many men followed him, and he founded a number of coenobitic monasteries for them, retreating himself further and further into the wilds. There he suffered the torments of strange noises and temptations, but he attributed all these to Satan's vindictiveness, and remained true to his vow of solitary communion with God.

## A long life

Antony lived to be 105, for much of this time seeing only one man who brought him bread every six months. He left instructions that his body was to be buried in an unmarked grave, because he wanted to remain as 'hidden' in death as he had tried to be in life.

We may not agree with such severe, self-imposed solitude, yet this is how not only Antony but many members of the ancient Egyptian and Syriac churches understood their way to God. It is not the actual practicalities, but the commitment to a Christian's perceived way that is more important. If we truly believe that God is leading us along a certain route, then we should give him our best. It does not matter what others may say: God has his own dealings with them. Nor does it matter if we agree 100 per cent with God: if he is having his way with us, he will work so gently and persuasively on us, until we grow into full agreement with him. Quite possibly there would be times in his tempted, tortured, wilderness days, when Antony remembered his early, pampered life, or the monasteries he had founded, where at least kindred spirits were within earshot of one another. But he stayed in the will of God and, though his grave may remain a secret between him and his Lord, his long life's work is known the world over.

## Others' missions

Antony's is a lesson to us not to criticize another Christian's life, even though it may be very different from our own. For Antony, solitude was apparently what God was asking of him. For us, God may want us in the thick of things; we may feel hard-pressed, overworked and starved of privacy. But God's evaluation of 'hard-pressed' may be streets away from ours. There's a prayer that includes a petition for 'Courage, gaiety and a quiet mind'. We need all three of these to do God's work, wherever he has put us, and whatever he is asking of us.

It's a prayer we can make at any time, in any place.

## Suggested Hymns

Father God, I wonder how I managed to exist; Forth in thy name, O Lord, I go; Not for our sins alone; Will you come and follow me?

# The Conversion of St Paul  25 January
## Set Apart for God  Acts 9:1–22; Ps. 67; Gal. 1:11–16a; Matt. 19:27–30

> *'But when God, who had set me apart before I was born and called me through his grace, was pleased to reveal his Son to me, so that I might proclaim him among the Gentiles...'*
> *Galatians 1:15–16a*

### A dramatic turn-around

From being the most violent persecutor of the Jesus-followers, Paul became the most ardent of Christian missionaries. He travelled further, suffered more vicissitudes, and preached more than any of the other apostles. But as he met up with Jesus on the Damascus Road, all that was still to come.

Jesus had taken Paul's (Saul's) persecution personally: 'Why do you persecute ME? ... I am Jesus, whom you are persecuting' (Acts 9:4–5). And Paul, with the warrants of arrest in his pocket, must have wished himself further away.

### After the healing

Jesus did not retire and leave Paul to work out his own salvation, after Ananias had restored his sight. Paul tells the Galatians that the Lord went on to give him special, personal revelations. God knew his man. He knew that the super-abundance of energy that Paul had shown in a negative way, would, when channelled positively, get the gospel-message spreading far and fast. 'He knew me before I was born,' marvelled Paul, as he came to realize how long ago God had 'set him apart'.

## God is no respecter

God is no respecter of persons (Acts 10:34, AV). What he could do for Paul, he can do for us. Probably he has already begun to move in our lives, but he hasn't finished. In the Christian life, there is no 'retirement'; we are serving, frontline troops until the day we die. Are we frail, or somewhat incapacitated? Don't worry, God knows what we can do. He will never ask us anything beyond our capabilities, but from each of us he expects our best efforts with the equipment we have.

## The value of scripture

The value of scripture is incalculable. Simply put, we need the Bible, and we need it all the time. We have a great advantage over Paul, in having the New Testament available, and in many versions we can understand. But we also need the personal, one-to-one revelations from God for our individual missions. He will give these, if we listen out for them, if we are open to what he is saying and doing in our lives.

It's the difference between knowing about God, and knowing God. Paul knew the old scriptures (the Old Testament) inside out; hadn't he been taught by the leading tutor of the day, Rabban Gamaliel (Acts 22:3)? Only a very few of the rabbis were promoted to the title of 'Rabban'. But though these scriptures had inculcated a deep respect for God in him, they hadn't stopped him persecuting the Christians. He could team up with Peter and the rest, and hear firsthand accounts of Jesus and his ministry, but this, though vital, was at one remove from the personal.

Jesus, whom he had encountered violently on the Damascus Road, led Paul into retreat in Arabia (Gal. 1:17), and gave him a one-to-one, personal-revelation tutorial.

Have we yet had our 'Arabia'? If not, it may be knocking on our door.

### *Suggested Hymns*

I am thine, O Lord; O Jesus, I have promised; Teach me, my God and King; To God be the glory.

# The Presentation of Christ in the Temple

(Candlemas)   **2 February**
**Spirit-Directed** Mal. 3:1–5; Ps. 24; Heb. 2:14–18;
Luke 2:22–40

*'It had been revealed to [Simeon] by the Holy Spirit that he would
not see death before he had seen the Lord's Messiah. Guided by
the Spirit, Simeon came into the temple . . .' Luke 2:26–27a*

## Openness to God

Simeon had had a revelation that the Messiah would come in his
lifetime. As his end drew nearer, surely he would become more
expectant, until the time came when the Spirit 'guided' him to the
temple and through the courtyards and colonnades, to where
Joseph and Mary were with the child, performing the rituals of
purification and presentation, in accordance with the law.

Had the old man given up on his revelation, or squashed the idea
of going to the temple that day, he would have missed the blessing
of God keeping his divine promise.

## Forty days

Candlemas, coming 40 days after Christ's nativity, has been cele-
brated at least since the sixth century. Processions of worshippers
carrying lighted candles would converge on the church, where the
priest would bless two bundles of candles: one of large candles to
be used in the church for the rest of the year; the other of smaller
candles, which the congregation lit for the duration of the service,
and then took away to be used in their homes. There were local
variations, where all the candles would be kept for church use,
particularly at baptisms.

Candlemas is the 'first light' of Christmas, marking the transition
into the run-up to Lent. In some churches, the Christmas crib and
decorations are kept up until today, rather than being removed on
or after Twelfth Night.

In the Eastern Orthodox Church, today is kept as the 'Presentation of Christ in the Temple'. The Western Catholic Church
observes it as the 'Purification of the Virgin'. 'Candlemas', which
is the title now gaining popularity, covers both titles.

## The sword to come

In Simeon's words, Mary is given an inkling of the trauma to come. She stores up the news in her heart, but for now it's a day of quiet celebration.

So, too, for us. We know what lay ahead, for Mary and Jesus. But our futures are hidden, in the mercy of God. Today is a day of light, and we rejoice that the Light that came to lighten the Gentiles is continuing to do just that. We carry our little candles today, and as their flames meet up with all the others in the church, they light up this 'crossroads', between Christmas and Lent, which once again will culminate in Easter.

Will our light – the light of Christ inside us – light the way for others, when our Candlemas lights are blown out? That will depend on whether, like Simeon, we are open to what God is saying and doing in our lives.

### Suggested Hymns

For Mary, Mother of our Lord; I sing the Lord God's praises; Jesus, good above all other; The Light of the world in the darkness has shone.

## SS Cyril and Methodius, Missionaries to the Slavs
869 and 885    14 February
**Those Who Bring Good News** Isa. 49:1–6; Ps. 24;
Rom. 10:11–15; Luke 9:1–6

> *'And how are they to proclaim him unless they are sent? As it is written, "How beautiful are the feet of those who bring good news . . ." So faith comes from what is heard, and what is heard comes through the word of Christ.' Romans 10:15, 17*

### Gift of languages

Cyril and his elder brother Methodius were born in Thessalonica, and were both gifted linguists. The pope sent them into Russia, to convert the Khazars, and later into Moravia. From the start, they had no intention of imposing foreign practices and language on their converts, as had previously been tried by others with disastrous effect. So Cyril devised a script for the Slavs, which still bears his name (Cyrillic), and began translating the Bible into what is now known as 'Old (or Church) Slavonic'. The brothers' work had made news at Rome, and they were recalled for an audience with the pope. Unfortunately, by the time they reached Rome, Pope Nicholas I had died, and while they were there Cyril himself died, and was buried in the Church of San Clemente. Methodius returned to Moravia, where against strong opposition from the German bishops, he eventually completed the translation of the Bible in Slavonic which had been begun by Cyril.

## The last Russian Christian?

The work begun by Cyril and Methodius was to spread across the vast Russian lands; but as the brothers had struggled against animosity and prejudice, so Christianity in Russia was to have a hard ride. In the eighteenth century, Peter the Great attacked the power of the Church, but not religion itself. In 1917, Lenin attacked both. The Church in Russia largely went underground so effectively that in the 1960s Nikita Krushchev was confident enough to boast that he would live to see the 'last Christian in Russia' paraded on the television.

Krushchev has been dead for many years, and the Church in Russia has gone from strength to strength, although it is still suffering persecution in many areas.

## Modern-day missionaries

The modern-day Cyrils and Methodiuses are not hard to find: they are going openly into countries where the laws permit freedom of religion, while in those areas still restricted they are still going in – either taking secular jobs and witnessing by precept, or getting God's word across boundaries by whatever means they can – 'hazarding their lives for the gospel', as did the earliest Christians (Acts 15:26). One young missionary, back from the East, was asked by a professor of his home univesity, what right he had to try to convert people of other religions to the Christian faith? The young man replied, even as St Paul had defended his own mission long ago: 'The love of Christ compels me' (2 Cor. 5:14).

While there are men and women inspired to answer Christ's call to take the gospel to lands where it has not yet reached, the light of Christ will continue to overcome the darkness of unbelief.

## Suggested Hymns

Far round the world; From Greenland's icy mountains; Hills of the north, rejoice; Jesus shall reign, where'er the sun.

## George Herbert, Priest, Poet 1633   27 February
**Praise Our God** Mal. 2:5–7; Ps. 1; Rev. 19:5–9;
Matt. 11:25–30

> 'And from the throne came a voice saying, "Praise our God, all you his servants, and all you who fear him, small and great."'
> Revelation 19:5

### A good beginning

Born into the wealthy aristocratic Pembroke family in 1593, Herbert went up to Cambridge where, in 1618 he became Public Orator, and then a Member of Parliament, with a high-profile life at Court ahead of him. To his friends' surprise, he forsook this career for the Church; after spending some time with his friend Nicholas Ferrar at Little Gidding, his first and only vicariate began in the rural parish of Bemerton, near Salisbury, in 1630. Here, for three years, he proved an exemplary parish priest, finding time also to do much writing. *The Country Parson* and *The Temple* are perhaps his best-known works; these lines on 'Matins' and 'Evensong' are from the latter.

*Matins*

*I cannot ope mine eyes,*
*But thou art ready there to catch*
*My morning soul and sacrifice;*
*Then we must needs for that day make a match.*

*My God, what is a heart?*
*Silver, or gold, or precious stone,*
*Or star, or rainbow, or a part*
*Of all these things, or all of them in one?*

*My God, what is a heart,*
*That thou shouldst it so eye, and more,*
*Pouring upon it all thy art,*

*As if thou hadst nothing else to do?*

*Indeed man's whole estate*
*Amounts (and richly) to serve thee;*
*He did not heaven and earth create*
*And studies them, not him by whom they be.*

*Teach me thy love to know;*
*That this new light, which now I see,*
*May both the work and workman show:*
*Then by a sunbeam I will climb to thee.*

### Evensong

*Blest be the God of love,*
*Who gave me eyes, and light, and power this day,*
*Both to be busy, and to play.*
*But much more blest be God above,*
*Who gave me sight alone,*
*Which to himself he did deny:*
*For when he sees my ways, I die;*
*But I have got his son, and he hath none.*
*What have I brought the home*
*For this thy love? have I discharged the debt,*
*Which this day's favour did beget?*
*I ran; but all I brought, was foam.*
*Thy diet, care and cost*
*Do end in bubbles, balls of wind,*
*Of wind to thee whom I have crossed,*
*But balls of wild fire to my troubled mind.*
*Yet still thou goest on.*
*And now with darkness closest weary eyes,*
*Saying to man, 'It doth suffice;*
*Henceforth repose; your work is done.'*

Herbert died in 1633, at the age of 40; but his writings live on, and some of his hymns are still firm favourites. These include the ones below.

## Suggested Hymns

King of glory, King of peace; Let all the world in every corner sing; Teach me, my God and King; The God of love my shepherd is.

# St Chad, Bishop of Lichfield, Missionary 672

## 2 March

**The Humble Prelate** Ecclus. 3:17–24; Ps. 84; 1 Tim. 6:11b–16; Luke 14:7–11

*'Pursue righteousness, godliness, faith, love, endurance, gentleness. Fight the good fight of the faith; take hold of the eternal life, to which you were called and for which you made the good confession in the presence of many witnesses.' 1 Timothy 6:11b–12*

### Scholar-monk

The youngest of four brothers, Chad was taught by St Aidan of Lindisfarne, from where he moved to Lastingham, the monastery in Yorkshire founded by his brother, Cedd. Cedd, its first abbot, having just died, Chad succeeded him in the office. Then for a time he became Bishop of York. However, confusion arose when a determined cleric, Wilfrid, returned from France claiming to have also been chosen Bishop of York. Rather than place the new Archbishop of Canterbury, Theodore, in the unenviable position of deciding which candidate had the prior claim, Chad quietly and graciously stepped down, and returned to the relative peace of Lastingham.

### First Bishop of Lichfield

Theodore didn't leave him rusticating for long. The King of Mercia had asked for a bishop, and Chad was chosen for the post, in the newly created diocese. His first act as bishop was to move the see from Repton to Lichfield. Today, Lichfield is still a large diocese, though it has had Southwell and Derby carved out of its northwestern flank; but in Chad's day it was very big, and he spent much time in travelling around it. He preferred to walk from church to church, but Theodore thought this was beneath the dignity of a bishop. In St Chad's Cathedral at Lichfield today can be seen a roundel depicting the archbishop assisting Chad to mount a horse for his missionary travels!

In 672, the plague swept through Mercia, carrying off hundreds of victims including Chad; but his name lives on not only in the cathedral but in many churches of the Lichfield diocese.

## Fighting the good fight

We may live for many years, or a few. We may travel extensively, or minister locally. We may have a 'successful' mission, or one that is frustrating and disappointing. Whatever it is, it will be our fight of faith, meant for us, and for which we shall be answerable to God. We should not waste time in comparing our lot with anyone else's; they are not running in our track; their finishing-line is in front of them, not of us. Our work is to run our race, to fight our fight, as well as ever we can. A runner who makes a practice of skipping from one track to another, is not going to win the race. Nor is a fighter who jumps out of one ring and into some other fighter's ring, going to win his own fight. God has tailored our race and our fight for us.

Doesn't that make us feel special?

It should, because, in God's eyes, we are.

### Suggested Hymns

Fight the good fight; I, the Lord of sea and sky; Inspired by love and anger; You may cross the barren desert (Be not afraid).

# St Patrick, Bishop, Missionary, Patron of Ireland
c.460   17 March
**For the Healing of the Nations** Isa. 51:1–11; Ps. 96;
Rev. 22:1–5; Matt. 10:16–23

> *'Then the angel showed me the river of the water of life, bright as crystal, flowing from the throne of God and of the Lamb through the middle of the street of the city. On either side of the river is the tree of life with its twelve kinds of fruit, producing its fruit each month; and the leaves of the tree are for the healing of the nations.' Revelation 22:1–2*

### The young cowherd

Patrick has become so synonymous with the Emerald Isle, that it comes as a shock to some to learn that he was born in England, probably of Roman stock, and possibly called Patricius Magonus Sucatus. Around the year 403, in his early teens, he was captured by Irish raiders and taken as a slave to Ballymena, where he worked long hours as a cowherd. While tending the animals, Patrick learned how to pray, and eventually he stowed away on a ship trading in dogs, and escaped to Gaul, where St Germanus of Auxerre took him in hand at the monastery of Lerins.

## The Irish dream

Yet his heart was in Ireland, albeit the land of his slavery; and once Germanus had consecrated him bishop, Patrick returned to Ireland in the year 432. His first challenge appears to have been a confrontation with the pagan King Laoghaire, at Tara, Co. Meath. Patrick converted the king's daughter, but made many enemies in the process. In 444, he set up his see at Armagh, from where he tirelessly made many missionary journeys over the island. At Crom Cruach, he demolished a pagan idol, and his fearless preaching converted many to Christ. For years, he had a vision of constructing the Irish Church along the well-established diocesan system of Gaul, but this proved too ambitious at the time for the Irish to take on board.

At Saul, on Strangford Lough, Downpatrick, the saint died, in the year 460 or 461. He had not accomplished all he had set out to do, but he had brought Christian healing to an island that would not be forgotten.

Today, our prayers are no less necessary for the ongoing, gradual progress of that beautiful island towards a lasting peace.

## He did what he could

'She has done what she could', was Jesus' lovely verdict on the woman (Mary?) who bathed his feet with expensive ointment, shortly before his passion. And it's a verdict that can be applied also, surely to Patrick's Irish ministry. At the end of the day, if we truly have done all we can, we should not worry over what we might have done, but thank God for giving us strength for all we have accomplished in his name.

It is perhaps strange that so many patron saints, Patrick included, have come to be linked with countries other than those where they were born; yet the tree of life in John's vision bore its fruits for the healing of all nations. Patriotism has many worthwhile virtues, but the Christian gospel knows no geographical boundaries.

Around the throne of God a band; For all the saints; Hail, glorious Saint Patrick; I bind unto myself today.

# The Annunciation of Our Lord to the Blessed Virgin Mary   25 March
**The Power of the Most High** Isa. 7:10–14; Ps. 40:5–10; Heb. 10:4–10; Luke 1:26–38

> *'The angel said to her, ''The Holy Spirit will come upon you, and the power of the Most High will overshadow you, therefore the child to be born will be holy; he will be called Son of God.'' '*
> *Luke 1:35*

### The holy child

What was the young virgin to think? Today, we can only give thanks that Mary's faith overrode everything else, and caused her to give her trusting 'Fiat', so that the angel's words would come to pass. It is a lesson in faith. When our times of testing come, even though we may not recall Mary and her courage, may we also be given strength to move more closely into the will of God.

To say 'Yes' to God, when he seems to be asking something desperately impossible of us, is not heroic; it is a simple act of faith. Let's not get hung-up about how virtuous we are. When Mary would reflect on the angel's message, she would realize that what God was asking of her was to accept what he was going to do: she would be the instrument through whom God would work. His would be the dynamic force, the energy, the movement. All that would be required of Mary, was her faithful acquiescence.

All? Yes, it was a big task, but God was asking for her trust. He would do the hard work.

### The right focus

When we have focused aright, that is what God is saying he will do in our lives. But so often we let the magnitude (and the mechanics) of the challenge claim our attention. God will take care of the size – almost certainly it doesn't look as big to him – and he will direct the mechanics as well. Most importantly, he can see the end-result. He knows the challenge can work out to a successful conclusion. God is not a sadist: he doesn't issue challenges that are incapable of being met. What's more, he issues them in such a generous way that we feel we've been a vital part of the success! How's that for encouragement! And so long as we give the glory to him, he will continue giving us more and more challenges, until the biggest one of all: that step from here to eternity; and, even there, it's God who does the hard work.

### The birth – and then?

Mary's challenge didn't end with the birth of Jesus. Simeon, at her purification, told her of the sword that would pierce her heart in time to come; the wise men in bringing myrrh foretold the sadness of the tomb; Herod's massacre of the Innocents saw Mary having to trek over 200 miles into Egypt; throughout Christ's ministry (now minus her husband) Mary saw the suspicion and animosity that her Son had to face; yet still she was there, at Calvary, for her stiffest challenge yet; and there, in his own agony, Jesus paid a beautiful tribute to her faithfulness in giving her into the care of John.

No, Mary didn't have the stamina of a prize-fighter, nor the physique of a long-distance runner.

She just had faith: oodles of faith.

### *Suggested Hymns*

Angelus ad virginem; For Mary, Mother of our Lord; Maiden, yet a mother; O purest of creatures, sweet Mother, sweet Maid.

## St George, Martyr, Patron of England c.304
### 24 April (transferred from 23rd)
**The Great Martyr** 1 Macc. 2:59–64 or Rev. 12:7–12; Ps. 126; 2 Tim. 2:3–13; John 15:18–21

> 'Remember Jesus Christ, raised from the dead, a descendant of David – that is my gospel, for which I suffer hardship, even to the point of being chained like a criminal. But the word of God is not chained. Therefore I endure eveything for the sake of the elect, that they may also attain the salvation that is in Christ Jesus, with eternal glory.' 2 Timothy 2:8–10

## Who was St George?

After the Crusaders reintroduced the story of George to England, this country adopted him as her patron saint in place of Edward the Confessor. But there are so many legends attached to George that mystery rather than fact predominates as regards his history. It may be that he was a Cappadocian knight martyred at Lydda in or around AD 304, in the Diocletian persecution. In the East, he is known as 'The Great Martyr'. Certainly churches in England were being dedicated to him prior to the Norman conquest.

## The dragon-slayer

Was George the dragon-slayer confused with Michael the Archangel, who was victorious in the heavenly war with the dragon Satan (Rev. 12:7–12)? It is possible, but the tradition relating to George seems not to have lost momentum through the centuries. It tells us that George, the Cappadocian knight, was riding through Libya when he happened on the city of Sylene, a community in turmoil, due to the insatiable hunger and venom of a man-eating dragon who lived in the nearby swamp. The Sylenians had been keeping the beast at bay by feeding it with sheep. When George arrived, the mutton supply was exhausted, and, in desperation, the king was about to sacrifice his daughter.

George struck a bargain with the king. He would do battle with the dragon. If he won, the whole population of Sylene must become Christians. The king agreed and proved a man of his word: George killed the beast, and around 15,000 Sylenians embraced Christianity. Legend even tells us that it took four ox-carts to carry away the body of the dragon.

## Defying the emperor

Yet another legend has George a Roman soldier in the army of Diocletian. One day, the emperor called in heathen priests to predict the future. They brought animal entrails to 'help' them in their divination, and one or two of the soldiers present were seen to cross themselves. Enraged, Diocletian published an edict ordering Christian clergy to sacrifice to pagan gods. George tore down the edict from the palace door, and suffered martyrdom as a punishment.

## A brave man

So many legends, so many possibilities; yet common to all is that George was a brave man. Edward III declared the saint Patron of the Order of the Garter, and from that time on he seems to have been unchallenged as England's patron saint.

### Suggested Hymns

And did those feet in ancient time; Faith of our fathers, living still; I vow to thee, my country; O faith of England, taught of old.

## St Mark the Evangelist   25 April
**Worldwide Gospel News** Prov. 15:28–33 or Acts 15:35–41; Ps. 119:9–16; Eph. 4:7–16; Mark 13:5–13

> *'As for yourselves, beware, for they will hand you over to councils, and you will be beaten in synagogues, and you will stand before governors and kings because of me, as a testimony to them. And the good news must first be proclaimed to all nations.'*
> *Mark 13:9–10*

### Mark the evangelist?

There are several references to 'Mark' in the Bible, and in early Christian literature. It is possible that they refer to one and the same man: more than that, we cannot say. John Mark's mother's house was an early meeting-place of the Church in Jerusalem; and since the second Gospel (thought by most to be the first of the canonical Gospels to be written) was written by a Jew, it was probably this 'Mark' also who wrote it. The young man who was so nearly captured at the scene of Jesus' arrest in Gethsemane, and who is only mentioned in this Gospel, is thought to be an autobiographical reference.

### Peter's amanuensis

According to early tradition, Mark was in Rome with Peter, and took down Peter's reminiscences. Thus the second Gospel bears the freshness of an eyewitness account; it is also the most explicit of the Gospels in recording the shortcomings, ignorance, impulsiveness and incomprehension of the disciples, particularly of Peter.

## Paul's companion

A 'Mark' accompanied Paul in his early ministry, and then appeared to desert him, which seems to have bothered Paul not a little. When Mark wanted to go on the apostle's next journey, Paul objected, and chose Silas instead, leaving the more generous and diplomatic Barnabas to take Mark with him to Cyprus. However, later on when Paul was in Rome under house-arrest, we find that all has been forgiven, and that Mark has rejoined him (possibly dividing his time between Peter and Paul, who seem to have been in Rome at the same period).

## The gospel

Mark set out to illustrate how Jesus came to suffer, fulfilled the prophecies, and triumphantly rose from the dead. There are no birth or infancy stories. Mark is interested in the ministry of Jesus, and what it meant for the world. It is Mark who gives us one of Jesus' broadest hints as to when the Second Coming will take place, namely, when the gospel has been proclaimed to all nations (Mark 13:10).

He writes quickly, and the action keeps moving, from healings, to preaching, to teaching, and back to miracles and Jesus' command over the forces of nature. Mark is not the deeply thinking theologian of the fourth Gospel, nor the carefully crafting writer of the third, nor the dramatic lover of the miraculous, which characterizes Matthew's writing. He simply gets down the facts as the eyewitness (Peter) has dictated them. Yes, the disciples were often wrong-footed: it is all there, as the ex-fisherman of Galilee recalls the highs and the lows of the time Jesus shared with the Twelve.

Mark's Gospel needs to be read at a sitting, to appreciate it fully; and his feast day is the best of all times to do just this.

## *Suggested Hymns*

A man there lived in Galilee; I bind unto myself today; Jesus calls us, o'er the tumult; Tell me the old, old story.

## SS Philip and James, Apostles  1 May
**Loyal, but Little Known** Isa. 30:15–21; Ps. 119:1–8;
Eph. 3:1–10; John 14:1–14

*'Of this gospel I have become a servant according to the gift of
God's grace that was given to me by the working of his power.'*
*Ephesians 3:7*

### Who were they?

It may seem strange, but in such a small coterie of twelve apostles,
so little is known about most of them. At least from John's Gospel
we know that Philip, called by Jesus to be a disciple, went and
found Nathanael (possibly Bartholomew) and brought him to Jesus.
It was Philip, too, who asked Jesus however they were going to
feed the crowd of 5,000. And Philip questioned Jesus (probably at
the Last Supper) about God, which led to some of the most beautiful
teaching of our Lord (John 14:8ff.).

This James is usually called 'James the Less', or 'James the son
of Alphaeus', to distinguish him from James the son of Zebedee
and brother of John. He could also have been 'James the Younger',
whom Mark tells us witnessed the crucifixion.

Philip and James have shared the same feast day since AD 560, when
a church in Rome where their relics repose, was dedicated on this day.

### Servants of the gospel

Like Paul, in today's epistle, Philip and James were 'servants of the
gospel'. Unlike Paul, we know very little about them. We ourselves,
as servants of the gospel, may have high- or low-profile ministries. It
does not matter which; the main thing is that we prove faithful in our
calling. Quality counts above quantity, every time. That's not to say
that if we are given opportunities to do more, share more, teach
more, witness more and go further, we are to decline the offers. If
God has opened a door, he doesn't want us to ignore it.

For all we know, Philip and James may have had very active
ministries in the early Church. One day, we may know more of
them. But for now it is sufficient to know that they were loyal to
Jesus and true to their calling. Like them, we are servants: and
servants don't seek personal recognition; they work for the good
name of their Master.

## God's grace

God's grace called Paul from being a persecutor of the Christians. The same grace had called Philip and James to accompany Jesus on his earthly ministry. We are where we are today because of this same grace. How we show it to others is a matter between ourselves and God. But we have a duty to show it, to put it to work in this world. The world is not yet so full of divine grace it can do without our input. Grace by its very nature is unselfish, and impossible to hoard or to use for one's own benefit.

That's why it's almost always associated with God. Just try defining it in purely human, physical terms, and you won't get far.

The Lord gives grace.

And the Lord can take grace away.

Blessed be the name of the Lord that we are the recipients of such a wonderful gift.


### Suggested Hymns

Amazing grace! How sweet the sound; God of mercy, God of grace; Grace! 'tis a charming sound; Let saints on earth in concert sing.


# St Matthias the Apostle   15 May (transferred from 14th)
## A Trusty Steward Acts 1:15–26; Ps. 15; 1 Cor. 4:1–7; John 15:9–17

> 'Think of us in this way, as servants of Christ and stewards of God's mysteries. Moreover, it is required of stewards that they should be found trustworthy.' 1 Corinthains 4:1–3


### The lot fell on Matthias

It could have fallen on Joseph called Barsabbas. There had to be a 'winner' and a 'loser'. That sounds hard, and we can surely believe that losing the toss didn't disturb Joseph's faith. What had been the conditions? That the candidates were in good spiritual standing, had been with Jesus from the beginning, and had witnessed his resurrection. This probably means that they had been among the 70 or so disciples sent out by Jesus on mission, so they would be accustomed to preaching, teaching and healing. They had work experience.

So the disciples cast losts. In this way, they felt that God not only made the difficult choice, but that he was seen to make it. And the lot fell on Matthias. And that's practically all we know of Matthias in the biblical text. For a time in the early Church a document circulated known as the 'Acts of Matthias', from which we learn that this apostle travelled to countries where cannibalism was practised. On his arrival there, Matthias was blinded and thrown into prison. Then God miraculously restored his sight, and he was released from the prison by Andrew (whether the 'Andrew' of the Gospels is not clear). We do not know how Matthias met his death.

## Trustworthy and faithful

But he had shown himself a trusty and faithful steward of the gospel. It is easy to take the 'outer circle' of disciples for granted: those faithful men (and, for all we know, also women) who had formed an important part of the mission team, though without the 'perks' of the Twelve who according to the gospel record were included in special events such as teaching sessions and the Last Supper. It is more difficult to maintain fervour and commitment when one is on the periphery of a group. And on this feast day of the one who made the transition from periphery to inner circle, let us pay tribute to all those unknown but faithful disciples.

We may be in an inner circle, or on the periphery, or perhaps we've never pondered the question. Does it really matter? If we're in God's will, we're in the right place. But if we're unhappy, frustrated, unfulfilled, perhaps God is telling us he wants us somewhere else, doing other work. If we dare to ask him, he will tell us, in his good time. Like Matthias, we may discover in Christ new fields for an expanding mission.

## *Suggested Hymns*

A charge to keep I have; O Jesus, I have promised; Soul of my Saviour; You shall cross the barren desert (Be not afraid).

# St Barnabas the Apostle  12 June (transferred from 11th)
**A Good Companion** Acts 11:19–30; Ps. 112; Gal. 2:1–10; John 15:12–17

> 'News of this came to the ears of the church in Jerusalem, and they sent Barnabas to Antioch . . . for he was a good man, full of the Holy Spirit and of faith.' Acts 11:22, 24

## A man of conviction

Barnabas had great faith; it had been tested in the days after Paul's conversion, when those with long memories had labelled Paul the arch-persecutor of the Church, and were unwilling to believe that the leopard had changed his spots. Barnabas believed, and made no secret of it, sticking up for Paul against all comers.

We first meet Barnabas the Cypriot, when he generously sold his property to give to the poor. From here, he appears to have just gone on growing in the faith. The Jerusalem Church sent Paul and Barnabas out on mission, and it was a great success. There was a blip, when the two apostles disagreed over Mark's apparent defection; again, it was Barnabas who took Mark with him on a mission to Cyprus, while Paul set off on another mission, this time with Silas.

According to tradition, Barnabas was martyred at Cyprus, in or around the year 61. A small chapel there, with pantiled cupola and cross, marks the tomb of this apostle, who is honoured as the founder of the Cypriot Church.

## A staunch ally

Barnabas was a staunch ally to have at one's side; and the Barnabases of today are following in worthy footsteps. Are we being Barnabases in our parish, our deanery, our diocese? Are we championing those whose faith or credentials are being assailed by others? Do we have the courage to stand up and speak out for them? Do we value our friendships to the point where, like Barnabas, we will support them against all comers? We don't have to agree with everything they say or do (because we hope their friendship will survive our own shortcomings); but the name of the game is encouragement rather than criticism.

We don't have to look far for Barnabas-opportunities: encouragement is in much shorter supply than need. If we look back over our lives, can we not see where someone's encouragement made a big difference? The strength it gave us to carry on; the impetus it gave to go beyond what we had thought was possible?

We are used to being extra-vigilant against the onslaughts of Satan. If we employ equally diligent energy into giving encouragement wherever we can, we are in effect dealing Satan a double, two-edged blow.

And that can't be anything but good news.

### Suggested Hymns

Brother, sister, let me serve you; Can I see another's woe; Help us to help each other, Lord; Lord, for the years.

## Corpus Christi (Day of Thanksgiving for the Institution of the Holy Communion)   15 June
**Life For Ever** Gen. 14:18–20; Ps. 116:10–end; 1 Cor. 11:23–26; John 6:51–58

> '[Jesus said], "Those who eat my flesh and drink my blood abide in me, and I in them. Just as the living Father sent me, and I live because of the Father, so whoever eats me will live because of me." ' John 6:56–57

### The vital Eucharist

Jesus' teaching in this sixth chapter of John's Gospel may have been given at the Last Supper, or it may have been intended as a preparation for the disciples. Or John may have 'lifted' it from a post-resurrection appearance teaching of Jesus. We do not know. Since it was so new, so distinctive – and so shocking – it was bound to disturb those who were hearing it, especially those hearing it for the first time.

The Roman world at that time was an amalgam of pagan cults, in which food and wine was offered to the deities at orgies and celebrations. But Jesus' institution of the Eucharist could not have been more different from these. He is not taking bread and wine from his followers, but giving it to them. He is not asking sacrifice from them; he is giving himself as a sacrifice. He is not demanding human or animal blood to be shed; but is shedding his own blood, offering his own body. Such self-sacrifice had never been seen before. But then, the world had not been saved before.

Hell had not been invaded before. Satan had not been mortally wounded before. The old covenant had not been replaced by the new before; and eternal life in glory with God had not been on universal offer before.

All this hung on Jesus' institution of the Eucharist. The disciples were mystified then; and only after the resurrection, ascension and the giving of the Holy Spirit at Pentecost, did realization dawn that to keep the sacrifice of Calvary operative – to 'show the Lord's death till he comes' – the Eucharist must continue until the End of Time.

## A great investment

Ex-fishermen, tax-collectors and the like were invested with the task of explaining this deep theology to people who had either grown up with the animal sacrifices of the temple, or the pagan cults with their meaningless orgies, or a stoic indifference to religion of any kind.

Difficult? About as difficult as it is for Christ's followers today to explain to non-believers what the Eucharist means. Could Jesus have chosen another way for us to remember? Doubtless he could, but he chose the Eucharist because it was simply the BEST way.

One of the most beautiful of the ancient eucharistic prayers comes from the Egyptian tradition:

> To thee have we offered this bread, the likeness of the Body of the Only-Begotten ... wherefore we also making the likeness of the death have offered the bread, and beseech thee through this sacrifice to be reconciled to all of us and to be merciful, O God of truth; and as this bread had been scattered on the top of the mountains and gathered together came to be one, so also gather thy Holy Church out of every nation and country and every city and village and house and make one living catholic church ... (From the Prayer of Oblation of Bp Sarapion)

### Suggested Hymns

Author of life divine; Once, only once, and once for all; O thou, who at thy Eucharist did pray; We hail thy presence glorious.

# The Birth of John the Baptist  24 June
**'His Name is John'** Isa. 40:1–11; Ps. 85:7–13; Acts
13:14b–26 or Gal. 3:23–29; Luke 1:57–66, 80

> *'Then they began motioning to his father to find out what name
> he wanted to give him. He asked for a writing-tablet, and wrote:
> "His name is John". And all of them were amazed.' Luke 1:62–63*

## 'You will name him John'

The angel had told Zechariah, 'You will name him John', nine
months before (v. 13). And Zechariah and Elizabeth were as faithful
in obeying the angelic command, as Mary and Joseph would be in
the naming of Jesus.

Is there another miracle in these verses that is often overlooked?
'John' (like 'Jesus') was quite a common name, so there was nothing
unusual in the name itself. But it had been chosen by God, and so
it would be. Yet Zechariah was struck dumb, because the whole
thing seemed so tremendous. Therefore, he could not declare the
child's name audibly; and the inference was, he could not write;
hence the 'motioning', the sign-language (as though he were also
deaf). The attitude, 'Does he take sugar?' is not a modern phenom-
enon; many people are unable to relate normally to the handicapped. If indeed Zechariah could not normally write, then his
inscribing of the declaration (as though a fait accompli) on the
writing-tablet was surely a miracle.

One way and another, it was far more than merely the birth of
'another John'. Yet the rejoicing would be there, as at any safely
delivered birth: the elderly parents would not know that their child
would have a short life and a brutal death. But even now they knew
he was special . . .

. . . So special, that each of the four Gospels begins its account
of the ministry of Jesus with the part played by John the forerunner,
the rough man from the wilderness who was fearless in facing up
to priests and Pharisees, scribes and Sadducees, soldiers and
lawyers. He had a word for each of them; an uncompromising
word, that the axe was already laid at the root of the tree. Judgement was about to begin, and the only way to meet it was by
repentance and forgiving of sins.

## The bare essentials

We tell ourselves today that we need so many 'bare essentials'. Were John the Baptist here, no doubt he would consider many of these as luxuries. Eating locusts and wild honey, and drinking no wine, John wore only the simple loincloth, and startled people not only by his strict asceticism but also by his passionate, uncompromising message.

Yet he was one of the humblest men around. 'He must increase, I must decrease,' he said of the coming Messiah. And when Jesus came asking for baptism, John protested as much as he dare: 'I need to be baptized by you, and do you come to me?' (Matt. 3:14).

John was the last – and, for all his humility, probably the greatest – of the prophets: blessed before he was born, even while still in Elizabeth's womb, it is fitting that his birthday has been honoured by the Church with greater significance than his death.

### Suggested Hymns

Firmly I believe and truly; On Jordan's bank the Baptist's cry; The great Forerunner of the Lord; To God be the glory.


## SS Peter and Paul, Apostles   29 June
**Safe in God's Hands** Zech. 4:1–6a,10b–14; Ps. 125; Acts 12:1–11; Matt. 16:13–19

> *'Suddenly an angel of the Lord appeared and a light shone in the cell. He tapped Peter on the side and awoke him, saying: "Get up quickly". And the chains fell off his wrists.' Acts 12:7*

### Martyrs at Rome

Tradition has it that both Peter and Paul suffered martyrdom at Rome, in or around AD 64, and this day has been kept as their joint festival from very early times. Peter is honoured as the first Bishop of Rome, and by many as the leading apostle of the early Church. But others give the latter honour to Paul: certainly, going on the canonical texts, Paul travelled more than any of the other apostles, and probably suffered more.

Of their time at Rome, we know so little. Acts 28 tells us that Paul was kept under house-arrest for two years. It is unlikely that his case ever came before the emperor. His time appears to have been filled by teaching and preaching to the local Jews and Gentile believers, and in writing.

Peter is said to have been persuaded by his friends to leave Rome and seek sanctuary in the country, when renewed persecution flared up in the city. As he headed out through the suburbs, he met a man walking into Rome.

'Quo vadis [Where are you going]?' Peter asked the stranger.

'I'm going to Rome to be crucified, again,' came the quiet reply.

And Peter, in shame, turned back to face the persecution, and a martyr's death.

## Safe in the Lord's care

God had accomplished what 30 years before had looked impossible: he had got his key men to Rome. His hand had been on them, guiding and protecting. In our reading from Acts, we saw how Peter had been so secure in the knowledge that God was with him, he had been able to disregard his chains, his guards, and the conditions of his prison; and to sleep so soundly that the angel needed to prod him into consciousness before he could get him moving. Luke doesn't tell us how long Peter had been in the cell; only that the rescue came on the night before he was due to appear before Herod. The news that James (the Great) had been killed, had not kept Peter awake (the 'James' in Acts 12:17 is usually taken to mean 'James the Less', the son of Alphaeus, and is so defined in some versions). Peter probably knew the church was keeping a round-the-clock prayer-vigil for him. But in any case his trust in God stopped him from resorting to fear or panic.

What a difference from the man who, only three years or so before, had been so terrified in his own home-waters, he had woken up his Master, sleeping peacefully on a cushion, crying: 'Teacher, do you not care that we are perishing?' (Mark 4:38)!

Now it is the people down at the church in John Mark's house, who are wrong-footed. Praying so hard for Peter, they can't believe at first that he has walked free from the prison (Acts 12:15). The serving-girl Rhoda has hard work convincing them that Peter is at the door; just like Mary Magdalene tried to tell the disciples on Easter morning that Christ had risen.

God is still testing our faith today, in many, many ways because we, too, sometimes fail to see the wood for the trees.

Give me the faith which can remove; Light's abode, celestial Salem; O, for a faith that will not shrink; Oh, the love of my Lord is the essence.

## St Thomas the Apostle  3 July
**Apostle to India** Hab. 2:1–4; Ps. 31:1–6; Eph. 2:19–22; John 20:24–29

> *'So then you are no longer strangers and aliens, but you are citizens with the saints and also members of the household of God, built upon the foundation of the apostles and prophets, with Christ Jesus himself as the cornerstone.' Ephesians 2:19–20*

### The doubter

'Thomas the Twin (Didymus)' has come down to us through history as 'the Doubter'. He was a pessimist, at least in his early ministry. When Jesus set his face to go into Judaea and heal Lazarus at Bethany, Thomas knew only too well that they would be entering hostile territory, but very bravely he put loyalty to Jesus before danger: 'Let us also go, that we may die with him' (John 11:16). But this courage is often overlooked as we focus on his very openly expressed doubts about Jesus' resurrection: 'Unless I see the marks of the nails in his hands, and put my finger in the mark of the nails and my hand in his side, I will not believe' (John 20:25). Again, if we'll only realize it, there is courage here; not everyone would, given the chance, have the nerve to put these words into action.

Thomas was left a whole week (but only a week) with his doubts; and then when his risen Lord specially, personally confronted him and urged him to 'prove' his doubts, Thomas very honestly and convincingly declared his belief: 'My Lord and my God!' (John 20:28). It was the first time in the Gospels that Jesus had been called 'God'.

### To India

Tradition has it that after Pentecost Thomas went to India. Still today many Indian Christians call themselves 'Christians of St Thomas'. He is thought to have been buried at Mylapore, near

Madras, where a sixth-century cross bears his name in an inscription.

When Paul talks of 'strangers and aliens' in today's reading, he is referring to the Gentiles who before Christ had been forced to accept circumcision if they desired to embrace Judaism. Now, thanks to Jesus, they can come to God through his Son, without becoming Jews, without the need for circumcision, and certainly without feeling they are second-class citizens.

Not all the apostles would go into 'alien' territory as far from Jerusalem as Thomas did when he went to India; but after Pentecost and the gift of languages, the Christian Jews would of necessity see their patriotism in a new light. The full acceptance of Gentile status in the Church would not come overnight, and many would be the heart-searchings and debatings in its birth-pangs.

But come it did. And apostles such as Thomas helped to speed it on its way.

## No difference

Even today, society in general is having problems with the universal accepting of different creeds, colours and cultures. What are we, as an integral part of the Church, doing about this question?

### Suggested Hymns

All people that on earth do dwell; In Christ there is no east or west; There's a wideness in God's mercy; When I needed a neighbour.


## St Mary Magdalene  22 July
**The Urge of Love** S. of Sol. 3:1–4; Ps. 42:1–7;
2 Cor. 5:14–17; John 20:1–2, 11–18

> 'For the love of Christ urges us on, because we are convinced that one has died for all; therefore all have died. And he died for all, so that those who live might live no longer for themselves, but for him who died and was raised for them.' 2 Corinthians 5:14–15

## Love's strength

'Love' is that beautiful thing that we know so much about; the quality we cannot live without; the joy and colour that make life worth living; and yet the hardest thing to express in words. Watch a young (or not so young) couple who are head-over-heels in love, and there's more love-language spoken with their eyes and smiles, than articulated. The two Wesley brothers, John and Charles, often talked of 'unspeakable love' when referring to God and his dealings with us – and surely the prime expression of 'love in action' was when God loved the world so much that he sent his Son ... (John 3:16).

Mary Magdalene had been converted by that love; converted, it is believed, from a life of prostitution and immorality. She had been given physical, mental and spiritual freedom, when Jesus' love blotted out her former sins and enabled her to start over, with the slate wiped so clean, it was as though she had never sinned.

## A turn-around

It was such a turn-around from her former life. Here was the ex-prostitute an integral part of Jesus' mission-team back-up, working alongside women like Mary the Mother of Jesus, Joanna and Salome, learning every day how to act and speak the gospel of Jesus. It wouldn't really matter (though it probably hurt quite a lot from time to time) that people with long memories taunted her about her purple past. To Mary, that was over and done with, and gratitude to Jesus showed in her deep love and commitment.

## Easter morning

This love and commitment brought Mary to the tomb on Easter morning, and her reward was to be the first to see (and to believe in) her risen Lord. The men she told did not believe her, but that made no difference to her faith. She would always be the first to believe in the Easter Jesus. Her conversion had been vindicated: in coming to the tomb and accepting with joy and faith the good news, she had shown her love and devotion.

## Our commitment

We probably have had just as many sins washed away in Jesus' blood as Mary: different sins, it is true; but sins, nevertheless. Does our gratitude for this forgiveness drop into forgetfulness along with the sins? Or do we continue to brood in doubt that the sins have really been forgiven? Or, like Mary (often called the 'Apostle to the

Apostles'), do we show Jesus every day just how much we value his forgiveness, and love him with an 'unspeakable' love translated into action?

### Suggested Hymns

All in an Easter garden; Love divine, all loves excelling; Magdalene, thy grief and gladness; Thine be the glory, risen, conquering Son.

## St James the Apostle   25 July
### The First Apostolic Martyr Acts 11:27—12:2; Ps. 126; 2 Cor. 4:7–15; Matt. 20:20–28

> *'But we have this treasure in clay jars, so that it may be made clear that this extraordinary power belongs to God and does not come from us. We are afflicted in every way, but not crushed; perplexed, but not driven to despair; persecuted, but not forsaken; struck down, but not destroyed.'* 2 Corinthians 4:7–9

### One of the 'inner circle'

Called 'the Great', to distinguish him from James the Less, the son of Alphaeus, today's saint was a Galilean fisherman, the brother of John; and, with John, Peter and Andrew, one of the inner circle of Christ's disciples. He was present at the transfiguration, and at the arrest in Gethsemane; a witness of the resurrection, and there at Pentecost when the Holy Spirit was given.

James became the head of the church in Jerusalem, and as such was in the firing-line when Herod turned his venom on the believers. He was the first of the apostles to suffer martyrdom, in or around the year 44. 'About that time King Herod laid violent hands upon some who belonged to the church. He had James, the brother of John, killed with the sword' (Acts 12:1–2). And then he went after Peter, but God rescued Peter from prison; read all about it in Acts 12!.

### Clay jars

Our bodies, as Paul says in today's lesson, are merely 'clay jars', and the treasure we hold in them is not destroyed even though the jars may be smashed.

Death merely releases the treasure to where it ultimately belongs with God. And so James's death in Jerusalem was as though a precious seed had been sown: seed that went on growing and ripening as the Church not only expanded in Judaea, but began to spread out into many other countries. The Jews, as a nation, had feared 'the Great Sea' (the Mediterranean); but now they found that the freedom inside them – the indestructible Spirit of God – swept them far out across the Great Sea, with the gospel of Christ.

## Satan's obtuseness?

When will Satan realize that persecution brings renewed growth? The more the Church is attacked, the stronger faith grows. Does the devil in his obtuseness not see this? Oh, yes, he's not as dim as we'd like to think. His answer is to encourage apathy and lukewarmness first, and only if that fails overt persecution; this is a much more insidious and devious weapon. And we don't need to look far to see it operating today. The answer for Christians is to meet this attack with renewed vigour, renewed strength in Christ, for the greater our strength, the greater our joy (Neh. 8:10), because the joy – the joy of the Lord – is the best antidote to indifference and coldness. James's death fanned the faith of believers into a joyful strength that took them far and wide.

### Suggested Hymns

A charge to keep I have; Colours of day; Give me oil in my lap; Soldiers of Christ, arise.

# Transfiguration of our Lord  7 August (transferred from 6th)
**'My Chosen'** Dan. 7:9–10, 13–14; Ps. 97; 2 Pet. 1:16–19; Luke 9:28–36

> 'While [Peter] was saying this, a cloud came and overshadowed them; and they were terrified as they entered the cloud. Then from the cloud came a voice that said, "This is my Son, my Chosen; listen to him!"' Luke 9:34–35

## Today's revelations

If we expect today's revelations to be carbon copies of the trans-figuration, we shall be disappointed. God does not deal in carbon copies. But he does deal in revelations. In the lives of millions of folk today, God is revealing himself, his word, his truth. If we miss out on what he is revealing, it is not healthy for our souls.

So, how can we grasp these opportunities? Well, it helps if we can learn the lessons God gave us in the record of that first-century transfiguration.

## Effort

First, there needs to be effort on our part. God didn't give the beautiful experience to the disciples at their breakfast-table, or while they went about their housework. Jesus had them trekking up a mountain, using physical energy as well as displaying their loyalty to him. They might have wondered why and where they were going, but obediently they went. God may be calling us to do something or to go somewhere, outside and beyond our under-standing. Not to go, may be to miss a blessing.

## Glimpses from the past

There were Moses and Elijah, conversing from the past, in the present, about the future, with Jesus. If we consider the past as past, we may be missing out on important lessons from God. He was showing Peter and the others, not only that Moses and Elijah were still alive, and recognizable, but that they were integrated and involved in what was going on, and in what was going to take place. We have lessons to learn from the past, that should not be mothballed and consigned to history.

## Jesus is here

It may seem obvious, but we need constantly to be aware that Jesus is always here with us; he is there, as we trek up the mountain; he is there, as we learn from the past. All the time, his light is available and shining, for the Holy Spirit within us never goes short on energy.

And because he is here, we are not to fear, no matter where God takes us, or what happens to us. Jesus is here. What do we do about it? God is very uncompromising: 'He is my Son, my Chosen; listen to him!' Jesus is not here with us as a sleeping partner. He has taken no divine 'vow of silence', leaving us to muddle through as best we can. He is speaking today, through his Spirit, on every facet of our lives.

Every one. Jesus is not only interested in every created being; he is waiting for us to listen to what he has to say, about everything we say and do.

'Surely not!' sneer the scoffers.

Oh, yes! For we are dealing with the Lord who knows every hair on our heads.

### Suggested Hymns

In days of old on Sinai; O Jesus, I have promised; Round the Lord in glory seated; 'Tis good, Lord, to be here.

# Assumption of the Blessed Virgin Mary  15 August
**Fullness of Time** Isa. 61:10–11 or Rev. 11:19—12:6, 10; Ps. 45:10–17; Gal. 4:4–7; Luke 1:46–55

> *'But when the fullness of time had come, God sent his Son, born of a woman, born under the law, in order to redeem those that were under the law, so that we might receive adoption as children.' Galatians 4:4–5*

## Born of a woman

Hailed forever as the mother of God's Son, according to one tradition, Mary had spent her childhood in the temple. We meet her in the Gospels as a young virgin, betrothed to Joseph; and it is her trusting 'Fiat' that at the annunciation accepts God's will, however it may be manifested. In a crowded Bethlehem, she gives birth to Jesus, and within days is hearing Simeon's prophecy that her heart will be pierced by a sword. The visit of wise men from a far country sparks off Herod's paranoia regarding the 'King of the Jews', and Mary and Joseph obey God's instruction to take the child to Egypt for safety.

## The growing boy

We catch up with Mary again when she is back in Nazareth, for she and Joseph take the 12-year-old Jesus to the temple for his bar mitzvah. He worries his parents by staying behind to converse with the doctors of the law; and Mary continues to wonder what the child she is mothering will grow to become. Then, at some point before he reaches the age of 30 or so, Jesus loses his earthly father, and Mary continues to be the beautiful mother she is, encouraging Jesus to show his glory at the Cana wedding-breakfast, and accompanying him throughout his earthly ministry.

## At Calvary

She is still there, when most of his other friends have forsaken him, at the foot of the cross; and Jesus shows the precious bond between him and his mother, when even in his agony he commends her into the keeping of his beloved disciple.

Mary is there at Pentecost, at the descent of the Holy Spirit; and we may believe that she continued active in the Jerusalem Church, though it is possible that she went with John to Ephesus.

## Today

Today the Eastern Orthodox Church observes the Dormition of the Virgin (the Falling Asleep), while the Western Catholic Church (and not a few Anglicans) celebrate her bodily assumption into heaven.

Was Mary assumed? We have no biblical or other evidence for this. It would not have been the first assumption. Enoch 'walked with God, and was not; for God took him' (Gen. 22:24, AV); and Elijah went up to heaven in a fiery horsedrawn chariot (2 Kings 2:11). Certainly, Jesus loved his mother very specially, and perhaps because of this we can reverently believe that he may not have wanted her physical body to suffer corruption.

However Mary entered Paradise, we may surely believe that, beautiful as ever, she is very specially still with her Son.

### *Suggested Hymns*

I sing the Lord God's praises; I'll sing a hymn to Mary; Maiden, yet a mother; Mary immaculate, Star of the morning.

## St Bartholomew the Apostle   24 August
**A Strange Beginning** Isa. 43:8–13; Ps. 145:1–7; Acts 5:12–16; 1 Cor. 4:9–15; Luke 22:24–30

> '[Jesus said], "The greatest among you must become like the youngest, and the leader like one who serves. For who is greater, the one who is at the table or the one who serves? Is it not the one at the table? But I am among you as one who serves."'
> Luke 22:26–27

### 'What? From Nazareth?'

Bartholomew is generally equated with the 'Nathanael' mentioned in John's Gospel, who was brought by Philip to Jesus and did not have the most promising of beginnings. Told by Philip that Jesus hailed from Nazareth, Bartholomew was scathing in his cynicism that nothing good could surely emerge from Nazareth. Jesus disarmed the cynic by telling him him he was an Israelite with no deceit. Amazed, Bartholomew asked how he knew him, and Jesus replied that he had seen him under the fig-tree. From that moment on, Bartholomew was a loyal member of the Twelve, and a witness of Jesus' resurrection.

### After Pentecost

Tradition has it that after Pentecost Bartholomew travelled with the gospel to India and Armenia; and that while in Armenia he suffered martyrdom under King Astyages, being flayed alive and then beheaded. Sometimes he is portrayed in symbolism with a butcher's knife. Later, his relics were translated to Benevento in Italy.

### Honest men

While Thomas had his doubts, Peter his impulsiveness, James and John ambition, Bartholomew shows a cynicism that is further proof (were any needed) that the men who wrote the Gospels have given us a record of great accuracy and honesty. The Twelve were not perfect, nor did they show brilliant qualifications for the work to which Jesus called them; but he saw their potential, and instructed and moulded their characters until he could return to glory and leave the work of evangelism in their hands.

Bartholomew was probably right in his assessment of the people of Nazareth. Certainly when Jesus went back there to preach, he received a rough reception, and we are told he could only heal a very few people, because of the unbelief that was so prevalent. There had apparently been no ructions so long as he remained 'the carpenter's son' – one of them – but what they saw as pretensions of grandeur soon provoked hostility. The narrow-minded Nazarenes have twenty-first-century counterparts whom one does not need to seek far before finding today.

### 'As one who serves'

Bartholomew was content to be a servant of the Master who served. His cynicism had been cut away like a tumour under the surgeon's scalpel.

How is Jesus dealing with us today? It may not be cynicism he needs to work on, but if we are open to his examination, the treatment will be thorough, and the cure certain.

### *Suggested Hymns*

I, the Lord of sea and sky; Love divine, all loves excelling; Love is his word; You will cross the barren desert (Be not afraid)

# Birth of the Blessed Virgin Mary  8 September
**Wonderful Planning** Mic. 5:2–4; For the Psalm: Judith 16:3–16; Rom. 8:28–30; Matt. 1:1–16, 18–23

> *'We know that all things work together for good for those who love God, who are called according to his purpose. For those whom he foreknew he also predestined . . . and . . . called . . . and those whom he called he also justified; and . . . glorified.'*
> *Romans 8:28–30*

### What God has prepared

God has gone to infinite pains to prepare a wonderful progression to glory for those he has known prior to birth. And he has known us all in this way, for he has created us all. God is no respecter.

We all have the possibility of being . . . a Paul, a Peter, a John? Yes, for we are all called to share and spread the gospel.

But can we be a Mary? Surprisingly, yes, in a way. We cannot bear the Saviour of the world, for Mary has already performed that unique role, for which she was foreknown, predestined, called, justified and now glorified. But Jesus has marvellously said that those who follow him will be to him as a mother, a sister, a brother (Matt. 12:50; Mark 3:35; Luke 8:21). And we have only to see how Jesus loved his mother to know how he cherishes those who do his Father's will.

## Mary's birth

There are those who believe that Mary was immaculate, sinless, from birth. Whether or not this was so matters less than the fact that God loved her enough to choose her as the mother for his Son. So that Jesus could touch our lives at every point, he needed to be born and to know the helplessness and dependency of childhood. He needed to experience human vulnerability from the cradle to the grave. Had it not been so, there could be times in our lives when we'd feel unable to touch him, to feel his presence near. As it is, he is with us in every circumstance and situation under the sun.

And Mary played a unique and vital role in it all. Her parents, according to tradition, were Joachim and Anne (Anna), whose feast day is on 26 July. Joachim is thought to have been born in Nazareth, and married Anne when both were quite young. For many years they longed for a child, but none was born. In deep anguish, Joachim retired into the wilderness for prayer for 40 days, during which time an angel appeared to Anne (who was also praying) and promised a child who would be honoured the world over. Anne, in her joy, replied that any child she bore – boy or girl – would be devoted to God.

Anne gave birth to Mary when she was about the age of 40, and it is believed that both she and Joachim lived to see the birth of Jesus. Wouldn't we love to know so much more about this couple who cherished the mother of our Lord! God willing, we may, one day.

But today, as we give thanks for the birth of Mary, can we spend some time in reflecting on how much she and Jesus meant to each other, and, by extension, to Christians of 2006.

For Mary, mother of our Lord; I'll sing a hymn to Mary; Jesus, good above all other; Mary immaculate, Star of the morning.

## Holy Cross Day   14 September   **This Great Name**
Num. 21:4–9; Ps. 22:23–28; Phil. 2:6–11; John 3:13–17

> *'Therefore God also highly exalted him and gave him the name that is above every name, so that at the name of Jesus every knee should bend, in heaven and on earth and under the earth, and every tongue should confess that Jesus Christ is Lord, to the glory of God the Father.' Philippians 2:9–11*

### The Calvary cross

On this day, in AD 335, the Chapel of the Holy Sepulchre in Jerusalem was dedicated. According to a much later tradition, Helena, mother of the Emperor Constantine, had discovered the cross of Jesus while on a pilgrimage to the Holy Land in 326.

But the importance of today lies not in whether it is possible to see or touch the actual wood of Christ's cross, as in what the cross stands for: the day on which Jesus killed death by undergoing death for us: the sacrifice that made possible the glorious resurrection of Easter and the hope of glory.

Why did it have to be so terrible? Because, ever since the Fall of Adam, the world had been sliding further and further out of kilter with God. It needed nothing less than the power of God in Jesus to reverse the slide; and if that meant undergoing the worst death on the worst weapon of torture of the day, it would be so.

### God's love

The love of God went beyond all comprehension, to accomplish for humanity what we could not do for ourselves. We had done nothing to merit such magnanimous love: it was the free grace of God; free, that is, to us, but costly in divine terms.

And yet, on Easter Day the very disciples nearest to Jesus found it hard to believe. Jesus, in his parable of Dives and Lazarus, had forecast that folk would not believe even though someone rose from the dead, and he was proved so right. Yes, the disciples were persuaded when the risen Christ (wounds and all) appeared among them. Yes, believers began to realize the wonderful truth in their thousands, when the Holy Spirit descended at Pentecost. Yes, millions more have since believed and continue to believe.

But millions more have managed to believe that history is wrong, white is black and truth is a lie. What can we do, to make a difference? How can we persuade the doubters that the cross of Christ is not two pieces of wood probably lost for ever, but a commitment, a way of life, to be taken up out of sheer love for the Man who once said: 'Take up your cross, and follow me'?

Well, we shall not compel anyone to believe, but our life, our witness, our love, and the light of Christ that we can shine into others' lives, may just make our Lord real to them.

But it won't, unless we truly make the effort.

### Suggested Hymns

Beneath the cross of Jesus; How sweet the name of Jesus sounds; In the cross of Christ I glory; Jesus, the name high over all.

## St Matthew, Apostle and Evangelist   21 September
### Friend of Sinners Prov. 3:13–18; Ps. 119:65–72;
2 Cor. 4:1–6; Matt. 9:9–13

> *'As Jesus was walking along, he saw a man called Matthew sitting at the tax booth, and he said to him, "Follow me." And he got up and followed him.' Matthew 9:9*

### An immediate 'put-down'?

Matthew's quick and trusting response to Jesus' call was soon tested. In his joy, he gave Jesus a meal at the house, to which many of his workmates came. But the jollity was soured, when the Pharisees sneered at the guests' low standing in society; even at their crimes. And Jesus, as if testing his newest disciple even further, did not 'whitewash' the company, but implicitly agreed that he was eating with men of low profession and low morality! Yet Matthew stayed the course, and made good, trusting in Jesus not to paper over his shortcomings, but to convert them into something beautiful for God.

The Jews regarded tax-collecting as an accommodation to the

Roman army of occupation; and it probably did attract men of questionable morality. But Jesus took on Matthew in the full knowledge not only of what he was, but also of what he could become. And – yes – it's the same with everyone he calls. We are not perfect when he chooses us; we're still not perfect while we're working out our mission; but our Lord has faith that we shall be perfect one day.

## The evangelist

If, as is generally believed, the tax-collector of Capernaum and the Matthew whose name is associated with the first Gospel are one and the same (though Mark and Luke give his name as Levi), Jesus' trust was justified. Matthew the evangelist writes as a Jew for Jewish readers. Loyal to the Master who didn't desert him, Matthew writes of a Saviour who will keep faith with all whom he calls. He emphasizes, too, that this Saviour is the Saviour of the world; it is from Matthew that we hear of the Magi, the first Gentile visitors to the young Jesus; and it is Matthew who, of all the gospel-writers, mentions the 'church', founded by Jesus, which will never be overcome by the devil (Matt. 16:18).

Matthew also gives us the best ordered sermon of the Gospels, a large portion of uninterrupted teaching of Jesus, known as the Sermon on the Mount (chs. 5—7; much of this material also appears in Luke, but scattered hither and yon in his Gospel).

## Sheep and goats

Perhaps because he was a 'brand picked from the burning', Matthew is keen to note Jesus' teaching on those who stray from the path; and it is only in this Gospel that we find the parable of the Last Judgement, dealing with the sheep and the goats (Matt. 25:31ff.).

And the grand finale of his writing comes in his record of Jesus' Great Commission, to 'Go . . . and make disciples of all nations' (Matt. 28:19).

According to tradition, Matthew suffered martyrdom in Ethiopia; but his Gospel survives to give us much material for prayer and encouragement.

Go, tell it on the mountains; Loving Shepherd of thy sheep; Put thou thy trust in God; Take up thy cross, the Saviour said.

# St Michael and All Angels   29 September
**Welcomer into Paradise** Rev. 12:7–12; Ps. 103:19–22; Heb. 1:5–14; John 1:47–51

> *'And war broke out in heaven, Michael and his angels fought against the dragon. The dragon and his angels fought back, but they were defeated, and there was no longer any place for them in heaven. The great dragon was thrown down, that ancient serpent which is called the Devil and Satan, the deceiver of the whole world; he was thrown down to the earth, and his angels were thrown down with him.' Revelation 12:7–9*

## Archangel Michael

Michael is seen as the chief of the archangels, in this heavenly war. Two others – Gabriel and Raphael – are also mentioned in the Bible. Gabriel announced the birth of Jesus, and Raphael restores sight to Tobit. In Enoch, however, there are seven archangels, and their various functions are described:

Uriel, who is over the world and over Tartarus;
Raphael, who is over the spirits of humankind;
Raguel, who fights in the world of the lights;
Michael, who oversees much of humankind and of chaos;
Saraqael, who oversees the sinful spirits;
Gabriel, who is over Paradise, serpents and cherubim;
and Remiel, who is over the resurrection.

## Michael – and Moses

There is a strange reference to Michael, in the little Book of Jude, where we find the archangel contending with the devil over the body of Moses. It is a glimpse – as is John's vision in Revelation – of the drama that Jesus' triumph at Calvary brought about in the heavenly realms. On earth, the scenes of that weekend were dramatic enough, but the spiritual realm was apparently stirred as never before.

And Michael was there, in the centre of the action.

Jesus had told his arresters, in the Garden of Gethsemane, that he had 12 legions of angels standing by, to employ *force majeure* at a split-second's notice. It is on days such as this, when the angelic realm is brought into sharper focus, that we realize what an exciting place heaven (Paradise), the spirit world (call it what you will) must be. Michael and his angels are not sitting on velvet cushions, harping sweet chords day in and day out. They are violently alive and active . . .

. . . as we shall probably be, when we cross the line from breathing into really living.

## Michael's reception

After the crossing, it may well be Michael the Archangel whom we see first, as according to tradition it is Michael who receives the souls of the faithful into heaven. It is a blessed thought, that the war with Satan in heaven has already been fought, and won. When we get there, it will be the victor whom we see; the defeated devil will by then be a long, long way behind us.

### Suggested Hymns

Angel-voices ever singing; Around the throne of God a band; There is a land of pure delight; Ye holy angels bright.

# St Francis of Assisi, Friar, Deacon, Founder of the Friars Minor 1226   4 October
*Il Poverello* Mic. 6:6–8; Ps. 100; Gal. 6:14–18;
Luke 12:22–34

> *'May I never boast of anything, except the cross of our Lord Jesus Christ, by which the world has been crucified to me, and I to the world.' Galatians 6:14*

## The 'little poor man'

We remember Francis as '*Il Poverello*' (the little poor man), but he did not start out that way. Born into the family of a rich cloth merchant, Francis grew up in the 'fast set' of Assisi. Well into his teens, he thought that life meant riding around on a fine horse, gaily caparisoned, and feuding with his friends against the wealthy youth of neighbouring towns and cities. It wasn't until an unsuccessful skirmish against the lads of Perugia landed Francis in prison, that he had time to reflect that there must surely be more to life than such gallivanting.

Once free again, he was praying one day in the woebegone little church of San Damiano, when the crucifix seemed to speak to him: 'Francis, I want you to rebuild my church.' Nothing if not literal, Francis ran back home, selected a bale of his father's best scarlet cloth, sold it, and hurried back to the priest at San Damiano. Use this money to rebuild your church,' he said.

Pietro Bernadone was furious, and hailed his son to court, where the presiding bishop ordered Francis to repay his father. In a dramatic gesture, Francis stripped his clothes from his body, and declared that from henceforward he had only one father, God. Impressed by the young man's sincerity, the bishop clothed him with his own robe, but the question of the fine remained.

Francis paid back Pietro and rebuilt San Damiano with his bare hands. Then, donning a simple brown robe, he left home for a life of extreme poverty and simplicity. Soon others joined him, and the folk of Assisi became used to seeing the brethren begging for food each day. Francis would not permit even a house to live in, for he said houses meant possessions, and they were not to own anything.

## Out East

Francis and some of the brothers journeyed east, to convert, if possible, the Muslims. But, although the Sultan Malek al-Kamil received him courteously at Damietta in Egypt, few conversions occurred. Back in Italy, he obtained the Pope's permission to found the Order that became known as the Friars Minor. Under his tutelage, a wealthy woman, Clare Offreduccio founded what became known as the Order of Poor Clares.

## Accommodations

But as the number of Friars Minor grew, so did accommodations and modifications, as the newer recruits rebelled (ever so gently) against Francis's ascetic principles. Saddened, he eventually relinquished the leadership, but remained in the Order and personally true to his original vision.

Two years before his death, Francis received the stigmata, but humbly kept this secret, not wishing to singularize himself. The wounds were discovered by the brothers, when he died at the age of 45, in 1226.

## Suggested Hymns

All creatures of our God and King; Let all mortal flesh keep silence; O, for a closer walk with God; Thy way, not mine, O Lord.


# St Luke the Evangelist   18 October
**Only Luke** Isa. 35:3–6 or Acts 16:6–12a; Ps. 147:1–7; 2 Tim. 4:5–17; Luke 10:1–9

> *'Do your best to come to me soon, for Demas, in love with this present world, has deserted me and gone to Thessalonica, Crescens has gone to Galatia, Titus to Dalmatia. Only Luke is with me. Get Mark, and bring him with you, for he is useful in my ministry.'* 2 Timothy 4:9–11


## The last post

The Second Letter to Timothy was written by Paul from Rome during his second imprisonment, probably around AD 67. It is the last of the extant writings; Paul is now an old man, and the departure of Demas and the others has cut him to the heart. But on this feast day of St Luke, it is cheering to see that the Greek physician (who by this time is also probably 'full of years') is loyally standing by Paul: a good friend to have at any time, but especially when the rigours of age have to be borne, and one is under house-arrest, many miles from home.


## St Luke

The author of the third Gospel and the Book of Acts, Luke was a Gentile, and emphasizes the delaings Jesus had with non-Jews, and also the respect and consideration he showed to women, who otherwise had a pretty low status at the time. Luke is not a theologian, but he is at pains to present an accurate, factual account of what happened where, and who said what. Perhaps he derived the precious information for the birth stories from Mary. He joined Paul roughly midway in his mission (when the 'we-passages' in Acts begin), and proved a trusty companion. As Paul grew older, it probably made sound sense to have a medical man at his side.

## Verifiable

Luke is careful to include verifiable data in his writings: names of prominent Jewish and Roman officials, towns, countries and islands. He is saying, in effect: 'Check me out, compare mine with secular records of the time!' And where such comparisons have been made, Luke's account has been verified in every case. Therefore we can surely have confidence in accepting the other parts of his record.

After Paul's crucifixion in Rome, Luke is said to have travelled to Greece and died there in his mid-eighties. His remains – for long divided between Padua and Prague – have in the last decade been reunited. Pathological examinations of these bones have suggested that he suffered from emphysema, arthritis and a bad back, which could have been initiated or accentuated by the vicissitudes he shared with Paul on the missionary journeys.

On this, his feast day, let us take the opportunity of thanking God for all medical practitioners and personnel, whose dedication to healing and wholeness is so vital in the lives of so many.

### Suggested Hymns

A charge to keep I have; Be thou my vision; Help us to help each other, Lord; Thine arm, O Lord, in days of old.

## SS Simon and Jude, Apostles   28 October
**Loyal, but Little Known** Isa. 28:14–16; Ps. 119:89–96; Eph. 2:19–22; John 15:17–27

> 'So then you are no longer strangers and aliens, but you are citizens with the saints and also members of the household of God, built upon the foundation of the apostles and prophets, with Christ Jesus himself as the cornerstone . . .' Ephesians 2:19–20

## In the Gospels

Matthew and Mark list Simon among the Twelve, as 'the Canaanite', while Luke calls him 'the Zealot'. It is not clear whether he belonged to this Jewish patriotic group when Jesus called him; or if he joined it after Pentecost as a means of spreading the gospel further. Jude also was one of the Twelve, perhaps the same Judas who was related to Jesus, and the brother of James (and probably son of James, as Luke has it): the author of the shortest book in the New Testament is also called Jude, and may also be this apostle.

## Patron saint of lost causes

It was unfortunate that Jude's name was so similar to that of the betrayer; and this probably accounts for the fact that prayers were not often made to him. When they were, it was as a last resort, and so Jude came to be known as the patron saint of lost causes.

Legend has it that both Simon and Jude suffered martyrdom in Persia, although other traditions have Simon dying peacefully at Edessa.

## No strangers

James the brother of John met his death at the hands of Herod in Jerusalem (Acts 12:1), the first of the apostles to be martyred; but most if not all of the others died or were killed in lands far from their homes. Yet, as Paul tells us in today's text, there are no 'strangers or aliens' in the body of Christ. It does not matter where we are physically: spiritually, we are in him, as brothers and sisters; integral parts of his Bride, the Church. We 'belong' in Christ: the very thought should give us added assurance. In Christ, we can walk tall, on our home-ground, ground that is his, and so ours by virtue of our being 'Christ-ians', for all authority in heaven and on earth has been given to Christ.

'The heart has many a dwellingplace, but only once a home', is true for every follower of Christ. Our hearts are (or should be) in him, and as such able to weather whatever life brings. As Augustine said: 'Our hearts are restless', until they are abiding in Christ.

Travel and transport are so easy and prevalent today, we don't always realize the effort that the early apostles would need to make to take the gospel out into the world of the first century, nor the dangers they would face, nor the journeys that would so often be delayed for bad weather, bandits, snow on the high mountain-passes, or simply fatigue and exhaustion.

Today, though we know so little about them, as we give thanks for Simon and Jude, let us also consider if we are making the most of the opportunities God is giving.

### Suggested Hymns

Forth in thy name, O Lord, I go; Thou whose almighty Word; Ye servants of the Lord; Ye that know the Lord is gracious.

# All Saints' Day  1 November (or transferred to 5th)
**'Thank You, Father'** Wisd. 3:1–9 or Isa. 25:6–9; Ps. 24:1–6; Rev. 21:1–6a; John 11:32–44

> *'So they took away the stone. And Jesus looked upwards and said, "Father, I thank you for having heard me. I knew that you always hear me, but I have said this for the sake of the crowd standing here, so that they may believe that you sent me."'*
> John 11:41–42

## A long tradition

All Saints' Day as a celebration has a long tradition, but at its inception in the fourth century, it was held on the Sunday after Pentecost. Four hundred years later, a chapel to All Saints was dedicated on 1 November in St Peter's at Rome, and within a century this new date was being observed in much of Europe, including Britain.

They are the great ones, these saints of the Church, though none of them would have ascribed 'greatness' to their lives. But they have made their mark in Christian history, and their example is a beacon to light our way to God. As Moses and Elijah could appear and converse with Jesus about his passion, on the Mount of the Trans-figuration, may we not infer that all the saints not only know what is happening on earth, but can also on occasion play a part in our doings?

## The ever-hearing Father

In today's text, Jesus could no doubt have restored Lazarus to life after private, silent prayer to his Father; but he wanted the bystanders to realize where the resurrection power was coming from; and also, that God is ever-present, ever-listening out for every prayer we make. He doesn't only hear the prayers of great saints like Peter and Paul, but every prayer from every Christian, for we are all called to be saints. Those who have fought the fight, we honour today; honour them, who are cheering us on, we who are still on the track.

## In glory

Lazarus was resurrected to die again. The saints we honour now are in glory, with death very finally behind them. What are they doing, apart from watching us and cheering us on? We do not know. But for them, the proving-ground has been successfully negotiated, the obstacles have all been either circumvented or pushed out of the way.

## What makes a saint?

What makes a saint? This is an easy question to answer, for Paul has already spelled it out: 'Love, joy, peace, patience, kindness, generosity, faithfulness, gentleness and self-control' (Gal. 5:22–23). In other words, it is putting everything the Holy Spirit can give us, into practice; the hard part is remembering to take no credit for the exercise, but to give the glory to God.

Not some of the time, but all of the time.

### *Suggested Hymns*

Around the throne of God a band; For all the saints; Let saints on earth in concert sing; There is a land of pure delight.

## All Souls' Day (Commemoration of the Faithful Departed)   2 November

*Dies Irae*   Lam. 3:17–26, 31–33 or Wisd. 3:1–9; Ps. 23 or Ps. 27:1–6, 16–17; Rom. 5:5–11 or 1 Pet. 1:3–9; John 5:19–25 or John 6:37–40

> *'Blessed be the God and Father of our Lord Jesus Christ! By his great mercy he has given us a new birth into a living hope through the resurrection of Jesus Christ from the dead, and into an inheritance that is imperishable, undefiled and unfading, kept in heaven for you.' 1 Peter 1:3–4*

### In the year 998

At the end of the tenth century, Abbot Odilo of Cluny ordered the observance of the Faithful Departed on this day, in all houses of the Order. During the next three centuries, the rest of the Western Church followed suit. Still today in many churches the *Dies irae* will be included in the service, as it has been since medieval times. At the Reformation, the commemoration was quietly dropped; but following the dreadful carnage of World War One, it was restored in the proposed BCP of 1928. There have been too many wars since then, but the prevalence of this commemoration today is as a result not only of the numerous casualties of war, but from a desire to remember all the faithful departed: not today the haloed saints of stained-glass and oil-paintings – their special recognition took place yesterday – but the unsung saints of our friends and family circles, who in so many ways have helped us along our way to God.

### An opportunity to grieve

In modern society, where grief is largely hidden and traditional patterns of mourning have mainly been consigned to history, it is important to have a time specifically set aside where we can grieve, and share our remembrance, corporately in the context of worship. It is unhealthy to bottle up grief, or to restrict it behind closed doors. God has given us the capacity to grieve, and at times we all need to: not necessarily in a dramatic way, but quietly, reverently, in thanksgiving to God for lives which in his mercy he has allowed us to share, and which have meant (and still mean) so much to us.

## The sharing of memories

It is in the sharing of memories today, that real value lies. We know we can't bring our loved ones back; but in open, corporate thanksgiving to God, we can draw closer to them. They are here with us, as Moses and Elijah (longer 'dead') were with Jesus on the mount. Unlike Peter and the disciples, we cannot physically see them, but the eye of faith makes lovingly plain what the lesser eye cannot. They are here, rejoicing in our remembrance. And we can do what they, for all their limitless glory, cannot. We can still cry, and in our tears (which God not only observes but cherishes) we can release some of the grief that otherwise would cripple us and not advantage them.

They are here. By God's grace today there is a meeting of love, as Jesus stands among us, living and departed.

### Suggested Hymns

For those we love within the veil; Let saints on earth in concert sing; The day thou gavest, Lord, is ended; There are loved ones in the glory.


# A Sermon for Harvest Thanksgiving

*'The seed is the word of God.'* Luke 8:11

The Englishman stared in wonder at the rows of lettuces, stretching out in all directions as far as the eye could see. 'Just how big is this field?' he asked.

'Upwards of 600 acres,' came the laconic reply of his American host. 'The whole farm covers more than 10,000 acres, but there's plenty bigger round these parts.'

'Think of the seed for all that land!' marvelled the visitor.

I wonder if God ever had a similar thought, as he watched the unfolding of Jesus' ministry. True, the Holy Spirit would come at Pentecost, and would remind the disciples of every word that Jesus had taught. And God would raise up writers and evangelists to give future generations the New Testament as a rich seed-bank of gospel pearls. But would there be enough seed for worldwide evangelization? For without seed, there could be no harvest.

No, God would not need to exercise his mind over the logistics.

The nucleus of the harvest had been sown by Jesus, and thereafter every believer would have seed sufficient for his or her ministry. There would be enough. The seed is multiplying today into further and further harvest-fields, as the light of the gospel spreads and grows.

Is our local harvest festival then a mere horticultural display, a chance to sing hymns that have become firm favourites, yet which are sung only at this time of year? By no means. Harvest festival is a time to thank God for his rich material provision; a time also to reach out with prayer and harvest-gifts, to those (near and far) who are less privileged than ourselves, as well as a time to focus on the spiritual harvest of our life and ministry.

When the Revd Robert Hawker, of Morwenstow, Cornwall, instituted harvest thanksgiving as we know it, over a century ago, he was starting a tradition that was to grow and become an integral part of the Church's year. Even in an age where there is a plethora of food variety on supermarket shelves, we are still dependent on the harvest being safely gathered in, whether in Britain, Sri Lanka, Tanzania or the Bahamas. Still the balance of nature is poised so finely, that fire, flood, drought, typhoon or earthquake can quickly and drastically affect hundreds of thousands of acres of cereal or fruit crops, meat or fish stocks. Sooner or later, the lack percolates through to empty shelves in shops and supermarkets half-a-world or more away.

But the lack is not on a global scale, even then. 'As long as the earth endures, seedtime and harvest ... shall not cease,' God promised Noah (Gen. 8:22); and the Lord is faithful to his promise. Even the worst disaster is only 'local'.

So it is with the spiritual harvest. The severest persecution, the most terrible heresy, is only local. In that area the Church will take a battering, the harvest will seem to fail, but seed is already springing up and growing in another field. Satan, for all his venom, is not powerful enough to hit all of the harvest all of the time.

If this year our harvest is not too good, let us pray God to show us why; at the same time not forgetting to rejoice in the good harvest being reaped in another field. If we are presently reaping a wonderfully rich harvest, the message is clear: let's get out and share it as far and as fast as we can.

# A Sermon for Remembrance Sunday

*'I have fought the good fight, I have finished the race, I have kept the faith. From now on there is reserved for me the crown of righteousness, which the Lord, the righteous judge, will give to me on that day; and not only to me but also to all who have longed for his appearing.' 2 Timothy 4:7–8*

On Remembrance Sunday, there seems to be nothing at all 'good' about the fighting in our thoughts, the wars that have taken away those whom we miss so much. Yet there would be no warfare, unless those prepared to support what is good, fought against a perceived evil. So long as evil stalks the earth, it will encourage good men and women to fight against it, whether on the physical or spiritual front.

Why do we remember, today? Mainly because we cannot forget, and we should not forget the great sacrifice made by so many. 'The evil that men do lives after them; the good is oft interred with their bones' (Shakespeare, *Julius Caesar*) is patently untrue: courage and dedication, commitment and fortitude, these virtues are undying and immortal. They are never, never wasted, and are so much stronger than evil, that they will make it to eternity, leaving evil a long, long way behind.

Yet, despite the inevitability of war, there is also a desperate futility: so much loss, so little apparent gain. Will it always be so? Our Lord has not promised a sea-change, this side of the 'End': 'When you hear of wars and rumours of wars, do not be alarmed; this must take place, but the end is still to come' (Mark 13:7). We look at the carnage; God sees beyond it. We look at the buried grain, while God has the eventual harvest in view.

But so many lives go down in war! Yes, but even one life lost would be tragic. It was terrible that innocent children were massacred when Jesus had to flee Bethlehem for Egypt; we wonder at the futility of it each Christmas time, as the commemoration of the Holy Innocents impacts on our nativity joy.

'To everything there is a season, and a time for every purpose under heaven' (Eccles. 3:1, AV). A time for war? Yes, and a time for peace; and this side of eternity, both will come to pass. After some wars, comes peace when the sacrifice appears to have brought some reward. After others, peace still seems to be at a premium, and any advantage gained appears to be a misnomer. The pessimists declare that the world is on a helter-skelter of conflict, and all we can do is to career from one war to the next.

Are they right? Has the sacrifice of Christ really made so little difference?

It is true that some of the most dreadful wars in history have been over religion. Have we ever thought what a strange anomaly and irony it must present to non-believers, to have opposing sides declaring that they are fighting in the name of Jesus, for the right? How can we defend the honour of Christ's name here?

God allows these wars. He doesn't cause them, and it must surely grieve him to see Christians fighting each other. Only he knows how he can bring good out of evil. But he can. With human beings, it may be impossible, but not with God, for with God all things are possible.

While Satan is at work in the world, good will rise up against him. Yes, even if it needs to fight for its principles, and even if it means dying for them. And even if it means doing right in a wrong cause, for the good that is on earth is still bound by human limitations.

'Anyone then who knows the right thing to do and fails to do it, commits sin' (James 4:17). Justice and the 'right thing' will continue to take Christians into war, while the earth remains. But the fight is not only against 'flesh and blood' but against the perpetrator of the evil, Satan.

May we pray, as we remember the fallen, that we may be led to further the spreading of the gospel throughout the world, for this is the promise of Jesus that will bring in the End of Time, which is the End of War. That is the best of all tributes we can make to those who have gone on ahead.

# Sources and Acknowledgements

## Sources of quoted material

p. 26 Richard Rolle, *The Form of Perfect Living* (Thomas Baker, 1910).

p. 68 J. C. Ryle, *Practical Religion* (James Clarke & Co., 1959).

pp. 141–2 Hewlett Johnson, *Searching for Light* (Joseph, 1968).

p. 203 St John of the Cross, *The Dark Night of the Soul*, tr. E. Allison Peers (Image Books, 1990).

pp. 229–30 Dom Gregory Dix, *The Shape of the Liturgy* (Continuum, 2001).

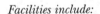

# Scripture Index

## Christian resource and education centre

\*13th century Manor House retreat  \*Meeting & seminar rooms
\*Self-catering listed cottages  \*Bungalows & dormitories
\*Prayer room  \*Restaurant with imaginative local food
\*Café-bar  \*Bookshop  \*Leisure facilities
\*Indoor heated pool  \*Formal gardens

*Chantmarle... A world where historic charm, peace, spiritual inspiration and contemporary convenience blend beautifully together to offer all the needs a Christian Residential Resource Centre could possibly have, nestled in 100 acres of beautiful Dorset countryside.*

*From arranging that meeting, big or small, prayer in groups or alone, to indoor or outdoor recreation after a hard day's work; from quiet contemplation to books, coffee or the internet; from spending time alone with God, with the family or with friends to the freedom of a child-friendly room, we have it all.*

*Whatever your needs, Chantmarle is the place to relax, unwind and meet with God in a setting that's historic, beautiful, peaceful and very welcoming. We look forward to meeting you soon!*

**Please visit our website: www.chantmarle.co.uk**

Bookings & enquiries: (01935) 83894; Fax: (01935) 83895
Email: resource.centre@chantmarle.co.uk
Chantmarle Manor, Frome St Quintin, Dorset DT2 0HD

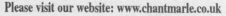

## ' The place to relax, unwind and meet with God'

# Subject Index

# Notes

........................................................
........................................................
........................................................
........................................................
........................................................
........................................................
........................................................
........................................................
........................................................
........................................................
........................................................
........................................................
........................................................
........................................................
........................................................
........................................................
........................................................
........................................................
........................................................
........................................................
........................................................
........................................................